The Man of Light in Iranian Sufism

وهذه صُورة الدّب الاصغر على ماترى في الكرة

وهذه صُورة الدّب الاصغر على ماترى في السَّماء

Ursa Minor

From *The Book of the 48 Constellations, Treatise on Uranometry*
by Abū'l-Hosayn al-Sūfi (d. 376/986).
(Paris, Bibliothèque Nationale; Arabic manuscript 5036)

The Man of Light
in Iranian Sufism

HENRY CORBIN

Translated from the French by
Nancy Pearson

SHAMBHALA
BOULDER & LONDON 1978

SHAMBHALA PUBLICATIONS, INC.
1123 Spruce Street
Boulder, Colorado 80302

A Far West Book
© 1971 by Henri Viaud
Translation © 1978 by Shambhala Publications, Inc.
All rights reserved.
Published by arrangement with Henri Viaud, Editions Presence,
"Aubard" St. Vincent sur Jabron, 04200 Sisteron, France.

ISBN 0-87773-114-4
LCC 77-6013

Distributed in the United States by Random House
and in Canada by Random House of Canada Ltd.

Distributed in the Commonwealth by Routledge & Kegan Paul Ltd.,
London and Henley-on-Thames.

Printed in the United States of America.

Library of Congress Cataloging in Publication Data

Corbin, Henry.
    The man of light in Iranian sufism.

    Translation of L'homme de lumiere dans le soufisme
iranien.
    "A Far west book."
    Bibliography: p.
    Includes index.
    1. Sufism—Iran.   I. Title.
BP188.8.I55C6713   297'4   77-6013
ISBN 0-394-73441-6

297.4
C791m

Contents

I. ORIENTATION   1
  1. The Pole of Orientation   1
  2. The Symbols of the North   4

II. THE MAN OF LIGHT AND HIS GUIDE   13
  1. The Hermetic Idea of Perfect Nature   13
  2. The *Noūs* of Hermes and the Shepherd of Hermas   26
  3. Fravarti and Walkyrie   28
  4. The Heavenly Twin (Mandeism and Manicheism)   33

III. MIDNIGHT SUN AND CELESTIAL POLE   39
  1. The Cosmic North and the "Oriental Theosophy"
     of Sohravardī (1191)   39
  2. Visions of the Pole in Rūzbehān of Shīrāz (1209)   52
  3. The Pole as the Abode of the Angel Sraosha   55

IV. VISIO SMARAGDINA   61
  1. Najmoddīn Kobrā (1220)   61
  2. Light and Spiritual Warfare   64
  3. The Trilogy of the Soul   66
  4. Like with Like   68
  5. The Function of the *Dhikr*   73
  6. The Green Light   76
  7. The Senses of the Suprasensory World   80
  8. The Orbs of Light   82
  9. The "Heavenly Witness"   84
  10. The Scales and the Angel   89

V. THE BLACK LIGHT   99
  1. Light without Matter   99
  2. The Doctrine of Photisms according to Najm Rāzī
     (1256)   103
  3. Black Light in the "Rose Garden of Mystery"
     (1317)   110

VI. THE SEVEN PROPHETS OF YOUR BEING   121
  1. Alāoddawleh Semnānī (1336)   121
  2. The World of Colors and the Man of Light   131
  3. The "Physiological" Colors according to Goethe   139

  NOTES   145
  BIBLIOGRAPHY   161
  INDEX   163

I. ORIENTATION

1. *The Pole of Orientation*[1]

Orientation is a primary phenomenon of our presence in the
world. A human presence has the property of spatializing a
world around it, and this phenomenon implies a certain relationship of man with the world, *his* world, this relationship
being determined by the very mode of his presence in the
world. The four cardinal points, east and west, north and
south, are not *things* encountered by this presence, but directions which express its *sense*, man's acclimatization to his world,
his familiarity with it. To have this sense is to orient oneself in
the world. The ideal lines that run from east to west, from
north to south form a system of *a priori* spatial evidences without which there would be neither geographic nor anthropological orientation. And indeed, the contrasts between Eastern
man and Western man, between Nordic man and Southern
man, regulate our ideological and characterological
classifications.

The organization, the plan, of this network has depended
since time immemorial on a single point: the point of orientation, the heavenly north, the pole star. Is it enough, therefore,
to say that spatialization, developed horizontally toward the
four cardinal points, is completed by the vertical dimension
from beneath to above, from the nadir to the zenith? Or rather

1

I. Orientation

are there not in fact different modes of perception of this same vertical dimension, so different in themselves that they modify the *orientation* of the human presence, not only in space but also in time? "Orientation in time" refers to the different ways in which man experiences his presence on earth, and the continuity of this presence within a kind of history, and the question as to whether this history has a *sense*, and if so, what sense? This in turn raises the question whether the perception of the heavenly pole, of the vertical dimension tending toward the cosmic north, is a uniform phenomenon, physiologically regulated by constant laws, or whether the phenomenon is not in fact regulated and diversified by the very mode of being of the human presence *orienting* itself? Hence therefore the primordial importance of the north and of the concept of the north: it is in accordance with the way in which man inwardly experiences the "vertical" dimension of his own presence that the horizontal dimensions acquire their *sense*.

Now one of the *leitmotive* of Iranian Sufi literature is the "Quest for the Orient," but this is a Quest for an Orient which, as we are forewarned (if we do not already realize), is not—and cannot be—situated on our geographical maps. This Orient is not comprised in any of the seven *climes* (*keshvar*); it is in fact the *eighth* clime. And the direction in which we must seek this "eighth clime" is not on the horizontal but on the vertical. This suprasensory, mystical Orient, the place of the Origin and of the Return, object of the eternal Quest, is at the heavenly pole; it is the Pole, at the extreme north, so far off that it is the threshold of the dimension "beyond." That is why it is only revealed to a definite mode of presence in the world, and can be revealed only through this mode of presence. There are other modes to which it will never be revealed. It is precisely this mode of presence that characterizes the mode of being of the Sufi, but also, through his person, the mode of being of the entire spiritual family to which Sufism—and especially Iranian Sufism—belongs. The *Orient* sought by the mystic, the Orient that cannot be located on our maps, is in the direction of the *north*, beyond the north. Only an ascensional progress can lead toward this cosmic north chosen as a point of orientation.[2]

A primary consequence already foreseen is, to be exact, a *dislocation* of the contrasts regulating the classifications of

Orient

1. A short reoccouring musical phrase represented w/ a given character situation or emotion in an opera (1st developed by Wagner)

2. A dominant theme or underlying pattern

exoteric geography and anthropology, which depend on outer appearances. Eastern men and Western men, Northern men and Southern men, will no longer be identified by the characteristics previously attributed to them; it will no longer be possible to locate them in relation to the usual coordinates. We are left wondering at what point the loss comes about in Western man of the individual dimension that is irreducible to classifications based on exoteric geographic direction alone. Then it may happen, just as we have learned to understand alchemy as signifying something quite different from a chapter in the history or prehistory of our sciences, that a geocentric cosmology will also be revealed to us in its true sense, having likewise no connection with the history of our sciences. Considering the perception of the world and the feeling of the universe on which it is based, it may be that geocentrism should be meditated upon and evaluated essentially after the manner of the construction of a *mandala*.

It is this *mandala* upon which we should meditate in order to find again the northern dimension with its symbolic power, capable of opening the threshold of the beyond. This is the North which was "lost" when, by a revolution of the human presence, a revolution of the mode of presence in the world, the Earth was "lost in the heavens." "To lose sight of the North" means no longer to be able to distinguish between heaven and hell, angel and devil, light and shadow, unconsciousness and transconsciousness. A presence lacking a vertical dimension is reduced to seeking the meaning of history by arbitrarily imposing the terms of reference, powerless to grasp forms in the upward direction, powerless to sense the motionless upward impulse of the pointed arch, but expert at superimposing absurd parallelepipeds. And so Western man remains baffled by Islamic spirituality, with its powerful call to recollection of the "pre-eternal covenant": and by the heavenly Assumption (*mi'rāj*) of the Prophet; he does not even suspect that his own obsession with the historical, his materialization of "events in Heaven," can be equally baffling to others. In the same way, the Sufi "Heavens of Light" will remain forever inaccessible to the most ambitious "astronautic" investigation, their very existence not even being suspected. "If those who lead you say, 'Lo! the Kingdom is in the sky!,' then the birds of heaven will be there before you . . . But the Kingdom is within you and also outside of you."[2a]

2. *The Symbols of the North*

And so, if we found ourselves writing the words *Ex Oriente lux* as an epigraph, we would be completely mistaken if we imagined we were saying the same thing as the Spiritual masters discussed in this work are saying, and if looking for the "Light of the Orient" we merely turned toward the geographical east. For, when we speak of the sun rising in the east, this refers to the light of the day as it succeeds the night. Day alternates with night, as two opposites alternate which by their very nature cannot coexist. Light rising in the east and light going down in the west are two premonitions of an existential option between the world of Day with its criteria and the world of Night with its deep and insatiable passions. At best, on the boundary between the two we have a twofold twilight: the *crepusculum vespertinum*, no longer day but not yet night; the *crepusculum matutinum*, no longer night but not yet day. This striking image, as we know, was used by Luther to define the being of man.

In our turn, let us pause to consider what a light can signify which is neither eastern nor western, the northern light: midnight sun, blaze of the aurora borealis. It is no longer a question of day succeeding night, nor night, day. Daylight breaks in the middle of the night and turns into day a night which is still there but which is a Night of light. *Et nox illuminatio mea in deliciis meis*. This already suggests the possibility of an innovation in philosophical anthropology: the need to situate and interpret in an entirely new way the opposition between East and West, Light and Darkness, in order finally to discover the full and unforeseen significance of the northern light, and consequently of Nordic man, the man who "is at the north," or who is going toward the north because he has come from the north.

But the north can only attain its full significance by a mode of perception which raises it to the power of a symbol, to being a symbolic direction, that is, to a "dimension beyond" which can be pointed to only by something that "symbolizes with" it. And so we are concerned with primordial Images preceding and regulating every sensory perception, and not with images constructed *a posteriori* on an empirical basis. For the *sense* of the given phenomenon depends on the primordial Image: the heavenly pole situated on the vertical of human existence, the cosmic north. And even in geographic latitudes where we should hardly think it possible for the phenomenon to occur, its archetypal Image exists. The "midnight sun" appears in many rituals of mystery religions, just as it suddenly bursts forth, in Sohravardī's work, in the midst of an ecstasy of which Hermes is the hero. Later Iranian Sufi masters refer to the Night of light, the dark Noontide, the black Light. And in the Manichean faith it is the flames of the aurora borealis that are visualized in the *Columna gloriae* as composed of all the particles of Light reascending from the *infernum* to the Earth of light, the *Terra lucida*, itself situated, like the paradise of Yima, in the north, that is, in the cosmic north.

Preceding all empirical data, the archetype-Images are the organs of meditation, of the active Imagination; they effect the transmutation of these data by giving them their *meaning*, and precisely in so doing make known the manner of being of a specific human presence and the fundamental *orientation* inherent in it. Taking its bearings by the heavenly pole as the threshold of the world beyond means that this presence then allows a world other than that of geographical, physical, astronomical space to open before it. Here "traveling the straight path" means straying neither to the east nor to the west; it means climbing the peak, that is, being drawn toward the *center*; it is the ascent out of cartographical dimensions, the discovery of the inner world which secretes its own light, which *is* the world of light; it is an innerness of light as opposed to the spatiality of the outer world which, by contrast, will appear as Darkness.

This innerness must in no way be confused with anything that our modern terms subjectivism or nominalism may be supposed to refer to; nor with anything imaginary in the sense of this word that has been contaminated for us by the idea of unreality. The inability to conceive of a concrete suprasensory reality results from giving too much importance to sensory reality; this view, generally speaking, leaves no alternative but to take the suprasensory universe as consisting of abstract con-

5

I. Orientation

cepts. On the contrary, the universe which in Sohravardī's neo-Zoroastrian Platonism is called the *mundus imaginalis* (*'ālam al-mithāl*) or the "heavenly Earth of Hūrqalyā" is a concrete spiritual universe. It is most certainly not a world of concepts, paradigms, and universals. Our authors never cease to repeat that the archetype of a species has nothing to do with the universals established in logic, but is the Angel of that species. Rational abstraction, at best, deals only with the "mortal remains" of an Angel; the world of archetype-Images, the autonomous world of visionary Figures and Forms, is on the plane of angelology. To see beings and things "in the northern light" is to see them "in the Earth of Hūrqalyā," that is, to see them in the light of the Angel; it is described as reaching the Emerald Rock, the heavenly pole, coming upon the world of the Angel. And this presupposes that the individual person as such, irrespective of anything collective, virtually has a transcendent dimension at his disposal. Its growth is concomitant with a visionary apperception, giving shape to the suprasensory perceptions and constituting that totality of ways of knowing that can be grouped under the term *hierognosis*. (Gk: hiero- sacred, holy)

As a corollary, the terms of reference presupposed by the mystical symbols of the north here suggest something like a psycho-spiritual realm of three dimensions, which the ordinary two-dimensional view cannot account for, since it is restricted to contrasting *consciousness* and *unconsciousness*. To put it more precisely, it has to do with two Darknesses: there is one Darkness which is only Darkness; it can intercept light, conceal it, and hold it captive. When the light escapes from it (according to the Manichean conception or the Ishrāq of Sohravardī), this Darkness is left to itself, falls back upon itself; it does not become light. But there is another Darkness, called by our mystics the Night of light, luminous Blackness, black Light.

Already in the mystical Recitals of Avicenna, an explicit distinction, dependent on the vertical orientation, is established between the "Darkness at the approaches to the Pole" (the divine Night of superbeing, of the unknowable, of the origin of origins) and the Darkness which is the extreme occident of Matter and of non-being, where the sun of pure Forms declines and disappears. The Orient in which the pure Forms rise, their *Orient-origin*, is the *pole*, the cosmic north. Here al-

6

§2. The Symbols of the North

ready the Avicennan recital explicitly shows us a twofold situation and meaning of the "midnight sun": on the one hand, it is
the first Intelligence, the archangel Logos, rising as a revelation over the Darkness of the *Deus absconditus*, and which, in
terms of the human soul, is the arising of *superconsciousness* on
the horizon of consciousness. On the other hand, it is the
human soul itself as the light of consciousness rising over the
Darkness of the subconscious.[3] We shall see how, in Najmoddīn
Kobrā's work, the colored photisms (in particular "luminous
black" and green light) proclaim and postulate an identical
psycho-cosmic structure. That is why *orientation* requires here a
threefold arrangement of planes: the day of *consciousness* is on a
plane intermediate between the luminous Night of *superconsciousness* and the dark Night of *unconsciousness*. The divine
Darkness, the Cloud of unknowing, the "Darkness at the approaches to the Pole," the "Night of symbols" through which
the soul makes its way, is definitely not the Darkness in which
the particles of light are held captive. The latter is the extreme
occident, and is Hell, the demonic realm. Orientation by the
Pole, the cosmic north, determines what is below and what is
above; to confuse one with the other would merely indicate
disorientation (cf. *infra* V, 1).

This orientation might well be what would enable us to val-
idate what Michel Guiomar so admirably foresaw. Our classical
oppositions expressed in the refusal of the hostile dawn or, on
the contrary, in the distress of twilight, of the "refused evening," might well turn out to be nothing other than pairs become unrecognizable, that is to say the divergence, in Mediter-
ranean and northern geographical areas, from one and the
same great original myth. This would imply an explosion of
this myth into two kinds of anguish, two refusals, two correlative kinds of powerlessness in the case of the man who has lost
his "polar dimension," that is to say of man no longer oriented
toward the heavenly pole and so faced with the dilemma of Day
succeeding Night, or of Night succeeding Day.

To speak of the polar dimension as the transcendent dimension of the earthly individuality is to point out that it includes a counterpart, a heavenly "partner", and that its total
structure is that of a bi-unity, a *unus-ambo*. This *unus-ambo* can
be taken as an alternation of the first and second person, as

7

I. Orientation

forming a dialogic unity thanks to the identity of their essence and yet without confusion of persons. This is why the polar dimension is heralded in the guise of a Figure whose recurrent manifestations correspond on each occasion to an absolutely personal experience of the spiritual seeker and to a realization of this bi-unity. So it is that in Iran in the twelfth century (sixth century of the hegira) this Figure reappears in contexts which differ but which in every case appertain to a metaphysics or a mystical experience of Light.

In northwestern Iran, Sohravardī (d. 1191) carried out the great project of reviving the wisdom or theosophy of ancient pre-Islamic Zoroastrian Iran; he set the seal on this achievement by dying as a martyr in Aleppo in the fullness of his youth, victim of the vindictiveness of the doctors of the Law. He called his theosophical system Ishrāq because he traced its source to an Orient and to the illumination of an Orient which is not the geographical east. Certainly the Sages of ancient Persia were above all others the representatives and guardians of this wisdom, but the fact that they are referred to as "Orientals" relates in the true sense to their orientation toward the Orient-origin of pure Light. Three centuries before the Byzantine philosopher Gemistus Pletho, Sohravardī's work made a link between Plato and Zarathustra, in a doctrine dominated by the name and wisdom of Hermes. And so the same figure which in Hermetism is that of the heavenly I, the *Alter Ego*, the eternal partner and companion, reappears in Sohravardī under the name of *Perfect Nature*.

A contemporary of Sohravardī in southwestern Iran, Rūzbehān of Shīrāz (d. 1209), the *imām* par excellence of the *"Fedeli d'amore"* in Iranian Sufism, declares in his *Diarium spirituale* that his decisive experience, his personal initiatic proof, was a series of visions referring to the heavenly Pole; it was by meditating on these that he finally understood how he was personally and secretly connected with the group of the masters of initiation symbolized by the stars stationed in the immediate vicinity of the Pole star.

Lastly, at the extreme east of the Iranian world, in Transoxiania, Najmoddīn Kobrā (d. 1220) guided the Sufism of Central Asia toward the practice of meditation with particular attention to the phenomena of light and *chromatic succession* that

will make clear to us the significance and pre-eminence of the
green Light. And in this context we meet again the homologue
of Perfect Nature, the Figure whom Najm Kobrā calls his
"Witness in Heaven," his "suprasensory personal Guide," "Sun
of the mystery," "Sun of the heart," "Sun of high knowledge,"
"Sun of the Spirit."

Concerning this Figure, Najmoddīn Kobrā teaches his disciple: "Thou art he"—and he illustrates his affirmation by adding the impassioned words of the lover to his beloved: "Thou
art myself (*anta anā*)." However, settling for the ordinary terms
"I" and "self" to describe the two "dimensions" of this *unus-
ambo* might well lead to a misunderstanding of the real situation. More often than not, Self designates an impersonal or
depersonalized absolute, a pure act of existing which obviously
could not act as second person, the second term of a dialogic
relationship. But the alternative, whether in experience or of
necessity, is not the supreme deity as described in dogmatic
definitions. *Deus est nomen relativum*: this essential and essentially individuated relationship is what is heralded in experience by the apparitional Figure we are attempting to recognize
here under different names. One cannot understand this relationship except in the light of the fundamental Sufi saying:
"He who knows *himself* knows *his Lord*." The identity of *himself*
and *Lord* does not correspond to a relationship of 1 = 1, but of
1×1: the identity of an essence raised to its total power by
being multiplied by itself and thus put in a condition to constitute a biunity, a dialogic whole whose members share alternately the roles of first and of second person. Or again the state
described by our mystics: when, at the climax, the lover has
become the very substance of love, he is then both the lover *and*
the beloved. But *himself* will not be *that* without the second person, without the *thou*, that is to say without the Figure who
makes him able to see himself, because it is through his very
own eyes that the Figure looks at him.

It would therefore be as wrong to reduce the two-
dimensionality of this dialogic unity to a solipsism as to divide it
into two essences, each of which could be *itself* without the
other. The seriousness of the misunderstanding would be as
great as the inability to distinguish between the Darkness or
demonic Shadow that holds the light captive, and the divine

I. Orientation

Cloud of unknowing which gives birth to the light. For the same reason, recourse to any collective schema can only be valid if the schema is taken as a descriptive process for indicating the potentialities that are repeated in every individual case, and above all the potentiality of the *I* which is not *itself* without its other "I", its *Alter Ego*. But such a schema by itself would never explain the real event: the intervention "in the present" of the "Perfect Nature," the manifestation of the "Heavenly Witness," the reaching of the *pole*. For the real event exactly implies a break with the collective, a reunion with the transcendent "dimension" which puts each individual person on guard against the attractions of the collective, that is to say against every impulse to make what is spiritual a social matter.

It is because of the absence of this dimension that the individual person lowers himself and succumbs to such falsifications. On the other hand, accompanied by the *shaykh al-ghayb*, his "suprasensory personal Guide," he is led and *directed* toward his own center, and ambiguities cease. Or rather, to suggest a more exact image, his "suprasensory Guide" and his individual person come to be situated in relation to one another as the two foci of the ellipse.

The divine and the satanic remain ambiguous so long as consciousness is unable to distinguish between what is its Day and what is its Night. There is an exoteric Daylight: so long as its conditions prevail, the "midnight sun" which is the initiatic light cannot show itself. This Day and this Night are unaware of one another and nevertheless are accomplices; the soul lives in this Daylight only because the Night is in itself. The ending of this ambiguity is the harbinger of the "midnight sun" with its horizons upon horizons: it may be the divine Night of superconsciousness irradiating the field of light of consciousness, and it may be the light of consciousness overcoming the Darkness of the subconscious, of the unconsciousness which was hemming it in. In both cases a burst of light rends the tissue of ready-made answers: the fictions of causal relationships, of linear evolutions, of continuous currents, everything that bolsters up what people have agreed to call the "sense of history." The sense of another history rising from Earth to Heaven is revealed: the history of an invisible spiritual mankind whose cycles of earthly pilgrimages refer to "events in Heaven," not to

10

the evolutionary fatality of successive generations. This is the secret history of those who survive the "deluges" that overwhelm and suffocate the spiritual senses, and who rise again one after another, time after time, into the universes toward which the same Invisible Forces guide them. This then is the *orientation* that has to be made clear: *where* is it leading, and *what* makes it such that the being who takes on the effort of this upward movement is, at the same time, the "being beyond" whose growing manifestation itself guarantees this progress? Hidden in this reciprocity, this act of correlation, is the whole secret of the invisible Guide, the heavenly Partner, the "Holy-Spirit" of the itinerant mystic (*sālik*), who, needless to repeat, is neither the shadow nor the "Double" as in some of our fantastic tales, but the Figure of light, the Image and the mirror in which the mystic contemplates—and without which he could not contemplate—the theophany (*tajallī*) *in the form corresponding to his being*.

These few remarks throw light on the way by which the present research must be pursued. The attempt must be made to establish the identity of this Figure under the various names that are given to its apparitions, for this very diversity supports us in the study of religious orientations which suggest the same type of individual initiation whose fruit is reunion with the Guide of light. The spiritual universe of Iran, before and after the advent of Islam, here becomes of the greatest importance. In its recurrent expressions (Zoroastrianism, Manicheism, Hermetism, and Sufism) this Figure points in one direction: to the light of the North as the threshold of the beyond, to the dwellings in the high North which are the inner abodes secreting their own Light. The mystic Orient, the Orient-origin is the *heavenly pole*, the point of orientation of the spiritual ascent, acting as a magnet to draw beings established in their eternal haecceity toward the palaces ablaze with immaterial matter. This is a region without any coordinates on our maps: the paradise of Yima, the Earth of light, *Terra lucida*, the heavenly Earth of *Hūrqalyā*. The ways of approach to it are pre-sensed in the splendor of a *visio smaragdina*, the outburst of green light characteristic, according to Najm Kobrā and his school, of a specific degree of visionary apperception. Its appearance may precede or succeed the "darkness at the approach to the pole,"

A visible appearance of God or A god to man

11

the crossing of which is the supreme ordeal of individual initiation; in other words the theme comes either as a prelude or as a sequel to the theme of the "black Light," as we shall hear it described below by two masters of Iranian Sufism. Since the theme is as fertile as it is exemplary, we shall only point out here some of the connections that open up before us. To go into them in detail would call for other lines of research.

The passing from the "black Light," from the "luminous Night: to the brilliance of the emerald vision will be a sign, according to Semnānī, of the completed growth of the subtle organism, the "resurrection body" hidden in the visible physical body. Exactly here the connection between the experience of colored photisms and the "physiology of the man of light" is unveiled: the seven subtle organs (*latīfa*), the seven centers typifying the Abodes of the seven great prophets in the man of light. The growth of the man of light thus recapitulates inwardly the whole cycle of Prophecy. The idea of this growth, which is the liberation of the man of light, can be read even in certain types of Iranian painting (from Manichean painting to the Persian miniature). Finally, the physiology of the man of light, whose growth is accompanied by colored photisms each having a precise mystical significance, is an integral part of a general doctrine of colors and of the very experience of color. We point this out briefly and at the end of this chapter because this is not the first time that a meeting takes place between the genius of Goethe and the Iranian genius.

*. . . For thou art with me . . . all the days
of my life.*

—Psalm 23 (22):4, 6

II. THE MAN OF LIGHT AND HIS GUIDE

1. The Hermetic Idea of Perfect Nature

Use of the word "syncretism" leads easily to abuse. It is used most often as a substitute for reasoned argument to avoid further consideration of some project nobly conceived to restore *in the present* doctrines generally accepted as belonging to a "bygone past." Yet nothing fluctuates more than the notion of "past"; it depends actually on a decision, or a pre-decision, which can always be *surpassed* by another decision which restores a future to that past. The whole history of gnosis throughout the centuries is rather like that. The restoration of an "oriental theosophy" (*hikmat al-Ishrāq*) by Sohravardī in the twelfth century was not exempt from such sweeping and undeserved judgment on the part of those who were able only to acquaint themselves rapidly and superficially with his work. Certainly, as with any other personal systematization, one finds elements in Sohravardī's system that are obviously identifiable—they belong to Hermetism, Zoroastrianism, Neoplatonism, the Sufism of Islam—but the organization of these materials into a new structure is directed by a central intuition, as original as it is consistent. This central intuition is made explicit in the form of a number of Figures, amongst which the role assumed by the Hermetic figure of the Perfect Nature (*al-tibā' al-tāmm*) is especially noteworthy. An essential

13

II. The Man of Light and His Guide

detail: the Arabic tradition of Hermetism is the only one that allows us to give this Figure its context. From it we learn that Perfect Nature is the heavenly *paredros*, the Sage's Guide of light. To understand its role and manifestation, it is necessary to picture to oneself the anthropology from which it is inseparable, an anthropology whose hero is the man of light, held captive by *Darkness* and struggling to free himself from Darkness. The entire ideology and experience centered on the manifestation of Perfect Nature thus presuppose the idea of the man of light and his living experience of the cosmic adventure. Only then can one understand how the couple comes to be joined in the *dialogic unity* of man of light and his Guide to which we find so many references in Arabic Hermetism down to the time of Sohravardī.

presupposition of the man of light

We can follow the presence of the idea of the "man of light" even further in the Sufism of Najm Kobrā, where the Arabic expressions *shakhs min nūr* and *shakhs nūrānī* are the equivalent of the Greek expression φωτεινός 'άνθρωπος. The Greek term figures in the Hermetic documents transmitted to us by Zosimos of Panopolis (third century), the famous alchemist whose teaching is based on the meditation of physical metallurgical operations as models or symbols of invisible processes, of spiritual transmutations.[4] This doctrine refers both to a Christian Gnosticism represented in this case by the "Books of the Hebrews," and to a Hermetic Platonism represented by the "Holy Books of Hermes." Common to both is an anthropology from which the following idea of the man of light emerges: there is the earthly *Adam*, the outer man of flesh (σάρ κινος 'άγθρωπος) subject to the Elements, to planetary influences, and to Fate; the four letters comprising his name "encipher" the four cardinal points of the earthly horizon.[5] And there is the man of light (φωτεῖνος 'άγθρωπος), the hidden spiritual man, the opposite pole to corporeal man: *phōs*. The homonyms φῶς, light, and φώς, man, thus bear witness in language itself to the existence of the man of light, the individual par excellence (the spiritual hero corresponding in this sense to the Persian *javānmard*). *Adam* is the archetype of carnal men; *Phōs* (whose own personal name was known only to the mysterious Nicotheos) is the archetype, not of humans in general, but of men of light, the φῶτες.

14

§1. *The Hermetic Idea of Perfect Nature*

Phōs, innocent and peaceful, pre-existed in paradise; the archons tricked him into clothing himself in the corporeal *Adam*. But the latter, explains Zosimos, was the man whom the Greeks called Epimetheus and who was advised by his brother Prometheus-*Phōs* not to accept the gifts of Zeus, namely, the bond which would enslave him to Fate, to the powers of this world. Prometheus is the man of light, oriented and orienting toward light because he follows his own guide of light. Those who have only physical hearing cannot hear him, for they are subject to the power of Fate, to the collective powers; only those who have spiritual hearing, that is, senses and organs of light, hear his summons and his advice. And this already, we notice, points to a physiology of the man of light and of his subtle organs.

As for more precise information about the Guide of Light, we gather it both from Zosimos and from the Gnostics to whom Zosimos himself referred. It is, in fact, the man of light who speaks through the mouth of Mary Magdalene when, in the course of the initiatic conversations between the Resurrected Christ and his disciples, she assumes the predominant role conferred on her in the book of the *Pistis Sophia*, the New Testament of the religion of the man of light: "The power which issued from the Savior and which is now the man of light within us. . . . My Lord! Not only does the man of light in me have ears but my soul has heard and understood all the words that thou hast spoken. . . . The man of light in me has guided me; he has rejoiced and bubbled up in me as if wishing to emerge from me and pass into thee."[6] Just as Zosimos places on the one hand Prometheus-*Phōs* opposite his guide of light who is the "son of God," and on the other the earthly *Adam* opposite his guide, the *Antimimos*, the "counterfeiter," so in the book of the *Pistis Sophia*: "It is I, declares the Resurrected One, who brought thee the power which is in thee and which issued from the twelve saviors of the Treasury of Light."

By the same inversion and reciprocity which in Sufism makes the "heavenly Witness" simultaneously the one Contemplated and the Contemplator, the man of light appears both as the one guided and the guide; this *communicatio idiomatum* forewarns us that the bi-unity, the dialogic unity, cannot be taken as the association of Phōs *and* carnal Adam,

15

(si z-ō-jē - conjunction, yoked together) the nearly straight-line configuration of 3 celestial bodies (as the Sun, moon & earth during a solar or lunar eclipse) in a gravitational system

II. The Man of Light and His Guide

who follows another guide. The Light cannot be compounded
with the demonic Darkness; the latter is Phōs's prison, from
which he struggles to separate himself and which will return to
its primordial negativity. The syzygy of light is Prometheus-
Phōs *and* his guide, the "son of God." This very fact also points
clearly to a structure, which has nevertheless been subject to all
kinds of misunderstandings. "The power which is in thee," in
each one of you, cannot refer to a collective guide, to a manifestation and a relationship collectively identical for *each one* of the
souls of light. Nor, *a fortiori*, can it be the macrocosm or universal Man (*Insān kollī*) which assumes the role of heavenly
counter-part of *each* microcosm. The infinite price attached to
spiritual individuality makes it inconceivable that salvation
could consist in its absorption into a totality, even a mystical
one. What is important is to see that it refers to an analogical
relationship presupposing *four* terms, and this essentially is just
what is so admirably expressed in the angelology of Valentinian
Gnosis: Christ's Angels are Christ himself, because each Angel
is Christ related to individual existence. What Christ is for the
souls of Light as a whole, each Angel is for each soul. Every
time one of these conjunctions of soul and Angel takes place,
the relationship which constitutes the pleroma of Light is reproduced.[7] The relationship is in fact so fundamental that it is
found again in Manicheism, and is also what, in Sohravardī's
"oriental theosophy," makes it possible for us to conceive the
relationship between the Perfect Nature of the mystic and the
archetypal Angel of humanity (identified with the Holy Ghost;
the Angel Gabriel of the Qorānic Revelation, the active Intelligence of the Avicennan philosophers). What this Figure represents in relation to the totality of the souls of light emanated
from itself, each Perfect Nature represents respectively for
each soul. The concept of this relationship is what we are
guided toward by the Hermetic texts in Arabic concerning Perfect Nature.

The most important of these texts known today is a work
attributed to Majrītī: the *Ghāyat al-Hakīm* (the "Goal of the
Sage"), composed no doubt in the eleventh century, but from
far more ancient material, since it informs us in detail about the
religion and ritual of the Sabeans of Harran.[8] There already
Perfect Nature is described as "the philosopher's Angel," his

pleroma - la Fullness, plenitude a in Gnostic Theosophy, the spiritual universe as the abode of God & of the totality of Divine powers & emanations
S. used in reference to Colossians ii, 9 where the Eng. versions from 1388 have 'fullness'.

16

initiator and tutor, and finally as the object and secret of all philosophy, the dominant figure in the Sage's personal religion. Again and again, the description sounds the fundamental note: his Perfect Nature can only reveal itself "in person" to one whose nature is perfect, that is, to the man of light; their relation is this *unus-ambo* in which each of the two simultaneously assumes the position of the *I* and the *self*—image and mirror: my image looks at me with my own look; I look at it with its own look.

> The first thing you have to do in relation to yourself,[9] is to meditate attentively on the spiritual entity (*rūhānīyato-ka*, "your angel") which rules you and which is associated with your star— namely your Perfect Nature—which the sage Hermes mentions in his book, saying: "When the microcosm which is man becomes perfect in nature, his soul is then the homologue of the sun stationed in Heaven, whose rays shed light on all horizons." Similarly, Perfect Nature rises in the soul; its rays strike and penetrate the faculties of the subtle organs of wisdom; they attract these faculties, cause them to rise in the soul, just as the rays of the sun attract the energies of the terrestrial world and cause them to rise in the atmosphere.

Thus it is suggested that between Perfect Nature and *its* soul, there will be a relationship—as formulated in the psalm composed by Sohravardī to his own Perfect Nature—such that the Bearer of the Child is simultaneously the Child who is Born, and vice versa.

> Wise Socrates declared that Perfect Nature is called the sun of the philosopher, the original *root* of his being and at the same time the *branch* springing from him. Hermes was asked: "How does one achieve knowledge of wisdom? How can one bring it down to this world below?" "Through Perfect Nature," he answered. "What is the root of wisdom?" "Perfect Nature." "What is the key to wisdom?" "Perfect Nature." "What then is perfect Nature?" he was asked. "It is the heavenly entity, the philospher's Angel, conjoined with his star, which rules him and opens the doors of wisdom for him, teaches him what is difficult, reveals to him what is right, in sleeping as in waking."[10]

We have just heard Hermes speak of the philosopher's Sun, and in Najm Kobrā, the homologue of Perfect Nature, the "Witness in Heaven," the suprasensory personal master, is described as the Sun of mystery, the Sun of the heart, and so forth; and in one of his ecstatic recitals, Sohravardī will tell us when and how this *sun* rises which is not the sun of the earthly east or west. Perfect Nature is so surely the ultimate secret that, as we read on, we are also told how it is the one part of mystical theosophy revealed by the Sages exclusively to their disciples and never mentioned, whether orally or in writing, outside their circle.

It follows that every account of the attainment of Perfect Nature represents an actual performance of the drama of initiation, whether enacted in the dream state or in the waking state. It is attained at the *center*, that is, in a place filled with Darkness which comes to be illuminated by a pure *inner Light*. One such account in the same work is Hermes' recital, where it is said:

> When I wished to bring to light the science of the mystery and modality of Creation, I came upon a subterranean vault filled with darkness and winds. I saw nothing because of the darkness, nor could I keep alight because of the violence of the winds. Lo and behold, a person then appeared to me in my sleep in a form of the greatest beauty.[11] He said to me: "Take a lamp and place it under a glass to shield it from the winds; then it will give thee light in spite of them. Then go into the underground chamber; dig in its *center* and from there bring forth a certain God-made image, designed according to the rules of Art. As soon as you have drawn out this image, the winds will cease to blow through the underground chamber. Then dig in its four corners and you will bring to light the knowledge of the mysteries of Creation, the causes of Nature, the origins and modalities of things." At that I said, "Who then art thou?" He answered: "I am thy *Perfect Nature*. If thou wishest to see me, call me by my name."[12]

The same account also appears, word for word, in a text attributed to Appollonius of Tyana (Bālīnās in Arabic). Here the ordeal of personal initiation consists of the efforts of the man of light, *Phōs*, before whom the Darkness of the primordial secret is transformed into a Night of light. It is in this effort toward the center, the *pole*, and "the Darkness at the approach to the pole," that the Guide of light, Perfect Nature, suddenly shows itself to him and tells him what to do to bring light into this Night: to dig for the Image which is the primordial revelation of the *Absconditum*. Having put his lamp under a glass,[13] as prescribed by Perfect Nature, the initiate enters the subterranean chamber; he sees a Shaykh, who is Hermes and who is *his own image*, sitting on a throne and holding an *emerald tablet* which bears an inscription in Arabic, the Latin equivalent of which is: *hoc est secretum mundi et scientia Artis naturae*.[14] The identification of the man of light and his Guide of light is established by making *Phōs* into the light-bearer, φωσφόρος, for it is both to him and through him that Perfect Nature, his guide, reveals that it is in itself the secret: the secret of the light of the inaccessible divine Night.

Thenceforth they are so intimately united that one and the same role is played in turn, even simultaneously, by Hermes and his Perfect Nature. This is what is suggested in Sohravardī's writings where Perfect Nature is described, particularly in the passionately lyrical psalm referred to above and in the "Sabean" liturgies conveying knowledge of the same characteristic situation. Hermes is the prophet of Perfect Nature; by initiating him to wisdom, his Perfect Nature taught him how to worship itself, taught him the form of prayer by which to call for it and cause it to appear (a Hermetic *dhikr*); this personal worship is what Hermes transmitted to the Sages, instructing them to perform among themselves, at least twice a year, this personal liturgy of their Perfect Nature. Thus we find a Sabean liturgy addressed to Hermes himself, invoking him in turn in the very same words in which he had been taught by his Perfect Nature to address it.[15] Here we have an experiential testimony, far better than a theory, provided by the performance of a prayer, of the relationship suggested by Sohravardī's own psalm, where he addresses Perfect Nature simultaneously as the one who gives birth and the one who is born. The same relationship, as we shall see, is implicit in the specifically Sufi notion of the *shāhid*, the witness-of-contemplation: the Sufi contemplates *himself* in contemplating the theophanic witness; the Contemplator becomes the Contemplated and vice versa, a mystical situation expressed by the wonderful Eckhartian formula: "The seeing through which I know him is the same seeing through which he knows me."

A particularly full and original development of the theme of Perfect Nature is found in a philosopher who lived a little before Sohravardī, namely Abū'l-Barakāt Baghdādī, a subtle and very individual thinker of Jewish origin, converted late in life to Islam, who died about 560/1165 at the age of ninety. Since we have dealt with him at greater length elsewhere,[16] we

II. The Man of Light and His Guide

shall only recall here how the theme of Perfect Nature seeps into his work in regard to the problem, inherited from Avicenna and the Avicennans, of the Active Intelligence. When the Active Intelligence of the Avicennans is taken to be the same as the Holy Spirit, and the latter the same, in the Qorānic Revelation, as the Angel Gabriel—in other words, the Angel of Knowledge as being the same as the Angel of Revelation—far from leading to a rationalization of the Spirit, it raises again, on the contrary, the whole problem of noetics in terms of angelology. Thereupon a further question arises: why should there be only one Active Intelligence? To answer this question calls for a decision as to whether all human souls are identical in species and essence, whether each soul differs from another in kind, or again whether they are not perhaps grouped essentially in spiritual families composing many different species.

> This is why the ancient Sages . . . initiated into things the sensory faculties do not perceive, maintained that for each individual soul, or perhaps for several together having the same nature and affinity, there is a being in the spiritual world which throughout their existence watches over this soul and group of souls with especial solicitude and tenderness, leads them to knowledge, protects, guides, defends, comforts them, leads them to victory; and this being is what they called *Perfect Nature*. This friend, defender and protector is what in religious terminology is called the *Angel*.

Although here the aspect of intimate union is not so explicitly stressed, the theme nevertheless faithfully echoes the Hermetic teachings; it defines the situation which will result, according to Sohravardī, from the relationship to be established between the Holy Spirit, the Angel of Humanity, and the Perfect Nature of each man of light. Whether it is referred to as the divine Being or as the archetype-Angel, no sooner does its apparition reveal the transcendent dimension of spiritual individuality as such, than it must take on individualized features and establish an individuated relationship. From that very fact, a direct relationship is established between the divine world and this spiritual individuality, independently of the mediation of any earthly collectivity. "Some souls learn nothing except from human masters; others have learned everything from invisible guides known only to themselves."

In Sohravardī's vast body of writings, there are three pas-

§1. The Hermetic Idea of Perfect Nature

sages in particular that throw light on the theme of Perfect Nature, not theoretically, but as a figure in a visionary experience or as one who speaks in answer to a prayer. The most explicit is in the *Book of Conversations*,[17] where Sohravardī undoubtedly alludes to the Hermetic text quoted a few pages back: a luminous form appears to Hermes; it projects or breathes into him the knowledge of gnosis. To Hermes' question, "Who then are you?" it answers, "I am your *Perfect Nature*." And in another passage[18] we find the invocation addressed by Hermes to his Perfect Nature amidst the perils that come to try him in the course of a dramaturgy of ecstasy, an allusive dramatization of an initiatic ordeal experienced in a secret personal world (wherein Hermes may then perhaps be a pseudonym for Sohravardī). Now the *hour* as well as the *place* of this visionary episode evoke the symbols of the North to indicate the passage to a world beyond the sensory world. This episode is the most striking illustration of the theme we are analyzing here: Perfect Nature, the guide of light of the spiritual individuality, "opens" its transcendent dimension by making possible the crossing of the threshold . . . (see also *infra* III). The "person" to whom the appeal is addressed in this initiatic ecstasy is the same Perfect Nature addressed in the psalm composed by Sohravardī, which is perhaps the most beautiful prayer ever directed to the *Angel*. In this sense it is a personal liturgy, conforming to the instructions which, say the "Sabeans," were a legacy from Hermes to the Sages:[19]

> Thou, my lord and prince, my most holy angel, my precious spiritual being, Thou art the Spirit who gave birth to me, and Thou art the Child to whom my spirit gives birth . . . Thou who art clothed in the most brilliant of divine Lights . . . may Thou manifest Thyself to me in the most beautiful (or in the highest) of epiphanies, show me the light of Thy dazzling face, be for me the mediator . . . lift the veils of darkness from my heart . . .

This conjunction is what the spiritual seeker experiences when he reaches the *center*, the *pole*; the same relationship is found again in Jalāloddīn Rūmī's mysticism and in the whole Sohravardian tradition in Iran, as we learn from the testimony of Mīr Dāmād, the great master of theology at Ispahan in the seventeenth century. It is a relationship in which the mystical soul, as Maryam, as Fātima, becomes the "mother of her

21

II. The Man of Light and His Guide

father," *omm abī-hā*. And this again is the meaning of the verse in Ibn 'Arabī: "I created perception in Thee only that therein I might become the object of my perception."[20]

This relationship, inexpressible except in paradoxical terms, is the one toward which the same fundamental experience consistently tends, notwithstanding the diversity of its forms. Again, Sohravardī dramatizes the search for this experience and its attainment in a complete short work: a visionary recital, a spiritual autobiography entitled *Recital of the Occidental Exile*. This recital is related not only to the texts of the Hermetic tradition, but also to a text eminently representative both of gnosis and of Manichean piety, the famous *Song of the Pearl* in the book of the *Acts of Thomas*. Although it is true that such a book could not but be relegated by official Christianity to the shadowy realm of Apocrypha, it can nevertheless be said to express the *leitmotiv* of all Iranian spirituality still alive in Sufism.[21] Some may see in the *Song of the Pearl* a prefiguration of Parsifal's quest; Mount Salvat, emerging from the waters of Lake Hāmūn (on the present-day frontier of Iran and Afghanistan) has been likened to the "Mountain of the Lord" (*Kūh-e Khwājeh*), where the Fravartis watch over the Zarathustran seed of the Savior, the *Saoshyant* to come; as the *Mons victorialis*, it was the point from which the Magi began their journey, bringing Iranian prophetology back to the Christian Revelation; it connects at last the memory of King Gondophares and of the preaching of the Apostle Thomas. What is certain is that on the one hand Sohravardī's *Recital of the Exile* begins where Avicenna's *Hayy ibn Yaqzān* ended, and that on the other hand the *Recital of the Exile* is so closely parallel to the *Song of the Pearl* that everything takes place as though Sohravardī himself had just been reading the story of the young Iranian prince sent by his parents from the Orient to Egypt to win the Pearl without price.

The young prince sheds the robe of light which his parents had lovingly woven for him; he arrives in the land of exile; he is the *Stranger*; he tries to go unnoticed yet he is recognized: they feed him the food of forgetfulness. And next comes the message carried by an eagle, signed by his father and by his mother, the queen of the Orient, and by all the nobles of

Parthia. Thereupon the prince remembers his origin and the Pearl for which he had been sent on his mission to Egypt. And then comes the "departure from Egypt," the exodus, the great Return to the Orient. His parents send two emissaries to meet him and bring him the robe he had left behind when he departed. He does not remember what it was like, having been a small child when he took it off:

> And behold, I saw it altogether in me and I was altogether in it, for we were *two*, separated from one another but nevertheless *only one*, of similar form . . . I saw also that all the movements of gnosis were taking place in it and I saw further that it was about to speak . . . I saw that my stature had grown to fit the way it was made and in its regal movements it spread over me.[22]

Without doubt the author thus expressed in the most direct way and with a happy simplicity the bi-unity of Perfect Nature (here represented by the robe of light) and of the man of light guided by it out of exile, a bi-unity which is in fact inexpressible in the categories of human language.

All these themes recur in Sohravardī's *Recital of the Occidental Exile*.[23] Here also the child of the Orient is sent into exile in the West, symbolized by the city of Qayrawān, which is the same as the city mentioned in the Qorān as the "city of the oppressors." Recognized by the oppressors' people, he is put in chains and thrown into a well from which he can only emerge at night for fleeting moments. He also experiences increasing powerlessness due to fatigue, forgetfulness, and disgust. Then comes his family's message from afar, carried by a hoopoe, inviting him to set out without delay. Thereupon, in the blazing light that awakens him, he departs in search of that Orient which is not the east on our maps but which lies in the cosmic north (just as the Iranian Sages, the guardians of the "oriental theosophy," derive their epithet "Oriental" from an Orient other than geographic east). To return to the East is to climb the Mountain Qāf, the cosmic (or psycho-cosmic) mountain, the mountain of the emerald cities, all the way up to the heavenly pole, the mystical Sinai, the Emerald Rock. Sohravardī's major works make this topology clearer to us (see *infra* III): this Orient is the mystical Earth of Hūrqalyā, *Terra lucida*, situated at the heavenly north. This is the very place where the meeting occurs between the pilgrim and the one who gave birth to him (and to whom the psalm quoted above is addressed), his Perfect Nature, the personal Angel, who reveals to him the mystical hierarchy of all those who go before him in the suprasensory heights and at the same time, pointing to the one immediately before himself, declares: "He contains me just as I contain you."

The situation is similar: in both recitals the exile, the stranger, faces up to the powers of oppression which try to force him to forget and to conform to the demands of their collective mastery. The exile was at first a heretic; but when the criteria are secularized and become social criteria, he is no more than a madman, a misfit. From then on his situation is curable and the diagnosis is not hindered by such distinctions. And yet mystical consciousness has available a criterion of its own which makes it irreducible to these delusive assimilations: the prince of the Orient in the *Song of the Pearl* and the *Recital of the Exile knows* where he is and what has happened to him; he has even tried to "adapt," to disguise himself, but he has been recognized; he has been forced to swallow the food of forgetfulness; he has been chained in a well; in spite of all that, he will understand the *message* and knows that the light which guides him (the lamp in Hermes' underground chamber) is not the exoteric *day*light of the "city of the oppressors."

One further example will be given here to support the fact that this is the *leitmotiv* of Iranian spirituality (the image of the *well* appears again constantly in Najm Kobrā). We have just referred to the parallel between the *Acts of Thomas* and Sohravardī's *Recital*. This same parallelism reappears elsewhere. A compilation which in its present form cannot have been made earlier than the seventh/thirteenth century, and which is presented as an Arabic elaboration of a Sanskrit text, the *Amrtakunda*, includes a short spiritual romance which in fact is none other than the text of a recital elsewhere wrongly attributed to Avicenna, entitled *Risālat al-Mabdā wa'l-Ma'ād*, "The Epistle of the Origin and the Return,"[24] a title borne by many philosophical works in Arabic and Persian and which from a gnostic point of view, can also be translated "Genesis and Exodus," that is, the descent to the earthly world, into occidental exile, and the *departure* from Egypt, the return *home*.

Here the stranger is sent on a mission by the lord of his country of origin (the Orient) and before his departure receives instructions from his lord's wise minister. The place of exile is the city where the people of the outer and inner senses and of the physiological energies appear to him as a crowd of active and agitated people. At last, in the heart of the city, he finds himself one day before the throne of the shaykh who rules the country. He comes near and speaks to him; the same gestures and words respond to his own gestures and words. He realizes that the shaykh is himself (see above, the initiate recognizing his own image in the image of Hermes). Then suddenly the promise made before his departure into exile is remembered. In his bewilderment, he encounters the minister who had given him his instructions and who now takes him by the hand: "Plunge into this water for it is the Water of Life!" On emerging from the mystical bath he has understood all symbols, deciphered all codes and finds himself once more before his prince. "Be welcome!" says the prince, "Henceforth you are one of us." And having cut in two the thread spun by a spider, the prince puts it together again, saying: 1 x 1.

This is also the *formula* that we suggested above, because he who deciphers it holds the key to the secret that preserves him both from pseudomystical monism (whose formula is $1 = 1$) and from abstract monotheism which is content to superimpose an *Ens supremum* on the multitude of beings ($n + 1$). It is the cipher of the union of Perfect Nature and the man of light, which the *Song of the Pearl* so excellently typifies: "We were *two*, separated from one another, and yet *only one*, of similar form."[25] Even without having to consider Avicenna as the author of this spiritual romance, it nonetheless confirms the meaning of his *Recital of Hayy ibn Yaqzān*. Although it has been so weakly interpreted as to make it impossible to discern in this Recital anything beyond an inoffensive philosophical allegory on the interpreter's level, it nevertheless has a deeper sense which shines through page after page, because, as in the other Recitals of the Avicennan trilogy, Hayy ibn Yaqzān points a finger to the same *Orient* to which Sohravardī's recitals redirect us.

II. The Man of Light and His Guide

2. *The Noūs of Hermes and the Shepherd of Hermas*

The archetypal Figure exemplified by the apparition of Perfect Nature assumes therefore in respect to the man of light, *Phōs*, throughout the entire ordeal of his exile, a role best defined by the word ποίμην, the "shepherd," the watcher, the guide. This is precisely a word which calls to mind both the prologue of the most famous of the Hermetic texts and that of a Christian text which is perhaps its echo. In each case the sequence of episodes is the same: first the visionary's meditation, his withdrawal to the *center* of himself, the moment of dream or ecstasy intermediate between waking and sleep; then the apparition and the interrogation; then the recognition. In the same way the *Noūs* appears before Hermes while "his bodily senses were held in bondage" during a deep sleep. It seems to him that a being of enormous size approaches, calls him by name and asks:

> "What dost thou wish to hear and see, and to learn and know through thought?" " But thou, who art thou?" "I am *Poimander*, the *Noūs* with absolute sovereignty. I know what thou wishest and I am with thee everywhere . . ." Suddenly everything opened before me in an instant, and I saw a boundless vision, everything having become serene and joyous light, and having seen this light, behold I was filled with love for it.[26]

Referring to the Coptic term from which the name Poimander is derived, it can be understood as the heavenly *Noūs*, as the shepherd or as the witness, but it is surely the same vision witnessed by those of the Iranian Spirituals who speak sometimes of Perfect Nature, as in Sohravardī's Hermes, sometimes of the witness in Heaven, of the suprasensory personal Guide, as in the works of Najm Kobrā and his school.

At one time the *Canon* of Christian Scriptures included a charming little book, the *Shepherd of Hermas*, especially rich in symbolic visions; today this little book, exiled like *Phōs* in person, finds a place only in the *Canon* of ideas of personal religion where it appropriately belongs beside the *Acts of Thomas*. Hermas is at home, seated on his bed in a state of deep meditation. Suddenly a strange-looking personage enters, sits down at his side and announces: I have been sent by the Most Holy Angel to live beside thee all the days of thy life." Hermas thinks that the apparition is trying to tempt him:

§2. The Noūs of Hermes and the Shepherd of Hermas

"Who art thou then? For I know to whom I have been entrusted." Then he said to me: "Dost thou not recognize me?" "No." "I am the Shepherd to whose care thou hast been entrusted." And while he spoke, *his aspect changed*, and behold I recognized *the one to whom I had been entrusted*.[27]

Whether or not one is willing to see in the prologue of Hermas a Christian replica to the Hermetic Poimander, the fact remains that Christology was not originally quite what it later became. It is not at all by chance that in the little book of Hermas the expressions "Son of God," "Archangel Michael," "Most Holy Angel," and "Magnificent Angel" are interchangeable. The vision of Hermas goes back to the conceptions dominated by the figure of *Christos-Angelos*, and the situation thus defined offers the following analogy of relationships: the shepherd of Hermas is related to the Magnificent Angel as, in Sohravardī, the Perfect Nature of Hermes is related to the Angel Gabriel, the Angel of Humanity, the Holy Spirit.

The theme of *Christos-Angelos* is also the theme of Christus-*pastor*, so well illustrated in primitive Christian art, where Christ is represented by the figure of *Hermes Creophoros* (with a lamb on his shoulders, his head haloed by the seven planets, the sun and the moon at his sides), or as Attis, with a shepherd's staff and a flute, viewed both in meditation and mystical experience (Psalm 23 and John 10:11-16) as a true *daïmōn paredros*, a personal protector, everywhere accompanying and leading the one in his care, as Poimander says: "I am with thee everywhere."[28] Hermas' exclamation on recognizing "the one to whom he has been entrusted" seems to allude to a spiritual pact concluded at the time of an initiation. Then also we are reminded of the specifically Manichean expression of the twofold theme: of Christ as the "Heavenly Twin" of Mani and of the "form of light" which each of the Elect receives on the day when he renounces the powers of this world. The conjunction of these two themes introduces us to the heart of the pre-Islamic Iranian representations; their later recurrences are evidence of the persistence of the archetype whose exemplifications always reproduce the same situation: the conjoining of guide of light with man of light effected in terms of *orientation* toward a primordial Orient which is not simply the geographic east.

27

II. The Man of Light and His Guide

3. *Fravarti and Walkyrie*

The Zoroastrian religion of ancient Iran offers us the homologue or rather the perfect, classic exemplification of what the Hermetic figure of *Perfect Nature* or of the *shepherd* heralds and represents. However, in analyzing it, one must beware of the difficulties of a twofold task. In the first place Perfect Nature as guide and heavenly partner of the man of light has heretofore appeared to us as essentially immune to any contamination by the Darkness. Is there not however a joint responsibility? As soon as it is clearly stated, a second question follows: what if the man of light fails to maintain his effort and falls victim to the Darkness, what if *Phōs* is finally captured and overcome by the earthly, carnal Adam? This question finds an answer first in the sequence of events in Zoroastrian individual eschatology and again in the interpretation of the colored photisms by Najm Kobrā and his school, according to whether the colors unveil or on the contrary conceal the suprasensory personal Guide. To guard against any possible misunderstanding, let us say immediately that what these answers show is that the act of seeing changes according to whether it is the act of the man of light, *Phōs*, or on the contrary the act of the carnal and maleficent Adam who, by projecting his own shadow on the heavenly Figure and by interposing thus this shadow, is himself the one that makes this Figure invisible to himself, that dis-figures it. It is within man's power to betray the pact, to cast a darkened look on the whiteness of the world of light, thereby hiding it from his own gaze, but this is the limit of his power, and this holds true in the case of the *shāhid* in Sufism as well as of the eschatological figure of *Daēnā* in Zoroastrianism.

In the second place, we shall have to define the relationship between two figures that are of equal value as archetypes, those which are designated respectively as *Fravarti* and *Daēnā*. We cannot go deeply into this theme here, but must confine ourselves to indicate how the problem arises and how certain texts allow us to foresee a solution in accordance with the schema verified up to now.

The *Fravartis*[29] are, in Mazdean cosmogony, feminine entities, heavenly archetypes of all the beings composing the Creation of light. Each being having passed from the heavenly or

28

subtle (*mēnōk*) state to the material and visible state (*gētīk*, a material state which in the Mazdean conception implies by itself
neither evil nor darkness, the latter being proper to the
Ahrimanian counter-powers, which are themselves a spiritual
order)—each being has his *fravarti* in the heavenly world which
assumes the role of his guardian angel. What is more, all the
Celestial beings, gods, angels and archangels, even Ohrmazd
himself, have their respective *fravarti*. Syzygies of light, "light
upon light." Ohrmazd reveals to his prophet Zarathustra that
without the concurrence and assistance of the Fravartis he
would not have been able to protect his Creation of light
against the assault of the counter-creation of Ahriman. Now,
the very idea of this warfare is dramatically unfolded when we
come to the Fravartis of human beings. In the prelude to the
millenniums of the period of *mixture*, Ohrmazd offered them
the choice from which their entire destiny originates: they
could either live in the celestial world sheltered from the rav-
ages of Ahriman, or else descend to earth there to be incarnated in material bodies and struggle against the counter-
powers of Ahriman in the material world.[30] Their answer to
this proposal was the *yes* which gives their name its full meaning, most significantly for our purpose: *those who have chosen*. In
practice the *fravarti* incarnated in the terrestrial world finally
became identified in religious representations purely and simply with the soul.

But then the question inevitably arises: how to conceive of
the bi-dimensional structure characteristic of the beings of
light, if the Fravartis "in person," the heavenly archetypes, by
descending to earth, are identified with the earthly "dimension"? In other words, if, in the case of humans, the archetype
or angel, on leaving the high ramparts of heaven, is the terrestrial person himself, does he not in his turn need some guardian angel, a celestial reduplication of his being? It seems that
Mazdean philosophy has in fact entertained this question. One
solution might be in some way to conceive of the earthly union
of Fravarti and soul as one in which the former remains immune from all Ahrimanian contamination.[31] However, when
we consider the fundamental situation that is the basis for the
entire meaning of human life as it is experienced once the
Fravarti and the soul are actually identified, the question is

Eschatology. that part of Theology
which deals w/ death

much too complex for a solution to be found in a mere philological inventory of existing texts.

A philosophical approach is itself called for by the eschatological· intervention of *Daēnā* (an Avestan name, whose form in middle Iranian or Pehlevi is *Dēn*). Etymologically she represents the visionary organ of the soul; ontologically, the light that makes seeing possible and the light which is seen. She *is* the pre-terrestrial vision of the celestial world and is thus *religion* and *faith* avowed, the very faith which was "chosen" by the Fravarti; she is also the essential individuality, the "celestial" transcendent "I," the Figure which, at the dawn of its eternity, sets the believer face to face with the soul of his soul, because *realization* unfailingly corresponds to *faith*. All the other interpretations of the personage of Daēnā culminate in this and thereafter cease to conflict with each other. Accordingly, there is the posthumous episode at the entrance to the Chinvat Bridge, the apparition of the "heavenly maiden," a primordial Figure, who is at the same time witness, judge, and retribution: "Then who art thou, whose beauty outshines all other beauty ever contemplated in the terrestrial world?" "I am thine own *Daēnā*. I was loved, thou hast made me more loved still. I was beautiful, thou hast made me still more beautiful," and embracing her devotee, she leads him into the Abode-of-Hymns (*Garotman*). This *post mortem* dialogue again reminds us of the reciprocity of the Giving-Birth/Being-Born relationship analyzed above. In contrast, he who has betrayed the pact concluded prior to existence in this world sees himself in the presence of an atrocious figure, his own negativity, a caricature of his celestial humanity which he has himself mutilated, exterminated: a human abortion cut off from its *fravarti*, which is to say a man without a *Daēnā*. The *Daēnā* remains what she *is* in the world of Ohrmazd; what the man sees who has cut himself off from her, who has made her invisible to himself, is fittingly his own *shadow*, his own Ahrimanian darkness, instead of his celestial mirror of light. This is the dramatic meaning of Mazdean anthropology.

A Mazdean text giving the best solution of the complex situation regarding the physiology of the man of light suggests to us a trilogy of the soul, that is, of the spiritual or subtle organism of man (his *menōkih*), independent of his material physi-

cal organism.[32] Firstly is the "Soul on the way" (*ruvān-i rās*), that
is, the one that is met on the *way* to the Chinvat Bridge, which,
eschatologically and esctatically, is the threshold of the beyond,
linking the *center* of the world with the cosmic or psycho-cosmic
mountain. There can be no doubt, therefore, that this indeed
refers to *Daēnā* guiding the soul in the ascent leading to the
northernmost of heights, the "Abode-of-Hymns," the region of
the infinite Lights.[33] And then there is the soul referred to in
the text as "the soul outside of the body" (*ruvān-i bērōn tan*), and
finally the soul which is "the soul in the body" (*ruvān-i tan*).
These latter two descriptions correspond to two aspects of the
same soul, that is of the Fravarti incarnated in a terrestrial organism, ruling the latter like an army commander (the *Espahbad* of the *Ishrāqīyūn,* the *hegemonikon* of the Stoics), and
sometimes escaping from the body in dream or in ecstatic anticipation to meet, during this fleeting exodus, the "Soul on the
way," that is, the *Daēnā* who guides it, inspires it, and comforts
it.

The totality represented by their bi-unity is therefore "light
upon light"; it can never be a composite of Ohrmazdian light
and Ahrimanian darkness, or in psychological terms, of consciousness and its *shadow*. It can be said that the Fravarti identified with the terrestrial soul is related to the angel *Daēnā* in
the same way as Hermes is related to Perfect Nature, Phōs to
his guide of light, Hermas to his "shepherd," the exiled prince
to the Robe of light. There is additional confirmation in that
the Iranian theme is highly reminiscent of Tobias and the
Angel. The theme is inexhaustibly fruitful, for it expresses a
fundamental human experience; wherever it is experienced
the same symptom reappears, telling of the feeling of individual transcendence prevailing against all the coercion and
collectivization of the person. Therefore it has homologues
both in the religious universes related to that of the ancient
Iranian religion, and in those of its successors, reactivating and
transvaluating the fundamental concepts.

In Mazdean terms, Daēnā-Fravarti, as the pre-existential
fate of man, represents and is the holder of his *xvarnah*; in
order to convey very briefly the full significance of this specifically Mazdean notion, it is best to recall the twofold Greek
equivalent which it was given: light of *glory* (δόξα) and *fate*

($\tau \acute{\upsilon} \chi \eta$). Now here precisely we have a representation that brings the Iranian and the Nordic theogony into accord. In both there are similar visions of celestial feminine entities bearing and keeping the power and destiny of a man: *Fravartis* and *Walkyries*. Perhaps these figures will finally give the lie to the austere critics who consider that to associate feminine features with the Angel makes the latter "effeminate." Such criticism in fact presupposes complete incapacity to conceive of the power in question; having lost the meaning of the Angel, man without a *fravarti* (which may be the state of mankind throughout an entire epoch) can no longer imagine anything but a caricature of this figure. In any case the theme of comparative research consociating Fravartis and Walkyries, would reveal all its potentialities only on condition of searching, even of calling, for its reflowering in the course of time. We recall here a conversation with the late Gerhard van der Leeuw, who himself, as a good phenomenologist, could do justice to Richard Wagner on this point. As he pointed out, and as we wholly agreed, though Wagner treated the ancient Sagas in a very personal manner, he at least had a penetrating and subtle comprehension of the ancient Germanic beliefs. In the figure of Brünnhilde he created a beautiful and moving figure of an Angel, "Wotan's thought," a soul sent forth by God; vis-à-vis the hero she is certainly the authentic *Fylgja*, holding his power and fate in her hand, her apparition always signifying the imminence of the beyond: "Who sees me bids farewell to the daylight of this life. Thous hast seen the fiery gaze of the Walkyrie; now thou must depart with her."[34] In the same way the Iranian ecstatic meets Daēnā only on the road to the Chinvat Bridge, on the threshold of the beyond; Hermes meets his Perfect Nature only in a moment leading up to the supreme ecstasy.

Any rationalist interpretation would go astray here in reducing this Figure to an allegory, on the grounds that it "personifies" the act and action of man. By no means is it an allegorical construct, but a primordial Image thanks to which the seeker perceives a world of realities which is neither the world of the senses nor the world of abstract concepts. This power from the depths necessarily recurs not only, as we have seen, in the "oriental theosophy" of Sohravardī, but even in the works of certain commentators on the Qorān (in Tabarī's great *Tafsīr* on *sūra* 10:9 there is to be found word for word the Avestan episode of the *post mortem* meeting with Daēnā), and more systematically still in Ismaelian Shī'ite gnosis. Ismaelian anthropology represents the earthly human condition as a boundary state between two things: potential angel or potential demon. At the climactic point, Ismaelian anthropology spontaneously links up again with the Zoroastrian representations. And indeed, it is the classical Mazdean trilogy that Nasīroddīn Tūsī reproduces in speaking of what becomes of the faithful adept after death: "His *thought* becomes an *Angel* proceeding from the archetypal world, his *speech* becomes a *spirit* proceeding from this Angel, his *action* becomes a *body* proceeding from this spirit." Once again in the same way, the vision of Daēnā at the Chinvat Bridge can be recognized feature for feature, this time in "the Angel in loveable and beautiful form who becomes the companion of the soul for all eternity.[35] And thus the gnosis of Islamic Iran[36] only serves to reactivate the features of a Figure who is likewise the pre-eminent figure in Mandeism and in Manicheism.

4. The Heavenly Twin (Mandeism and Manicheism)

In Mandean gnosis, every being in the physical universe has its counterpart in the heavenly Earth of Mshunia Kushta, inhabited by the descendants of a mystical Adam and Eve (*Adam kasia, Eva kasia*). Every being has his archetypal Figure (*mabda'* = *dmutha*) there, and the latter sometimes communicates with its earthly counterpart (as for example in the episode of the girl awakened and warned by "her sister in *Mshunia Kushta*"). After the *exitus* at death, the earthly person abandons his body and takes on the subtle body of his heavenly *Alter Ego*, while the latter, rising to a higher plane, assumes a body of pure light. When the human soul has completed its cycle of purifications and when the scales of Abathur Muzania bear witness to its perfect purity, it enters the world of Light and is reunited with its eternal Partner: "I go towards my likeness/And my likeness goes toward me;/He embraces me and holds me close/As if I had come out of prison."[37]

Similarly, the heavenly Partner (*qarīn*) or Twin (*taw'am*) is the dominant figure in the prophetology and soteriology of

Soteriology = spiritual salvation, esp. that 33
believed in xion theology to have been
accomplished thru Jesus

II. The Man of Light and His Guide

Manicheism. It is the angel who appears to Mānī when he is twenty-four years old and announces that it is time for him to manifest himself and bid men hear his doctrine.[38] "Greetings to you, Mānī, from myself and from the lord who sent me to you." The last words of the dying Mānī alluded to this:"I contemplated my Double with my *eyes of light*." Later, in their psalms, his community sing: "We bless your partner-Companion of light, Christ, the source of our good."[39] Mānī, like Thomas in those same *Acts* which include the *Song of the Pearl*, has *Christos Angelos* as his heavenly Twin, who informs him of his vocation, just as the prophet Mohammed was to receive the revelation from the Angel Gabriel (and the identification *Christos-Gabriel* is by no means unknown in gnosis.) Now, Christos Angelos is the same in relation to Mānī (in eastern Manicheism the Virgin of light is substituted for Christos Angelos), as is the *taw'am*, the "Heavenly Twin," in relation to each of the Elect respectively and individually. It is the Form of light which the Elect receive when they enter the Manichean community through the act of solemn renunciation of the powers of this world. At the passing away of one of the Elect, a psalm is sung in praise of "thy heavenly Partner who faileth not." In Catharism it is he who is called the *Spiritus sanctus* or *angelicus* of the particular soul, as carefully distinguished from the *Spiritus principalis*, the Holy Spirit referred to in invoking the three persons named in the Trinity.

That is why, since *Manvahmed* (the archangel Vohu Manah of Zoroastrianism, the Noūs) is without doubt according to the Eastern texts the element of light, and as such both outside and inside the soul, the situation can be correctly defined only by preserving the four terms required by the analogy pointed out above. The great *Manvahmed* is to the totality of the souls of light (the *Columna gloriae*) what *each* Manvahmed (not the collectivity) is to its terrestrial "I." Here again it can be said that each *Manvahmed* (or *Spiritus principalis*) as in Sohravardī Perfect Nature is related to Gabriel, the Holy Ghost and Angel of humanity. This Form of light thus fulfills the same function as Perfect Nature. Each one of the Elect is guided by it throughout life and beyond; it is the supreme theophany. It is the "guide who initiates him by causing conversion ($\mu\epsilon\tau\acute{a}\nu o\iota\chi$) to penetrate his heart; it is the *Noūs*-light coming from above, the

34

ray of the sacrosanct φωστήρ which comes to illuminate, purify, and guide the soul toward the Earth of light (*Terra lucida*) from which it came at the beginning of time, and to which it will return, reassuming its original form."[40] This wise guide is the Form of light which is manifested *in extremis* to the Elect, "the image of light in the semblance of the soul," the Angel bearing the "diadem and crown"; it is, for each of the Elect, the heavenly Sophia or Virgin of light (the dominant figure also in the book of the *Pistis Sophia*). And Manicheism explicitly gives this figure its Zoroastrian name, thus confirming the Zoroastrian vision where the *Daēnā* of a being of light comes to meet him after death in the form of a "maiden who guides him."[41]

All we have just tried to bring together here—too rapidly, too allusively—should be completed by reference to still other texts, more accessible no doubt than those alluded to above, as for instance the passages in the *Phaedo* and *Timaeus* of Plato and the commentary on these in the fourth chapter of the third *Ennead*, in which Plotinus speaks of the *daïmōn paredros* into whose care we are given, and who is the guide of the soul throughout life and beyond death. Mention should also be made of the beautiful development of the same theme in Apuleius (*De Deo Socratis*, 16), dealing with the higher group of *daïmōns* to each of whom the care of one human individual is entrusted and who serves as its witness (*testis*) and guardian (*custos*). No less essential for our purpose are the texts in which Philo of Alexandria calls the *Noūs* the true man, the man within man. We experience this *homo verus* who dwells in the soul of each of us, now as an archon and king, now as a judge awarding the crown after life's battles; on occasion he plays the part of a witness (μάρτυς), sometimes even of a prosecutor.[42] Finally, mention must be made of the notion of *sakshin* in two Upanishads.[43] "The man in man" is also the eyewitness, looking on at, but not involved in, not sullied by the actions and inner states of the man, whether in the waking state or the dream state, in deep sleep or in ecstasy. "Two friends with beautiful wings, closely entwined, embracing one and the same tree; one eats its sweet fruits; the other does not eat, but looks on." The *sakshin* is the guide; the human being contemplates it and is united with it to the degree that all his defects are effaced in it; it is the homologue of Perfect Nature, of the *shāhid* as the form of light.

The word "witness" (μάρτυς, *testis*, *shāhid*) has been mentioned several times, which already suggests what all these recurrences of the same Figure have in common—from the Zoroastrian vision of Daēnā to the contemplation of the *shāhid* in Sufism. Where this witness of contemplation becomes, as in Najm Kobrā, the theophanic witness of what is seen in vision, the function its name implies is made even clearer: according to whether the soul in vision sees it as light, or on the contrary "sees" only darkness, the soul itself testifies, by its vision, *for* or *against* its own spiritual realization. Thus the "witness in Heaven" is called the "scales of the suprasensory" (*mīzān al-ghayb*); the beauty of the being who is the witness of contemplation is likewise a means of weighing, since it proves the capacity or incapacity of the soul to perceive beauty as theophany par excellence.

All these texts converge toward the epiphany of the same Figure whose very diverse names reveal rather than conceal its identity: the philosopher's Angel or Sun, Daēnā, Perfect Nature, personal master and suprasensory guide, Sun of the heart, etc. All these signs of convergence provide the indispensable context for a study of the phenomenology of the visionary experience in Iranian Sufism, where perceptions of colored lights are the manifestation of the personal spiritual guide (*shaykh al-ghayb* in Najm Kobrā, *ostād ghaybī* in Semnānī). It was important to show that the examples of this experience are linked with one and the same type of essentially individual, personal spiritual initiation. Further, as the reunion of the man of light and his guide, his heavenly counterpart and the transcendent "dimension" of his person, this experience has seemed to us *oriented* and *orienting* in a definite direction, toward those "Earths" whose direction can be suggested only by symbols—the symbols of the North.

In effect we have tried to show the structure and premises on which the liberation of the man of light, Prometheus-*Phōs*, depends. The liberation as an event will now make clearer to us the *orientation* on which it depends. We shall need to recognize to what region the suprasensory guide forming a pair with its terrestrial "double" belongs, and in what direction it is re-

vealed, namely the region and direction from which *Phōs* originates and back to which his guide has to lead him. In the writings of Najm Kobrā, we find again the image of the *well* into
which the exile of the Sohravardian recital is cast. The *effective*
emergence from the well begins when a supernatural *green light*
shines at its mouth. Earlier we learned in Sohravardī both the
hour when the event takes place and the *direction* indicated by
this experience of radical individuation, experienced as a reunion with the personal Form of Light. Midnight Sun and
heavenly pole: the symbols of the *North* taken together will
show us the direction of the mystic *Orient*, that is, the Orient-
origin, which has to be looked for not on the earthly plani-
spheres, but at the summit of the cosmic mountain.

III. MIDNIGHT SUN AND CELESTIAL POLE

1. *The Cosmic North and the "Oriental Theosophy" of Sohravardī (1191)*

The Avestan term *Airyanem Vaejah* (Pehlevi *Ērān-Vēj*) designates the cradle and origin of the Aryan-Iranians in the center of the central *keshvar* (*orbis*, zone). Those who have attempted to determine its position on geographic maps have run into great difficulties; no convincing solution has been obtained in this way, for the first and good reason that the problem of locating it lies in the realm of visionary geography.[44] The data presented here relate to a primordial and archetypal Image, that is, to the primary phenomenon of *orientation* we referred to at the outset (*supra* I, 1). It is this Image that dominates and coordinates the perception of empirical data; it is not the other way round, that acquired data, geographical and cultural, produce the Image. The Image gives physical events their meaning; it precedes them, it is not they that give rise to it. This in no way implies that it is a question of mere "subjectivity" in today's loose usage of this word. It indeed refers to an organ of perception to which a definite plane or region of being corresponds as its *object*, a region which is represented in a later elaboration of Iranian philosophy as the heavenly Earth of *Hūrqalyā*. To *orient* ourselves personally, it will be best to inquire

39

III. Midnight Sun and Celestial Pole

first of all into the events that take place in Ērān-Vēj, of which the pertinent ones are as follows:

Ērān-Vēj is the place of the memorable liturgies celebrated by Ohrmazd himself, by the heavenly beings, by the legendary heroes. It was in Ēran-Vēj that Yima the beautiful, Yima the dazzlingly beautiful, the best of mortals, received the command to construct an enclosure, the *var*, where the elite of all beings, the most beautiful, the most gracious, would gather to be saved from the deadly winter unleashed by the demonic powers so that they might one day repeople a transfigured world. (*Vendidad* 2:21 ff.) This *var* or paradise of Yima is like a walled city, with houses, storerooms, and ramparts. It has a gate and luminescent windows *which themselves secrete an inner light* within, for it is illuminated both by uncreated and created lights. Its inhabitants see the stars, moon, and sun rise and set only once a year, and that is why a year seems to them only a day. Every forty years, from each pair of humans, another couple is born, consisting of a male and a female. "And all of these beings live the most beautiful of lives in the unchanging *var* of Yima."

Certainly we might be tempted to hear an echo in this description of a primaeval sojourn of the Iranians in a geographic far north, the memory of a dawn of thirty days preceding an annual sunrise. However, the indications are stronger that it in fact refers to the threshold of a supranatural beyond: there are uncreated lights; a world that secretes its own light, as in Byzantine mosaics the gold illuminates the enclosed space because the glass cubes are reinforced with gold leaf; a shadowless country peopled with beings of light who have reached spiritual heights inaccessible to earthly beings. They are truly beings of the beyond; where the shadow which holds the light captive ends, there the beyond begins, and the very same mystery is enciphered in the symbol of the *North*. In the same way the *Hyperboreans* symbolize men whose soul has reached such completeness and harmony that it is devoid of negativity and shadow; it is neither of the east nor of the west. Just as in Indian mythology also we hear of the people of the *Uttara-kurus*, the people of the northern sun, who have fully and ideally individualized features; a people composed of twins linked together, typifying a state of completeness expressed also by the form and the dimensions of their country: an earthly paradise

40

in the Far North whose shape, like the *var* of Yima, like the emerald cities Jābalqā and Jābarsā, like the Heavenly Jerusalem, is a perfect square.

Other events in Ērān-Vēj: Zarathustra (Zoroaster), having reached the age of thirty, yearns for Ērān-Vēj and sets out with a number of male and female companions. The nature of the spaces they traverse, the date of the migration (homologous, in the annual cycle of the calendar, with the dawn of a millenium)[45] show us something more and better than a positivist history: what we have here is a series of hierophanies. To long for Ērān-Vēj is to long for the Earth of visions *in medio mundi*; it is to reach the center, the heavenly Earth, where the meeting takes place with the Holy Immortals, the divine heptad of Ohrmazd and his archangels. The mountain of visions is the psycho-cosmic mountain, the cosmic mountain seen as homologous to the human microcosm. It is the "Mountain of dawns" from whose summit the Chinvat Bridge springs forth to span the passage to the beyond, at the very spot where the auroral meeting of the angel Daēnā and her earthly ego takes place. Here, therefore, the Archangel Vohu-Manah (Persian, *Bahman*, "Excellent Thought," $\epsilon'\nu\nu\omicron\iota\alpha$) enjoins the visionary-prophet to cast off his robe, that is, his material body and organs of sensory perception, because in Ērān-Vēj it is the subtle body of light that is the seat and organ of events. And it is there, *in medio mundi* and at the summit of the soul, that the Zarathustrian seed of light is preserved, which is the *Xvarnah* of the three *Saoshyants*, the future Saviors who by a cosmic liturgical act will bring about the transfiguration of the world.

These same categories of the transcendental active Imagination give form to the perceptions through which something in the nature of a "physiology of the man of light" is revealed. By making psycho-cosmic homologation possible, this imagination has served as the basis of symbolic constructions, designated by the term *mandala*, which serve to support the mental realizations achieved through meditation. Some of these constructions were gigantic, as we know. The famous *ziqqūrāt* of Babylonia typified the cosmic mountain with seven stories whose colors corresponded respectively to those of the seven Heavens; thus allowing the pilgrim, ritually, to climb to the summit, that is, to the culminating point which is the cosmic north, the pole round which the earth revolves. In each case, the local zenith could be identified with the heavenly pole. *Stupas* (as in Borobudur) are constructions of the same kind; their symbolic architecture typified the outer covering of the universe and the secret, inner world whose summit is the center of the cosmos. Lastly, involving the same homologies, there is the microcosmic temple, called by the *Ishrāqīyūn* the "temple of light" (*haykal al-nūr*), the human organism with its *seven* centers or subtle organs: the seven *latīfa* (*infra* VI, 1), or inner Heavens, resting one upon another, each with its own color, each identified as the microcosmic seat of one of the great prophets. Man and the world are thus wholly represented as evolving around a vertical axis; from this viewpoint, the idea of a horizontal linear evolution would appear totally devoid of meaning and direction—*unoriented*. The Abode-of-Hymns, the Earth of Hūrqalyā, the Heavenly Jerusalem, *descend* progressively in direct relation to the *ascent* of the man of light. The space enclosed in the 360-degree sphere is the homologue which on the cosmic scale materializes a secret, supernatural *corpus mysticum* of beings and organs of light.

Ērān-Vēj, the paradise of Yima, the spiritual realm of subtle bodies, has been a constant and absorbing theme of Iranian meditation for the adepts of Zarathustra in the distant past, the adepts of the Sohravardian theosophy of Light, and thinkers of the Shaykhi school in Shī'ite Iran. The idea of the center of the world, the legendary theme of the central keshvar determining the orientation of the other six *keshvars* arranged around it and later separated from one another by the cosmic ocean, has had a continuous philosophic development. The most important phase of this development is perhaps the moment when, in Sohravardī's "oriental theosophy", the Platonic Ideas are interpreted in terms of Zoroastrian angelology.

Between the world of pure spiritual Lights (*Luces victoriales*, the world of the "Mothers" in the terminology of *Ishrāo*) and the sensory universe, at the boundary of the ninth Sphere (the Sphere of Spheres) there opens a *mundus imaginalis* which is a concrete spiritual world of archetype-Figures, apparitional Forms, Angels of species and of individuals; by philosophical dialectics its necessity is deduced and its plane situated; vision of it in actuality is vouchsafed to the visionary apperception of the active Imagination. The essential connection in Sohravardī which leads from philosophical speculation to a metaphysics of ecstasy also establishes the connection between the angelology of this neo-Zoroastrian Platonism and the idea of the *mundus imaginalis*. This, Sohravardī declares, is the world to which the ancient Sages alluded when they affirmed that beyond the sensory world there exists another universe with a contour and dimensions and extension in a space, although these are not comparable with the shape and spatiality as we perceive them in the world of physical bodies. It is the "eighth" *keshvar*, the mystical Earth of Hūrqalyā with emerald cities; it is situated on the summit of the cosmic mountain, which the traditions handed down in Islam call the mountain of Qāf.[46]

There is ample supporting evidence that this was indeed the mountain formerly called Alborz (*Elburz*, in Avestan *Haraiti Bareza*), geographically, the name today designates the chain of mountains in northern Iran. But this orographical fact is irrelevant to the visionary geography of the ancient legends which tell us of the marvelous race inhabiting the mountain's cities: a race as ignorant of the earthly Adam as of Iblīs-Ahriman, a race similar to the Angels, androgynous perhaps, since without sexual differentiation (see the twins of the paradise of Yima and of the Uttara-kurus), and hence untroubled even by desire for posterity. The minerals in their soil and the walls of their cities secrete their own light (like the *yar* of Yima); they have no need of any outer light, whether from the sun, the moon, the stars, or the physical Heavens. These concordant signs establish the heavenly topography of this supernatural Earth on the boundary of the Sphere above the planetary Heavens and the Heaven of the innumerable Fixed Stars, which encompasses the entire sensory universe. The mountain of Qāf is this Sphere of Spheres surrounding the totality of the visible cosmos; an *emerald rock*, casting its reflection over the whole of the mountain of Qāf, is the keystone of this celestial vault, the pole.

Now, in the *Recital of the Occidental Exile*, whose very title points to the fundamental meaning of the "oriental theosophy," this is precisely the mountain which the exile must climb when he is summoned at last to return *home*, to return *to himself*. He has to reach the summit, the *Emerald Rock* that rises up before him like the translucent wall of a mystical Sinaï;

there, as we have already seen (*supra* II, 1), on the threshold of
the pleroma of Light, the pilgrim meets his Perfect Nature, his
Holy Ghost, in an ecstasy of anticipation corresponding, in the
Mazdean dramaturgy, to the meeting in the dawn with the celestial Person, at the entrance to the Chinvat Bridge. This
threshold opens onto the "climate of the Soul," a world made
wholly of a subtle "matter" of light, intermediate between the
world of the Cherubinic pure Lights and the world of *physis*,
which includes corruptible sublunar matter as well as the astral
matter of the incorruptible Heavens. This universe of *physis* in
its entirety forms the cosmic *Occident*; the other universe is the
Orient, which begins at the climate of the Soul, the "eighth"
climate.

Thus the paradisal Earth of Light, the world of Hūrqalyā, is
an Orient intermediate between the "lesser Orient," which is
the soul's rising to the highest point of its desire and consciousness, and the "greater Orient," which is the further spiritual
Orient, the pleroma of pure Intelligences, the soul's rising to
supra-consciousness. The twofold symbolic meaning of the midnight sun (*supra* I, 2) corresponds to this structure of Orient
rising upon Orient. Indeed, since the eighth climate, the celestial Earth of Hūrqalyā, is said to be in the *Orient*, and since the
direction indicated to us is that of the cosmic north, the "summit of the world," it certainly does not refer to the East as we
are accustomed to locate it on the terrestrial map. Here the
Orient *is oriented* toward the center which is the topmost point
of the cosmic dome, the *pole*: it is the Emerald Rock at the
summit of the mountain of Qāf. To reach it one has to succeed
in climbing the mountain just as the pilgrim reaches it in the
Recital of the Exile, by obeying a summons identical to the summons received by the exiled prince in the *Song of the Pearl* in the
Acts of Thomas (*supra* II, 1). This orientation pertains to a
visionary geography oriented to the "climate of the Soul," the
place of the emerald cities, illuminated by the brilliance of the
inner light that they themselves secrete. This *Suprasensory
Orient* governs the primary phenomenon of the Gnostic's orientation toward his country of origin. The *Orient-origin* identified
with the center, with the heavenly north pole, heralds access to
the beyond, where vision becomes real history, the history of
the soul, and where every visionary event symbolizes a spiritual

state; or, as the *Ishrāqīyūn* say, it is the climate "where what is bodily becomes spirit and what is spiritual acquires a body."[47]

Northern Light, original light, pure inner light coming neither from the east nor the west: the symbols of the north open spontaneously around that central intuition which is the intuition of the center. The exodus from the *well*, the ascent that leads to the Emerald Rock and toward the angel, Perfect Nature, begins in the darkness of night. The journey is marked by the vicissitudes which typify the states and the perils of the soul undergoing this initiatic test. The *midnight sun* bursts into flame at the approach to the summit—the primordial Image of inner light that figured so prominently in the ritual of the mystery religions (see *supra* II, 1: the light carried by Hermes into the heart of the underground chamber). This is how it comes to pass for Hermes, the hero of the eschatological ecstasy described by Sohravardī, from which we have already gathered evidence (*supra* II, 1) in support of the hermetic tradition, and which relates the vision wherein Hermes recognized his Perfect Nature in the beautiful and mysterious spiritual entity which manifested itself to him.

Sohravardī gives more particulars concerning this vision in one of his major works.[48] In this case, Hermes kept vigil all night long, meditating in the "temple of light" (*haykal al-nūr*, his own microcosm), but a sun shone in this night. When the "pillar of dawn" burst forth, that is to say, when the being of light broke down the walls of the "temple" that enclosed him (here we are reminded of the *columna Gloriae* of Manicheism in which reascent of the elements of light coincides with the descent of the Cross of Light), Hermes saw an Earth being swallowed up and with it the "cities of the oppressors" drowning in the divine wrath. This downfall of the sensory, material world, of the *Occident* of corruptible matter and its laws, recalls the scene described in the Recital of the occidental exile: here, the arrival at the *cosmic north*, at the Emerald Rock, threshold of the beyond, is heralded by the outburst of light of the "midnight sun" (as in Apuleius: *media nocte vidi solem coruscantem*). The midnight sun is the *illuminatio matutina*, the brilliance of dawn rising in the Orient-origin of the soul, that is, at the *pole*, while the cities of the oppressors are being swallowed up. Here the *aurora consurgens* rising at the Emerald Rock, at the keystone of the

45

heavenly dome, is the *aurora borealis* in the Heaven of the soul. Before this unknown horizon Hermes was full of fear and cried out: "Save me, you who have given birth to me!" (In Sohravardī's psalm, as we recall, he appeals to his Perfect Nature in the very same way.) And Hermes hears this answer: "Seize hold of the cable of the ray of light and rise to the battlements of the Throne." He climbs up, and lo! under his feet were an Earth and a Heaven. A Heaven and an Earth where, with Sohravardī's commentators (Shahrazōrī and Ibn Kammūna), we recognize the *mundus imaginalis*, the autonomous world of the archetype-Figures, the Earth of Hūrqalyā sheltered by the battlements of the Throne which is the Sphere of Spheres, the climate of the Soul revolving around the heavenly pole. In the Sabean texts of the pseudo-Majrītī we also read a description of the Perfect Nature as the philosopher's Sun; and Najm Kobrā will refer to the "witness in Heaven" as the suprasensory Sun, the Sun of the heart, the Sun of the spirit.

In regard to this Orient-origin, oriented vertically toward the pole as the threshold of the beyond, where the inner, the esoteric light shines in the divine Night, the "literal," geographic East would then typify the *daylight* of exoteric consciousness, as powerless in opposition to the divine Night of the Ineffable as against the nocturnal depths of the dark Psyche; hence the confusion between these two nights, since by its very nature this Day cannot co-exist with Night; it can exist only in the inevitable alternation of days and nights, of rise and decline. But here we have another light, that of the Emerald Rock. (In Isma'ilian Shī'ite gnosis, another symbolism will allude to the "sun rising in the west," from the side of night, but there it will refer specifically to the Imām who is the *pole*, the keystone and axis of the esoteric hierarchy.) The "midnight sun" typifies the inner light, that which is secreted by the abode itself (as by the *var* of Yima), in its own secret way. That is why, as we said, this suggests a new way of evaluating the Orient-Occident contrast: here "Nordic" man is no longer the nordic man of ethnology, but is the "Oriental" in the *polar* sense of the word, that is, the exiled Gnostic, the stranger who refuses the yoke of the "oppressors" because he has been sent to this world for a purpose which they cannot recognize. And that is why we have already had a premonition of the significance of this fun-

46

damental *orientation*, guiding vision and actualization in the direction of an ascent which conflicts with our habitual notions of dimensions of time, of evolution, of historical actuality.

Is not the sense of all myths of *reintegration* henceforth affected by this orientation? For the totality of man's being, the transcendent personal dimension he discerns in the northern light, in the "midnight sun," is not merely the sum total of orient and occident, of left and right, of conscious and unconscious. The man of light's ascent causes the shades of the *well* where he was held captive to fall back into themselves. Hermes does not carry his *shadow* with him; he discards it; for he rises up, and correspondingly the "cities of the oppressors" sink down into the abyss. And it is difficult, we must confess, to read with equanimity certain interpretations of the *coincidentia oppositorum* where complementaries and contradictories are apparently indiscriminately lumped together under the head of *opposita*. To deplore that Christianity is centered on a figure of goodness and light and entirely overlooks the dark side of the soul would be no less valid an evaluation if applied to Zoroastrianism. But how could reintegration consist in a complicity between, a "totalization" of Christ and Satan, Ohrmazd and Ahriman? Even to suggest such a possibility is to overlook the fact that even under the reign of a figure of light the satanic forces remain in operation—those for example who tried to prevent Hermes' escape from the depths of the well and his ascent to the battlements of the Throne. And it is exactly for this reason that one has to affirm that the relationship of Christ to Satan, Ohrmazd to Ahriman, is not complementary but contradictory. Complementary elements can be integrated, but not contradictory ones.

It would seem that the misunderstanding in the first place concerns the nature of the *Day* whose constraints are deplored, and consequently the remedies called for. From this point of view the distinction made clear to us by certain Iranian Sufi masters between luminous Night, or black Light, and unqualified black, blackness without light (*infra* V and VI), is essential to prevent us from going astray and to keep us *oriented* toward the pole. The Day whose constraints are deplored, and whose ambiguity is obvious because it obeys the demonic law of constraint, is the exoteric Day where ready-made notions are ac-

cepted and taken for granted. Deliverance from it lies in the
esoteric Night of hidden meanings, which is the night of superconsciousness, not of unconsciousness; for it is not the
Ahrimanian Night, but the Night Ineffable, the Night of symbols, which alone can pacify the dogmatic madnesses of Day.
Rational dogmatic excitement and irrational lunacy cannot
compensate for one another. The totality symbolized by the
"midnight sun" is the *Deus absconditus* and the Angel Logos, or,
in terms of Shī'ite gnosis, the *pole*, the Imām, which brings light
into the night of the inner world. Nothing short of total disorientation could result in confusing the night of the *Deus
absconditus* with the Ahrimanian night, the Angel Logos with a
revelation of Ahriman or a revelation complementary to
Ahriman. That is why the old Iranian *Zervānism* which has been
so complacently admired on the pretext that it implies a philosophy of unity transcending dualism, could only appear absurd
and grotesque in the eyes of the Zoroastrians. The word *eso-
terism*, so often misused, refers to the unavoidable necessity of
expressing the reintegration of the human being in symbols:
luminous night and midnight sun; twins of the paradise of
Yima; the man of light and his guide; the theme of androgyny,
the reunion of Adam and the celestial Sophia, to whom he was
"betrothed in his youth." But one essential fact has to be remembered: Faust, *renovatus in novam infantiam*, is reborn "in
Heaven," where the *Sophia aeterna* appears; the redemption of
Faust is not a "sum total" of Faust and Mephistopheles. The
counterfeiter, the *Antimimon*, is not *Phōs's* guide of light; it
brings contradiction; it is not complementary.

If the diversity of these expressions is stressed here, all too
briefly, it is because of the impression that the orientation required in this search by the very nature of its theme and
sources, encounters at every step the same difficulties deriving
from the same confusion or disorientation. This can but pro-
long and strengthen the laws of the exoteric Day against which
the Sohravardian Hermes exerts his effort to be free, by break-
ing with the pre-established and generally accepted view. One
cannot concoct "history" out of Hermes' visions. Nor can
Hermes and the prince of the *Song of the Pearl* be adapted to a
social context. To attempt to do so is, as it were, to prevent
them from *orienting* themselves, and from understanding *where*

they are, and to make them forget the well into which they have been thrown. The Daylight turned on them in this way is not the light of the Emerald Rock, and that is why this Day cannot enter into combination with the Night of Symbols. The bi-unity is Hermes *and* his Perfect Nature, it is not Hermes *and* the "City of the oppressors," nor Hermes *and* the well into which the oppressors have thrown him. He does not emerge alone from this well; still less does he emerge in a crowd and *en masse*; he emerges from it as a pair, that is to say, in the company of the guide of light, by whatever name, among his many names, he makes himself recognized.

That is why the possibility of reaching the cosmic north, the Emerald Rock, is essentially linked to the bi-unitary structure of human individuality, potentially including a transcendent dimension of light (Hermes and his Perfect Nature, the Manichean adept and his Form of light, etc.). The powers of doubt and forgetfulness, under the different names that cover them up through the ages, the powers of the exoteric Day and the powers of the Night without light, do all they can to stifle and annihilate this potentiality. This is why one may no longer even glimpse the nature of the luminous Night, the black Light spoken of by certain Sufis, and which is in no way a mixture of divine Light and demonic shadow. To say that what is below is an imitation of what is above is not to say that what is below *is* what is above. The *night* of rejected demonic depths, or on the contrary the horror of the *day* inspired by the fascination of these depths—these perhaps are the two impotences to which occidental man succumbs. It is not by compounding them that one finds the luminous Night of the "Oriental," that is to say, of the "northern man," nor the night of the intra-divine heights (*infra* V and VI).

The stress laid on the symbol of the *pole*, on the double constellation of the *Bear* and the *Pole star* in the hierognosis of Sufism, succeeds in convincing us of this. We find here the same homologation as in the cosmic mountain whose *pole* is the culminating point. The same law of psycho-cosmic structure makes the mental circumambulations around the heart, for example, homologous to those made around the Temple, and to the rotation of the heavenly dome about its axis. Projected on the zenith, the primordial Image of the *center* that the mystic experiences in himself, around which he inwardly revolves, then allows him to perceive the Pole star as a cosmic symbol of the reality of inner life. Inner sanctuary and Emerald Rock are then simultaneously the threshold and place of theophanies, the pole of orientation, the direction from which the guide of light appears. We shall see him appear in this way in the visions of a great Sufi master of Shīrāz, and it could likewise be analyzed by a phenomenology of prayer linked to the fact that the Mandeans, the Sabeans of Harran, the Manicheans, the Buddhists of Central Asia take the north as the *Qibla* (the axis of orientation) of their prayer.

But here again our phenomenology of the north, of the *pole*, should preclude any danger of the disorientation which, as we have just stressed, can manifest as the temptation to confuse the northern sun, the midnight sun, with a *coincidentia oppositorum*, as an artificial isolation of contradictions instead of complementaries. Since this fictitious conciliation remains in fact on the exoteric level, the "break away" demanded by the vertical dimension oriented toward the north is not consummated. Hermes departs from the "Occident," but it is not by carrying his *shadow* along with him that he rises to the battlements of the Throne. Because the north, the pole, is "above," it allows the recognition of *where* the shadow is, be it the individual shadow of the lower functions of the *psyche*, or the collective shadow of the "city of the oppressors." But how could this justify saying that *what makes* the shadow *visible* and shows in what direction it lies could also be the very same *shadow*? Far from it, what indicates *where* the shadow is, is characterized as being itself *shadowless*. If the cosmic north is the threshold of the beyond, if it is the paradise of Yima, how could it be the place of Hell? Hermes rises; he leaves the *Infernum* in its place, below him, in the world which he has left. There is neither ambivalence nor ambiguity; the opposition between Zoroastrianism and Zervānism has been recalled above, and if something of the latter survived and bore fruit in the gnosis of Islam, it was thanks to a shifting of level, a radical alteration of its dramaturgy, freeing the field precisely for the orientation here envisioned.

Certainly there are mythological data in which the *north*

takes on a meaning contrary to that which we are analyzing here. But there could then be no question of ambivalence unless the *subject* remained identical. One should therefore have started by constructing, more or less fictitiously, and by substantializing, a collective Psyche, in order to affirm its permanence and identity in the alternation of its contrary tendencies. The ambivalence of the symbol of the *north* would depend on this one subject, signifying now the threshold of the paradise of life, now the threshold of darkness and hostile powers. Unfortunately, would one not thereby fall into the trap of this invented and complacently accepted picture of the situation? For what exists in fact, really, concretely and substantially, is not a collectivity but individual souls, that is, persons each of whom can help another to find his own way out of the well; but as soon as there is a wish by some to impose their way on others, the situation becomes once more that of the "city of the oppressors" in the Sohravardian tale. This notion of a collective Psyche, involving the disorientation of symbols, is again only a result of the forgetting and consequent loss of the ascending vertical dimension, for which an evolutionary horizontal extension is substituted. The vertical dimension is individuation and sacralization; the other is collectivization and secularization. The first is a deliverance both from the individual and from the collective shadow. If Hermes had accepted to remain at the bottom of the well, he also, we must conclude, would have taken the cosmic north, the pole, for Hell. But this is by no means to say that Heaven is Hell; what he would have perceived would have been nothing but the collective shadow projected on the pole and preventing him from seeing it, that is, from seeing his own person of light (as the unbeliever in the Chinvat Bridge sees only his own caricature instead of seeing Daēnā; as the Sufi novice sees only darkness until the green light shines at the mouth of the well). If the region of the pole *is* what it foretells to the Sufi, it can foretell the contrary only if a shadow darkens it, the shadow precisely of those who refuse to make the ascent to which Sufism invites them. To cast off the shadow is not to return toward the shadow; orientation cannot be disorientation.

III. Midnight Sun and Celestial Pole

2. *Visions of the Pole in Rūzbehān of Shīrāz (1209)*

Some of the visions described by Rūzbehān of Shīrāz in his *Diarium spirituale* illustrate the symbolism of the *pole* in a particularly explicit way.[49] In a dream, or rather in a state intermediate between waking and sleeping, the totality of creatures is revealed to him as though they were assembled within a house; there are many lamps which give off a bright light, but a wall prevents him from reaching them. Then he mounts to the terrace of the house which is his own dwelling place; there he finds two very beautiful personages who appear to be Sufi shaykhs and in whom he recognizes *his own image*—a very significant detail. Together the three partake of a kind of mystical repast, consisting of pure wheat bread and oil so subtle that it was like a pure spiritual substance. Subsequently, one of the two shaykhs asks Rūzbehān if he knows what this substance was. As he does not know, the shaykh informs him that it was "oil from the *constellation of the Bear*[50] which we gathered for you." After emerging from his dream Rūzbehān continues to meditate upon it, but it took him some time, he confesses, to understand that there had been in it an allusion to the *seven poles* (*aqtāb*, more generally the seven *abdāl*) in the heavenly pleroma, and that God had dispensed to him the pure substance of their mystical station, that is to say, had admitted him to the rank of the *seven* masters of initiation and intercessors who are invisibly apportioned to our world.

> Then [he writes], I concentrated my attention on the constellation of the Bear and I observed that it formed *seven* apertures through which God was showing himself to me. My God! I cried, what is this? He said to me: these are the *seven* apertures of the Throne.

Just as Hermes in Sohravardī's recital is invited to climb to the battlements of the Throne, so here Rūzbehān, being admitted to the number of the seven *Abdāl* surrounding the *Pole* (in Shī'ite terms the "hidden Imām"), is introduced to the summit of the mysterious and invisible spiritual hierarchy, without which life on earth could not continue to exist. The Idea and the structure of this mystical hierarchy which dominates Sufi theosophy and especially, in Shī'ism, Shaykhi theosophy, correspond to the idea and structure of an esoteric astronomy; the one and the other exemplify the same archetypal Image of the

52

world. Rūzbehān adds these further details which confirm that what he perceives in his vision of the *pole*, of the cosmic north, is indeed the threshold of the beyond and the place of theophanies:

> Every night [he writes], I continued afterwards to observe these apertures in Heaven, as my love and ardent desire impelled me to do. And lo! one night, I saw that they were open, and I saw the divine Being manifesting to me through these apertures. He said to me, "I manifest to you through these openings; they form seven thousand thresholds (corresponding to the seven principal stars of the constellation) leading to the threshold of the angelic pleroma (*malakūt*). And behold I show myself to you through all of them at once."

Thus the visions of Rūzbehān illustrate a twofold theme: that of the *pole* and that of the *walāyat*, the "initiation" whose keystone is the *pole*, grouping and graduating around him the members of a pure *Ecclesia spiritualis*, who remain unknown to ordinary men and invisible to their eyes. The use of the Arabic term *qotb*, "axis" (*najmat al-Qotb*: the pole Star), here evokes the image of the mill pivot fixed into the lower stationary millstone, and passing through a central opening in the higher mobile millstone, whose rotation it governs. The heavenly dome is the homologue of this mobile element, while the pole Star represents the aperture through which an ideal axis passes. The stars closest to the pole Star participate in its pre-eminence and are invested with special energy and significance (the invocations to the constellation of the Bear in certain Gnostic or magical documents testify to it). These seven stars have their homologues in the spiritual Heaven. We have just seen Rūzbehān describe them as the "seven poles," whereas these seven mysterious personages are usually designated as the seven *Abdāl* who, from cycle to cycle, are substituted in succession for one another. Just as the constellation of the Bear dominates and "sees" the totality of the cosmos, they are themselves the *eyes* through which the Beyond looks at the world.[51]

It is at this point that this twofold theme and the spiritual doctrine of Rūzbehān conjoin. In the latter we find the theme common to the entire speculative mysticism of Sufism, especially stressed in Ibn 'Arabī, of the *Deus absconditus*, the "hidden Treasure," aspiring to reveal himself, to be known. However, this very revelation gives rise to a dramatic situation in which the divine Being and the being in which and through which he reveals himself are simultaneously implicated, for God cannot look at an *other* than himself, nor be seen by an *other* than himself. The *Awliyā*, the "initiates," graduated in the different spiritual degrees, are precisely the *eyes* at which God looks, because they are the eyes through which He looks. Through them our world remains a world at which God "looks," and this is the meaning of the mysterious affirmation that if they were not, if there ceased to be the *pole* (the hidden Imām) who is the keystone of the invisible Heavens which they all combine to form, our world would collapse in final catastrophe. It is rather difficult certainly to find in our languages two terms that faithfully render the meanings of the words *walāyat* and *Awliyā*.[52] The idea of "initiation," that of a sodality of "initiates," invisible and permanent from cycle to cycle of prophecy, by substitution of one for another individuality, seems best fitted to awaken their resonances. The theme is especially important in Shī'ite imāmology; and it is also Shī'ite Sufism that offers the best possibility of a study in depth. And these terms suggest another connection. Literally the word *Awliyā* means "Friends": the Persian expression *Awliya-e Khodā* means the "Friends of God." The very same term was applied to themselves in the fourteenth century by an entire family of Spirituals in the West. All inhabit the same heights inaccessible to those who are unaware of their *orientation*, like the "Friend of God" in *Oberland*, the "high country," where Goethe's inner vision will nevertheless know how to find these heights, in a great poem which remained unfinished: *die Geheimnisse* (the Secrets).

There are many traditions referring to this people of "initiates" unknown to the very men whom they exist to protect. Rūzbehān developed these traditions in the prologue to his great work on "the Paradoxes of the mystics." They are generally said to be 360 in number, corresponding to the 360 divine Names, the 360 days and nights of the year, the 360 degrees of the Sphere measuring the day-night cycle. All the variations of this number have symbolic meanings. To pick one of the simplest forms, we will quote the following:

> God [writes Rūzbehān], possesses on earth *three hundred eyes* or persons whose heart is consonant with the heart of *Adam*; *forty* whose heart is consonant with the heart of *Moses*; *seven* whose

heart is consonant with the heart of *Abraham*; *five* whose heart is consonant with the heart of *Gabriel*; *three* whose heart is consonant with the heart of *Michael*; *one* (the *pole*) whose heart is consonant with the heart of *Seraphiel*.[53]

The sum of 356 persons is raised to the total of 360 by four figures of prophets who, according to Islamic esotericism meditating on the Qorānic revelation, have the common characteristic of having been carried off *alive* from death: Enoch (that is to say Idrîs, identified with Hermes), Khezr, Elijah, and Christ.

3. *The Pole as the Abode of the Angel Sraosha*

A few years ago, a learned Zoroastrian carefully investigated this symbolism of the *pole* and its spiritual constellation. The extreme interest of his study lies in the fact that it opened a new path leading from the Zoroastrian religion to the Sufism of the Islamized Iran.[54] In fact, the work of Sohravardī has already shown us the path, which he himself and in person opened intentionally and historically. Here the dominant figure, the very one which shows the way in question, is that of a *Yazata* or "Angel" of the Avesta,[55] who, although not belonging to the supreme heptad of the Amahraspands (the Immortal Saints, the "Archangels"), occupies a particularly outstanding rank, namely the angel *Sraosha* (Pehlevi *Srōsh*, Persian *Sorūsh*), who has become identified in Islamized Iran with the angel Gabriel. He is represented as a priest-angel, with the youthful features common to all Celestials, and our learned Parsee identifies him as the Angel of initiation (*walāyat*), the angel Sraosha's prerogatives, the *situs* of his abode, the specificity of his function, are all features that would seem to imply the existence in Zoroastrianism itself of an esoteric doctrine professed by the representatives of a cult in which he was the central figure.

The Avesta (*Yasht* 57) has him dwelling in triumph on the summit of the highest of mountains (*Haraiti Bareza*, the *Alborz*). We have already learned that this very abode is "self-illuminated within, and adorned on the outside with stars"; and it is the cosmic mountain described in an Avestan hymn (*Yasht* 12:25) as the mountain around which the sun, the moon, and the stars revolve. Neryoseng, who translated the hymn into Sanskrit, identifies it with Mount Meru. The Avesta and traditions here enrich this theme of the cosmic mountain with a new detail: the fact that there at its summit, at the pole, at the pole star, is the abode of the Angel Sraosha. From that point on, the development of our research allows us to understand the following for ourselves: since hierocosmology places the dwelling of the angel of Initiation in the cosmic north, and since hierognosis perceives in his person the *pole*, it goes without saying that the arrival at the summit of mystic initiation has to be experienced, visualized and described as arrival at the pole, at the cosmic north. And here exactly is where we can glimpse a link of continuity between Zoroastrian spirituality centered on the angel Sraosha and the spiritual universe of Sufism centered around the pole. We in fact quoted above, while pointing out the existence of variants in regard to the number and naming of the persons, the traditions which bring out the esoteric hierarchies, the invisible supports of our world centered around the *pole*. On the one hand, the pole is therefore the *situs* of the angel Sraosha (who thus would correspond to the angel Seraphiel); on the other hand this is the qualification given in Sufism to the great shaykh of a period (even the shaykh of a Sufi community, a *tarīqat*, insofar as the latter is taken as the homologue of a microcosm), and for this reason the pole is considered in Shī'ite Sufism as representing the hidden Imām.

Another point of interest in the Zoroastrian scholar's research was that he drew attention to a parallelism between Sufi hierocosmology and certain Taoist concepts; and it is also in Central Asian Sufism that the idea of the *walāyat* is the most firmly rooted and amplified (notably after Hākim Termezī, d. 898, in whose writings the number of the forty *Abdāl* is particularly significant). The Taoist traditions refer to *seven* spiritual rulers "localized" in the constellation of the Bear. The "Classic of the Pivot of Jade" gives a spiritual doctrine told in its very title, which refers to the North Star, "the pivot of Heaven revolving on itself and carrying all the heavenly bodies along with it in its round dance." And it never ceases to suggest remarkable correspondences with Sufi esoteric concepts. On both sides we note in fact that the spiritual hierocosmos exemplifies the same schema as the cosmos of astronomy: the world is arranged like a tent resting on a central axis and four lateral pil-

§3. The Pole as the Abode of the Angel Sraosha

lars (*awtād*). The function of the personages who exemplify the latter is to revolve around the world every night and to inform the *Qotb* what situations require his help. Better still, symbolic numerology shows a truly striking concordance between the numerical configuration of the mystical palace of Ming-Tang (the hall of light which is at once a temple and an astronomical observatory) and the arrangement of the figures in the mystical hierarchy already enumerated here.[56]

Thus, on the one hand, the angel Sraosha watches over the sleeping world; he is the guardian angel and the head of a brotherhood of migrants who "keep watch" on the world and for the world; they are described by a term referring to their holy poverty, the Avestan term *drigu* (Pehlevi *drigōsh*, Pāzend *daryōsh*), the equivalent of which in modern Persian is *darwīsh*, "dervish," the name by which all Iranian Sufis are still referred to today: the "poor in spirit." On the other hand, this brotherhood represents a group which is invisible to ordinary men and which exemplifies the very image of the cosmos unfolded, resting like a tent on its axis and at its peak Sraosha's own abode, the cosmic north "secreting its own light." The symbols of Taoism, Zoroastrianism, and Sufism are all in accord with this same representation.

And so the "heavenly Earths" from which we have already (*supra* II) seen Forms of light appear and descend toward their earthly Doubles are all, like Hūrqalyā, the "eighth" climate, regions of the cosmic north, which means thresholds of the beyond. In Manicheism there is the Earth of Light, *Terra lucida*, situated in the kingdom of light. It is governed by a divinity of eternal light, surrounded by twelve Splendors. Like Hūrqalyā, like the Paradise of Yima, all the beauties of our terrestrial Earth are included in it, but in the subtle state, as pure light without an Ahrimanian shadow. And just as, when the Manicheans take as their *Qibla* the sun and the moon, it does not mean that they are worshipping the sun and the moon but that they look upon them as the pre-eminent visible representatives of the world of light, so when they take the north as *Qibla* it means that they are turning toward the *Terra lucida*, the dwelling of the king of Light. We have already mentioned the ideal world of the Mandeans, *Mshunia Kushta*, a world intermediate between our world and the universe of light; this is a world peopled by a divine race of superhumans, beings with a subtle body invisible to us, descendants of the hidden Adam (*Adam kasia*), and we learned that among them each earthly being has his Twin of light. This *mundus imaginalis* also has its guardian spirit (its *dmutha*), its king of light, Shishlam Rba, just as Hibil Ziwa is the guardian spirit of the Earth (and there are striking analogies between the *actions* of Hibil Ziwa and those of the young prince in the *Song of the Pearl*). Now, the Mandeans also believe that this Earth of light is in the north, separated from our world by a high mountain of ice; while they make it clear that it is "between Heaven and Earth," this belief points out precisely that what is in question is not the earthly north, but the cosmic north.[57] The theme of the Green Island (*al-Jazīrat al-khodrā*) should also be recalled here, the Green Island being the dwelling of the "hidden Imām."

No doubt it would take a whole book to bring together all the evidence showing the significance of the Orient as supra-sensory Orient, Orient-origin, Orient that consequently has to be looked for in the heights, on the vertical axis because it is identified with the pole, the cosmic north, as being a threshold of the worlds beyond. This *orientation* was already given to the Orphic *mystēs*. We find it in the poem of Parmenides where the poet undertakes a journey toward the Orient. The sense of two directions, right and left, the Orient and Occident of the Cosmos, is fundamental in Valentinian Gnosis. *But to make one's way to the right, toward the Orient, still means to go upward*, that is to say in the direction of the pole, because in fact the Occident typifies the world below, the world of sensory matter, whereas the Orient typifies the spiritual world. Ibn 'Arabī (1240) symbolically glorifies his own departure for the East; the journey which took him from Andalusia toward Mecca and Jerusalem, he saw as his *Isrā*, comparing it to an *ekstasis* which repeats the Prophet's ascent from Heaven to Heaven, up to the "Lotus of the boundary."[58] Here the geographic, "literal" East becomes the symbol of the "real" Orient which is the heavenly pole described in Sohravardī's recital of the Exile as the ascent of the mountain of *Qāf* to the Emerald Rock.

Another very great Iranian Sufi master, 'Alī-e Hamadānī (d. 786/1385), in a treatise on dreams, speaks of the *Orient* which is the very ipseity (*bowīyat*) of the world of Mystery, that is

58

to say of the supra-sensory world, of that Orient where the Perfect Ones rise. Elsewhere he speaks of this same Orient as the ipseity of the invisible world which is the source of the emanation of being, *descending* to the *Occident* of the world of bodies, by the eight degrees or Abodes of the worlds of the *Jabarūt* and of the *Malakūt*.[59] In the same way, when Avicenna asks Hayy ibn Yaqzān (who plays in respect to him the part played by Perfect Nature in respect to Hermes) what his country is, the answer refers to the Heavenly Jerusalem, Hayy ibn Yaqzān, the personification of the Active Intelligence, is an "Oriental"; he belongs to that "Orient" the steps to which he shows to the philosopher, his disciple, mounting one above the other from the world of earthly matter.[60] This idea of the Orient in the Avicennan Recitals is thus perfectly in accord with Sohravardī's idea expressed in his own "oriental theosophy"; the "Orientals" are those who, coming from above, return there after passing through the inner initiation described in the Recital of the "occidental" exile.

They arrive at this "oriental knowledge" (*'ilm ishrāqī*) which is not a re-presentative knowledge, but an immediate Presence of the known, in the way that he who knows himself is present to himself. The Latin equivalent would be the expression *cognitio matutina*, used in Renaissance Hermetism and which already figures in St. Augustine's terminology. Whereas the evening knowledge, "occidental," *cognitio vespertina*, is the outer man's knowledge—knowledge of the outside of things—the morning knowledge, "oriental," *cognitio matutina*, is the knowledge of the man of light, having attained the "abode which secretes its own light," that is to say the Emerald Rock, this being the knowledge which is self-consciousness. This *cognitio matutina* is in a sense *cognitio polaris*, the aurora borealis in the Heaven of the soul. There exactly is discovered the way of access to the deepest sense of the Sufi saying recalled here from the beginning: "he who knows himself knows his Lord," that is: knows his heavenly *pole*.

There is indeed a correlation between the discovery of the ego, the ego in the second person, the *Alter Ego, thou*, and the upward vertical direction—between internalization (the discovery of the Heavens of the soul) and orientation toward the heavenly pole. If Sohravardī's "oriental theosophy" explodes

III. Midnight Sun and Celestial Pole

the schema of Ptolemaic astronomy and the Peripatetic theory of the Intelligences, it is because the universe of spiritual beings postulated by both of them is not on the scale of the multitudes of the Heaven of the Fixed Stars, the "infinite Lights" on which Sohravardī's meditation was fixed. But by visionary apperception he assimilates the visions of Zarathustra and of the blessed king Kay Khosraw (one of the legendary kings of ancient Iran, born in Ērān-Vēj), and goes beyond the schema of the astronomy of his own time through the vision of the suprasensory Heavens, or what in Sufism is called the "esoteric of each Heaven" (*bātin al-falak*), the very Heavens which mark the stages of the Prophet's heavenly ascent or the ascent of the mountain of Qāf. The identification of the "esoteric" Orient, that is to say of the suprasensory Orient, cosmic north, heavenly pole, is conditioned by the effective passing to the inner world, that is to say to the eighth climate, the Climate of the Soul, the Earth of Light, Hūrqalyā.

In the same way, Najmoddīn Kobrā emphasizes this by developing the theme that like can only be known by like.

> Do not believe that the Heaven you contemplate in the suprasensory is the visible outer Sky. No, in the suprasensory (i.e., in the spiritual world) there are other Skies, more subtle, bluer, purer, brighter, innumerable and limitless. The purer you become within, the purer and more beautiful is the Sky that appears to you, until finally you are walking in divine purity. But divine purity is also limitless. So never believe that beyond what you have reached there is nothing more, nothing higher still." (§ 60)

And here is a still more radical statement of the principle of innerness, making every spiritual reality something as inherent in the mystic as his own life and his own death:

> Know that the soul, the devil, the angel are not realities outside of you; you *are* they. Likewise, Heaven, Earth, and the Throne are not outside of you, nor paradise nor hell, nor death nor life. They exist in you; when you have accomplished the mystical journey and have become pure you will become conscious of that. (§ 67)

Now, to accomplish this mystical journey, is exactly what *internalize* is, that is, to "come out toward oneself"; that is what the *exodus* is, the journey toward the Orient-origin which is the heavenly *pole*, ascent of the soul out of the "well," when at the mouth of the well arises the *visio smaragdina*.

IV. VISIO SMARAGDINA

1. *Najmoddīn Kobrā (1220)*

It seems that Najmoddīn Kobrā was the first of the Sufi masters to focus his attention on the phenomena of colors, the colored photisms that the mystic can perceive in the course of his spiritual states. He took great pains to describe these colored lights and to interpret them as signs revealing the mystic's state and degree of spiritual progress. Some of the greatest masters of the Iranian Sufism issuing from this Central Asian school, notably Najm Dāyeh Rāzī, Najm Kobrā's direct disciple, and Alāoddawleh Semnānī who followed his *tarīqat*, have in their turn illustrated this experimental method of spiritual control which implies at the same time an appreciation of the symbolism of colors and their mutations.

This is certainly not to say that their predecessors were unfamiliar with visionary experiences. Far from it. But the anonymous short work of a shaykh (which must have been written later than Semnānī, since it refers to him by name) bears witness to an "orthodox" teacher's alarm at what seemed to him an innovation.[61] Sohravardī himself, at the end of his most important work, wherein his aim is to restore the "oriental, theosophy," gives a detailed description of the experiences of light, of *photisms*, that a mystic can have; however, colors and their symbolism are not yet referred to.[62]

61

IV. Visio Smaragdina

The descriptions do not refer to physical perceptions; Najm Kobrā alludes several times to these colored lights as something seen "with the eyes closed." They have to do with something related to the perception of an *aura*. There is indeed affinity and correspondence between physical colors and auric (or *aural*, "auroral") colors, in the sense that physical colors themselves have a moral and spiritual quality and that what the aura[63] expresses corresponds to it, "symbolizes with it." This correspondence, this symbolism, is precisely what makes it possible for a spiritual master to establish a method of control by which to discriminate between suprasensory perceptions and what we would call today "hallucinations." Technically, one should speak of it as visionary apperception. The phenomenon corresponding to it is primary and primordial, irreducible, just as the perception of a physical sound or color is irreducible to anything else. As for the organ of this visionary apperception and the mode of being in which it can function, these questions relate precisely to the "physiology of the man of light," whose growth is marked by the opening of what Najm Kobrā calls the "senses suprasensory." To the extent that the latter are the *activity* of the subject himself, of the soul, we shall conclude this study by briefly outlining an interconnection with Goethe's theory of "physiological colors."

It has to be understood, of course, that in the schema of the world presupposed and verified here by mystical experience, the terms light and darkness, clarity and obscurity, are neither metaphors nor comparisons. The mystic really and actually *sees* light and darkness, by a kind of vision that depends on an organ other than the physical organ of sight. He experiences and perceives the state from which he aspires to free himself as shadow and darkness, as powers which attract him downward; he perceives as light all the signs and premonitions heralding his liberation, the direction from which it comes, all the apparitions that attract him upward. There is nothing questionable about the *orientation* of the world experienced in the vertical dimension: at the summit the heavenly pole, at the nadir the well of darkness where the element of light is held captive (just as, in the Mazdean schema, the light is in the north, the shadow and darkness are in the south). That the entire schematization is in perfect consonance with the Manichean cosmogony and at the same time with the Sohravardian recital of the *Exile*, and with the *Song of the Pearl* in the *Acts of Thomas*, is what the first paragraph of Najm Kobrā's great book tells us: "Learn, O my friend, that the *object* of the search (*morād*) is God, and that the *subject* who seeks (the subject who makes effort, *morīd*) is a light that comes from him (or a particle of his light)." (§1)[64] In other words the "seeker," the hero of the Quest, is none other than the captive light itself, the man of light, φωτεινὸς ᾿άνθρωπος.

This is the first *leitmotiv* of Najm Kobrā's great work. This particle of light aspires to free itself, to rise again to its origin. What is depicted in those of the Persian miniatures where the Manichean influence can be detected (*infra* VI, 1) is thus exactly the same as what Najm Kobrā perceives through visionary apperception. A flame comes down from the Heavens to meet the flame leaping up from the Earth, and at their fiery meeting-point Najm discerns or foresees the presence of the "heavenly Witness," the "suprasensory Guide," who is revealed in this climax as the homologue of Perfect Nature, the *Noūs*, the ποιμήν, the guide of light of Prometheus-Phōs. There is a correlation between the escape of the man of light, the colored photisms, and the manifestation of the heavenly guide. This correlation itself intimates the condition which must precede all such experience: men must separate themselves from the veil that blinds them.

> Now, this veil is not outside themselves; it is a part of them, and is the darkness of their creatural nature. (§1)
>
> My friend, shut your eyelids and look at what you see. If you tell me: I see nothing—you are mistaken. You can see very well, but unfortunately the darkness of your nature is so close to you that it obstructs your inner sight, to the point that you do not discern what is to be seen. If you want to discern it and to see it in front of you even with your eyes closed, begin by diminishing or by putting away from you something of your nature. But the path leading to that end is spiritual warfare. And the meaning of spiritual warfare is putting everything to work so as to repel the enemies or to kill them. The enemies in this case are nature, the lower soul, and the devil. (§2)

To reach the goal, one must first *orient oneself*: discern the shadow and where the shadow is. This shadow is composed of the three antagonists that have just been named. Spiritual warfare trains one to recognize the enemies, to know them by name, to distinguish the forms in which they appear, and to effect their transmutation. Actually these various works are carried out synchronically rather than successively; progress and results are correlative: separation from the shadow and the fall of the shadow, manifestation of the lights and of the Guide of light. This exactly will serve as a final warning not to abuse the idea and the word *shadow*: the guide of light is no more the shadow than he is a "positive" aspect of the shadow. This figure requires us henceforth to recognize *another* dimension of the person, not a negativity but a transcendence. Since Najm Kobrā's book is a spiritual journal rather than a didactic treatise, a *diarium spirituale* not unlike that of Rūzbehān, the best we can do is to single out certain of its leading themes; their lines converge. The three adversaries can only be destroyed at the price of an effort that attacks the discordant trilogy of the soul. The motive power to fuel this effort is the light itself, that is, the particle of light, the "man of light," effecting the conversion of like to like. The *dhikr*, as a spiritual technique, plays an essential role. The spiritual energy given off by the *dhikr* makes possible the emergence and ascent from the well; this theme recurs with an emphasis we have already pointed out. The stages of ascent are accompanied by the colored photisms that herald the growth of the subtle organs or centers of the man of light, attracted to and by the supernatural *green* light that shines at the mouth of the well. At the end of this ascent, the phenomena of light multiply, heralding the rejoining with the heavenly Witness, at the *pole*. Najm Kobrā's entire doctrine perfectly exemplifies the archetype of individual initiation peculiar to Sufism.

2. Light and Spiritual Warfare

To recognize the three adversaries means actually to catch sight of them, to *experience* the forms in which they appear. Far from merely constructing a theory, Najm Kobrā describes real events which take place in the inner world, on the "plane of visionary apperception" (*maqām al-moshāhada*), in an order of reality corresponding specifically to the organ of perception which is the *imaginative* faculty (*Imaginatrix*).[65] This exactly is where creatural nature, natural existence (*wojūd*), "is at first sight complete darkness; when it begins to be purified, you will see it take on before your eyes the appearance of a *black* cloud. So long as it is the seat of the Devil (*shaytān*) it has a *reddish* appearance. When its excrescences are corrected and annihilated and legitimate aspirations are implanted in their stead, you will see that its appearance gradually whitens and it becomes a *white cloud* (a *cumulus*). As for the lower soul[66], at its first appearance, its color is deep *blue*; it seems to be an upsurge, like that of water from a spring. If the soul is the seat of the Devil, it looks like a twofold upsurge of *darkness* and of *fire*, without the power to show anything else, for there is no good in devilry. Now, what pours forth from the soul overflows and spreads over the whole of a man's nature; this is why all spiritual teaching depends on the soul. When the soul is healthy and pure, what flows from it is Good, and Goodness germinates from natural existence; if what flows from it is Evil, Evil will germinate. The Devil is an impure fire mixed with the darkness of impiety in monstrous form. Sometimes he takes the shape before your eyes of a gigantic Negro, terrible to look upon. He makes every effort to enter into you. If you want to make him give up, recite in your heart: 'O Thou, the help of those who ask, help me (§7).' " For, as another great Sufi says: "Satan laughs at all your threats. What frightens him is to see a *light in your heart*,"[67] that is to say, when you become aware of what he is. Now as we have read (*supra* §67 quoted *in fine* III, p. 100-101), he, like any other spiritual reality, is not outside of you; his attempts to "enter into you" are but one phase of the fight which is being waged within you.

What this means precisely is that the shadow is in you: to separate yourself from the shadow is to bring about your own metamorphosis, and by this metamorphosis to make possible the conjunction of the two currents of fire rising and falling to meet one another.

> Natural existence is made up of four elements superimposed on one another, all of which are *darkness*: Earth, Water, Fire, Air; and you yourself are buried beneath them all. The only way to separate yourself from them is to act in such a way that every rightful part in you comes together with that to which it rightfully belongs, that is, by acting in such a way that each part comes together with its counter-part: Earth receives the earthy part, Water the watery part, Air the etheric part, Fire the fiery part. When each has received its share, you will finally be delivered of these

burdens. The three adversaries disturb the innate knowledge of the divine; they form an obstacle between the *heart* and the divine *Throne*; they prevent the conjunction of the *two rays of light*. Because of them, a man finds himself at first in a state of total spiritual blindness (§11).

What is at stake in metamorphosis is therefore wholly this: either, the soul having succeeded in separating itself, the man of light effects conjunction with his guide of light, his "witness in Heaven" (*shāhid fi'l-samā*); or else the soul succumbs to its darkness, remains in the embrace of its Iblīs, its demonic shadow. "To convert *one's own* Iblīs to Islam," as Abū'l-Ma'ārī and 'Attār expresses it, means to effect the destruction of the lower soul. The individual has no power to destroy Iblīs in the world, but he can separate his soul from Iblīs by destroying the shadow in his soul, for Iblīs can weld himself to the soul only in shadow. Everything depends therefore on the effort directed to the central adversary: the soul, with its Iblīs on one side, and natural existence on the other. The stages of metamorphosis are detected by means of the three different words used in the Qorān to qualify the soul; when the third of these qualities flowers, it can be taken that the *heart* (*qalb*) exists in actuality; the heart is the subtle center of light, the Throne in the microcosm, and by that very fact the organ and place of conjunction with the light of the Throne.

3. The Trilogy of the Soul

Three characteristics situate and constitute the trilogy of the drama of the soul. There is the extravagant lower soul: *nafs ammāra* (12:53), literally, the imperative soul, "the one which commands" evil, the passionate, sensual lower *ego*. There is the "blaming" soul: *nafs lawwāma* (75:2), "the one which censures," criticizes; this is self-consciousness, and is likened to the intellect (*'aql*) of the philosophers. Finally there is the "pacified soul": *nafs motma'yanna* (89:87); the soul which in the true sense is the heart (*qalb*), to which the Qorān addresses the words: "O pacified soul, return to your Lord, accepting and accepted."[68] This return, which is the reunion of the two fiery currents, is exactly what is described in one of Najm Kobrā's most significant visions.

The extravagant lower soul, the *ego* of the common run of

§3. The Triology of the Soul

men, remains such as it is so long as the effects of spiritual warfare have not made themselves felt. When the effect of continuous prayer, the *dhikr*, penetrates it, it is as though a lamp were lighted in a darkened dwelling. Then the soul attains the degree of "blaming soul"; it perceives that the dwelling is cluttered with filth and wild beasts; it exerts itself to drive them out so that the dwelling may be ready to welcome the light of the *dhikr* as its sovereign; this welcome will be the prelude to the opening of the pacified soul (§54).

And there are signs which make it possible to recognize respectively by visionary apperception each moment in this trilogy, each phase of metamorphosis. Thanks to these signs the Spiritual retains perfect awareness of himself.

> Know that the lower soul presents a sign that makes it recognizable by visionary apperception: it is a great circle that rises in front of you, entirely *black*, as it were of tar. Then it disappears, only to arise before you again later in the aspect of a black cloud. But lo and behold! gradually, at its arising, something is revealed at its edges resembling the crescent of the *new moon* when one of its horns appears in the sky through the clouds. Little by little, it becomes a complete crescent. When the soul has become conscious of itself to the point of self-judgment, behold it rises to the side of the right cheek in the aspect of a *glowing sun* whose heat may even be felt on one's cheek. Sometimes it is visualized by the ear, sometimes before the forehead, sometimes above the head. And this *blaming soul* is the intelligence (*'aql* referred to by the philosophers) (§55).
>
> As for the *pacified soul*, it also presents a sign which makes it identifiable by visionary apperception: sometimes it rises in front of you forming as it were the orb of a great fountain giving forth lights; sometimes you visualize it in the suprasensory realm as corresponding to the circle of your countenance, an orb of light, a limpid disk, similar to a perfectly polished mirror. At times this circle may seem to rise toward your face and the latter to vanish into it. Your face is then itself the pacified soul.[69] Sometimes, on the contrary, you visualize the circle at a distance, as though far removed from you in the suprasensory realm. There are then between you and the circle of the pacified soul a thousand stages; if you were to draw near to one of them, you would be set on fire (§56).

From here on the end is in sight. The path will be long and perilous; it is difficult to describe, that is, it is not easy to connect descriptions of the path in a logical and rational order in which no moment would overlap another. Najm Kobrā's *Diarium* offers us rather the possibility of developing the theme of each phase alternately, considering them successively from several points of view, amongst which priority is given to that which applies to the force that moves the mystical pilgrim along the Way. From another point of view, to perceive the effects of this spiritual energy in him will be a way of following the stages of the ascent and the concomitant growth of the "organs of light," which multiplies *eo ipso* the possibilities of visionary apperception, leading to the vision that proclaims the integration of bi-unity.

4. Like with Like

So far we have been given the names of three organs or centers: the soul (*nafs*), the intellect (*'aql*), the heart (*qalb*). Two other centers, the spirit (*rūh*) and the transconsciousness (*sirr*, the "secret") take their place in a whole where their meaning and function will be made clear to us later in the writings of Najm Kobrā's disciples (*infra* V, 2 and VI, 1). These are the centers of a subtle physiology, recognizable by the colored lights which symbolize them. These are the organs which allow the supreme principle to operate, in hierocosmology as in hierognosis: like seeks to unite with like. A substance sees and knows only its like; it can itself be seen and known only by its like (§70). This is the principle which, according to Najm Kobrā, governs the fundamental intuition and sets it in operation: what is sought is the divine Being; the seeker is himself a light coming from the divine Being, a particle of its light. The statement and application of the principle certainly awaken many consonances. We already hear it in Empedocles: "Fire can be seen only by fire." In the *Corpus Hermeticum* (11/20) where the *Noūs* declares to Hermes: "If you do not make yourself like God, you cannot understand God." In Plotinus (*Enneads* VI, 9, 11): "The Principle can be seen only by the Principle." In the West it leads us from Meister Eckhart to Goethe (*infra* VI, 2).

'Alī-e Hamadānī, the great shaykh responsible for the spread of Sufism in India, formulates it briefly in a way that is particularly striking:[70] The human being, he says, is a copy

68

transcribed from the great Qorān which is the cosmos. Everything that constitutes this cosmic Qorān—suras, verses, words, letters, vowel signs—has an esoteric and an exoteric aspect.

> In each part of a man which has been purified, its counterpart of the same nature is reflected, for nothing can be seen except by its like. Therefore, when the esoteric nature indicated by a man's inclinations and faculties has become pure, he contemplates therein whatever is of the same nature in the macrocosm. The same applies to the soul, the heart, the spirit, the transconsciousness, up to the arcanum (*khafī*), the innermost place where the divine Attributes which intoxicate are unveiled, and where it can be said *I am His hearing, I am His sight . . .*

The parts constituting the human being can even be regarded as fragments of their cosmic counterparts; each belongs to a whole from which it derives. Najm Kobrā thus establishes a real connection between the fire of passion and the infernal fire: the fire of voluptuousness, of hunger and thirst, of wickedness and sensuality are parts of the infernal fire. By feeding these fires a man increases his hell, for hell is not outside of him; man is his own hell (§130). Particles of different natures are mutually repellent; the particles imprisoned in man are attracted to their like. The attraction, in its physical aspect, is magnetism, in its psychic aspect, the yearning of like for like. Actually the first aspect is only the exoteric aspect of the second; Najm Kobrā is thinking of the second aspect when he has recourse to his favorite image of the precious stone longing for the world from which it was originally extracted.

For this attraction is *oriented*: toward the Heaven of the soul, the suprasensory Heaven, the inner Heaven, or perhaps it is better to say the "esoteric" Heaven, in case the word "inner" should give rise to the idea of a subjective "heaven" lacking any substantial reality. Orientation toward the Heaven of the soul, toward the *pole*, presupposes and brings about this inward movement which is the return to the vast world of the soul, the passage to the "esoteric." The subtle organ which envelops the heart and which Najm Kobrā calls the Holy Ghost in man is identified with this Heaven. The subtle organ designated as Spirit is the Heaven of the heart. The movement inward brings about the passage from this world to the world beyond, from the outer man to the man of light. As we have noted, the idea of the spiritual Heavens had already led Sohravardī to explode the schema of Ptolemaic astronomy, and the same idea opened the way to the Emerald Rock for Hermes and the expatriate in the Recital of the Exile. This passage, this *exodus*, is what authenticates and what is foreseen in the visions received by visionary apperception, in which there are an above and a below, Heavens and Earths: because oriented toward the pole, all this no longer has to do with the world of objects of sensory experience. The reascent of like towards its like (the ascent of the "column of Light") traversing the entire cosmos, the return of light to light, of precious stones to their origin: the anthropology which is its organ is the science that concerns the man of light and is oriented toward the *pole*. If this were not so, the *mi'rāj* of the prophet and the ascent out of the well are unintelligible and devoid of reality. If this is so, then mystical experience fills a function of cosmic salvation. Several essential passages in Najm Kobrā's treatises make this abundantly clear.

> The Holy Ghost in man is a heavenly subtle organ. When the concentrated power of spiritual energy[71] is lavished on him, he is reunited with the Heavens and the Heavens are merged with him. Or rather, Heavens and Spirit are one and the same thing. And this Spirit does not cease to soar, to increase, and to grow until it has acquired a nobility higher than the nobility of Heaven. Or again we could say: in the human being there are precious stones from every kind of mine, and everything that aspires to rediscover its own original mine is of the same nature as the latter (§59).

But Najm makes it clear that will and effort are necessary to set free this attractive energy.

> I have never contemplated Heaven *below* me nor *within* me, unless beforehand there had arisen in me an effort and this complaint: why am I not now in Heaven or greater than Heaven? For then the noble precious stones in exile were experiencing a consuming nostalgia for their original home and found it again at last (§59).[72]

It is therefore the terminal point of this reunion that guarantees the orientation: Earths and Heavens of the suprasensory realm, of the beyond whose threshold is the *pole*.

> Know that visionary apperception is twofold: there is perception of what is below and perception of what is above. Below is the vision of all that the Earth (and by Earth I mean here the su-

prasensory Earth *Terra lucida*, not the Earth which is in the physically visible world)—of all, I repeat, that the Earth contains by way of colors, oceans, luminaries, deserts, landscapes, cities, wells, fortresses, etc. Above, there is the vision of all that the Heavens contain: sun, moon, stars, constellations of the Zodiac, houses of the moon. Now, you see and discern nothing whatsoever except by means of something that is its like (or which is a part of it): the precious stone sees only the mine from which it originated, it yearns and is homesick for that alone. Therefore when you envision a heaven, an earth, a sun, or stars, or a moon, know that this is because the particle in you which comes from that mine has become pure (§60).

There follows the warning we have already read (*supra* III, 3 *in fine*) and which conditions all suprasensory experience: whatever the heavens you are contemplating, there are always other heavens beyond; there is no limit.

Mutual attraction and recognition of like by like: this law is exemplified in multiple variations throughout Najm Kobrā's doctrine and mystical experience. It is the basis of a *communicatio idiomatum* between the divine and the human, a reciprocity of states which is very characteristically projected and expressed in terms of spatialization and localization. Pure spiritual space arises from the state experienced, and the state experienced is a visitation of the divine Attributes. Here we may recall the Coptic Gnostic books of Ieu (third century),[73] in which the Emanations of the true God Ieu surrounding a Treasury, the *place* of the true God, are themselves the places or abodes of the τόποι; the soul of the mystic is welcomed there by the collectors of the Treasury of Light; under their guidance it leaps from one *place* to another, until it reaches the Treasury of Light. The *mahādir*, in Najm Kobrā's terminology, correspond exactly to those places or abodes known to the gnostics. "The divine Being has different places or abodes and they are the *places* of the Attributes. You distinguish them from one another by your own mystical experience, for when you rise to this or that place, your tongue involuntarily utters the name of that place and of its attribute."

Here again, therefore, there are signs and indications which make verification possible, as previously in the case of each of the places of the soul, and as there will be also for each of the colored photisms.

IV. Visio Smaragdina

> The heart participates in every divine Attribute, and there-
> fore in the divine Essence. This participation does not cease to
> grow, and the mystics differ from each other according to the
> extent of their participation. Since each Attribute has its seat in
> one of the places or abodes in question, and since the heart par-
> ticipates in each of the divine Attributes, they are epiphanized in
> the heart to the extent that the heart participates in these Attrib-
> utes. Thus Attributes are revealed to Attributes, Essence to Es-
> sence (or the Self to the Self). On the one hand, the Attributes (or
> places) contemplate the heart (cause it to be present to them). On
> the other hand, the heart contemplates the places of the Attrib-
> utes (makes itself present to them). Theophany is brought about
> first by theoretical knowledge, later by visionary apperception,
> whether the Attributes make themselves witnesses present to the
> heart, or whether the heart makes itself a witness and present to
> the *places* of the Attributes (§61).

This is a subtle passage and hard to follow at first, but extremely important, because it is the preliminary outline of and
introduction to the subsequent account of the relationship of
the mystic with his "heavenly Witness" which will develop at the
summit of his inner ascent. In this relationship the Contemplator (*shāhid*) is simultaneously the one who is Contemplated (*mashhūd*), the one who witnesses is simultaneously
the one who is witnessed, and this already indicates that the
idea of the "heavenly Witness" in Najm Kobrā is no different,
in essence, from the idea of the Witness of contemplation
which orients the spiritual view of other contemporary Sufi
masters.

Furthermore, this relationship results from the idea that
the seeker is himself a particle of the divine light that is being
sought; it illustrates the principle of the Quest and of the recognition of "like by like," which is amplified with extraordinary
power in other passages, calling us to witness this *reunion* which
is the culminating moment of personal initiation.

> There are lights which ascend and lights which descend.
> The ascending lights are the lights of the heart; the descending
> lights are those of the Throne. Creatural being is the veil between
> the Throne and the heart. When this veil is rent and a door to the
> Throne opens in the heart, like springs toward like. Light rises
> toward light and light comes down upon light, "*and it is light upon
> light*" (Qorān 24:35) (§62).

Everything that we are analyzing may well be condensed in

§5. *The Function of the* Dhikr

those few lines: a totality which is "light upon light," not light *and* shadow, in the perspective of the threefold psychic dimension, as we have again to emphasize in conclusion (*infra* IV, 10).

Here are further invaluable quotations:

> Each time the heart sighs for the Throne, the Throne sighs for the heart, so that they come to meet . . . Each precious stone (that is, each of the elements of the man of light) which is in you brings you a mystical state or vision in the Heaven corresponding to it, whether it be the fire of ardent desire, of delight or of love (see §83 quoted *infra* IV, 9). Each time a *light rises up from you, a light comes down toward you*, and each time a flame rises from you, a corresponding flame comes down toward you (see further §83) . . . If their energies are equal, they meet half-way (between Heaven and Earth) . . . But when the substance of light has grown in you, then this becomes a Whole in relation to what is of the same nature in Heaven: then it is the substance of light in Heaven which yearns for you and is attracted by your light, and it descends toward you. This is the secret of the mystical approach (*sirr al-sayr*, §63-64).

A truly fascinating description; but how does the Sufi reach this aim? The most effective means of realization offered to him is the *dhikr* (= *zekr*), continuous prayer. This is what can bring about the opening and then the growth of this substance of light which is in you, to such a degree that by attracting the heavenly Witness, its suprasensory Guide, the reunion will take place. The stages of growth of this organism of light will then be marked by the colored photisms, until the particle of divine light, the man of light within you, your φωτεινὸς ἄνθρωπος, suddenly bursts forth.

5. *The Function of the* Dhikr

Of all spiritual practices: meditation on the sayings of the Prophet and on the traditions of Sufism, meditated recitation of the Qorān, ritual Prayer, and so forth, the *dhikr* (*zekr*) is the practice most apt to free spiritual energy, that is, to allow the particle of divine light which is in the mystic to rejoin its like. The advantage of the *dhikr* is that it is not restricted to any ritual hour; its only limitation is the personal capacity of the mystic. It is impossible to study the question of colored photisms without knowing the spiritual exercise which is their source. Everything takes place, needless to say, in the *ghayba*,

73

the suprasensory world; what is in question here is solely the physiology of the man of light. Najm Kobrā set himself the task of describing the cases and circumstances in which the fire of the *dhikr* itself becomes the object of mystical apperception. As opposed to the fire of the Devil, which is a dark fire, the vision of which is accompanied by distress and a feeling of overwhelming oppression, the fire of the *dhikr* is visualized as a pure and ardent blaze, animated by a rapid upward movement (§8). On seeing it, the mystic experiences a feeling of inner lightness, expansion, and intimate relief. This fire enters into the dwelling place like a sovereign prince, announcing: "I alone, and none other than I." It sets fire to all that is there to be consumed, and sheds light on any darkness it may encounter. If light is there already, the two lights associate with each other and there is *light upon light* (§§9-10).

That is why one form of the *dhikr* above all other, leading in actuality to the acquisition of this pure and ardent flame, consists in repeating the first part of the *shahāda*, the profession of faith: *lā ilāha illā'llāh* (*Nullus deus nisi Deus*), and meditating upon it according the the rules of Sufism.[74] In Ismaelian Shī'ite gnosis, theosophical dialectic was already practiced with extreme subtlety by alternating the negative and affirmative phases composing the first part of the *shahāda*, in order to open up a path between the two abysses, the *ta'tīl* and the *tashbīh*, that is to say, between rationalist agnosticism and the literal realism of naive faith. By following this way, the idea of mediating theophanies is established, the hierarchy of the pleroma of light. While the transcendence of the Principle beyond being and non-being is preserved in Ismaelian gnosis, orthodoxy is blamed inasmuch as it falls into the most pernicious kind of metaphysical idolatry, the very one it was so anxious to avoid. In the Sufism of Najm Kobrā, the reiteration of the negative part of the *shahāda* (*nullus Deus*) is designed to be a weapon against all the powers of the *nafs ammāra* (the lower ego); it consists in denying and rejecting all pretensions to divine prerogatives, all claims inspired in the soul by the instincts of possessiveness and domination. In the positive part of the *shahāda* (*nisi Deus*) on the other hand the exclusive nature and powers of the One and Only One are affirmed.

Then there comes about the state alluded to in a saying

tirelessly repeated by the Sufis, and familiar to us because we have read it in St. Paul (*I Cor.* 2:9), where in fact it harks back to the *Revelation of Elijah*.[75] The mystic "sees what the eye has not seen, hears what no ear has heard, while thoughts arise in his mind which had never arisen in the heart of man," that is to say, of man who remains buried in the depths of natural existence. For the effect of the *fire-light* of the *dhikr* is to make a man clairvoyant in Darkness; and this clairvoyance foretells that the heart is being freed, is emerging from the *well* of nature; but (let us remember the Sohravardian *Recital of the Exile*) "only a heart that holds fast to the cable of the Qorān and to the train of the robe of the *dhikr*[76] escapes from the well of nature."

No doubt the practice of the *dhikr* in Najm Kobrā's school includes also a whole system of techniques: movements of the head, control of breathing, certain postures (in Semnānī for example, the seated position with crossed legs, right hand placed on left hand, the latter holding the right leg which is placed on the left thigh) possibly revealing Taoist influence.[77] By uninterrupted polarization of the attention on an object, the object finally imposes itself with such force, is imbued with such life, that the mystic is attracted and is, as it were, absorbed into it. This is the phenomenon Rudolf Otto found so striking when he had already discerned a clear parallel between the Sufi *dhikr* and the μνήμη τοῦ Θεοῦ or Ἰησοῦ practiced by the monks of Athos and in early Christian monasticism.[78]

The preponderant role of the Sufi *dhikr* is justified in that it establishes experientially the connection between the theme of the ascent from the well, the polar orientation of the spiritual seeker and the growth of his body of light. The polar orientation in this case signifies also and essentially an inward movement as the way of passing to the world beyond. Najm Kobrā describes by meticulous analyses and reference to his personal experience this process of internalization: it is a gradual deepening of the *dhikr* in three stages. As it was recalled above, the phenomena described relate not to the physical organism but to the physiology of the subtle body and its organs.

A first and still incomplete phase of penetration is marked by acoustic phenomena which may be painful and even dangerous: in such a case (as Najm was strictly advised by his shaykh), it is absolutely necessary to interrupt the *dhikr* until everything returns to normal (§§45 ff.) The two other phases are described as the fall or absorption of the *dhikr* first into the *heart*, then into the *sirr*, or "secret," the transconsciousness. "When the *dhikr* is immersed in the heart, the heart is then sensed as though it were itself a well and the *dhikr* a pail lowered into it to draw up water," or, according to another image of the same experience: the heart is 'Īsā ibn Maryam, and the *dhikr* is the milk that nourishes him. Thus we find again the theme of the birth of the spiritual Child (*supra* II, 1), a theme whose equivalent is reiterated by so many mystics and which led the Sufis to regard Maryam as the typification of the mystic soul (§49). Other descriptions given by Najm Kobrā speak of an opening produced by the *dhikr* on the top of the head, through which "descend on you first a darkness (of natural existence), then a fiery light, then the *green light* of the heart" (*ibid.*); or again, of a wound in the side through which the heart and its Holy Ghost escape like a horseman with his mount and make their way up to the divine places, (*mahādir al-Haqq*, the τόποι of the Gnostics, *supra*) (§50). Let us not necessarily infer that this indicates some outer stigmatization. None of this takes place in the outer sensory world, nor in the "imaginary" world, but only in the *mundus imaginalis* (*'alam al-mithāl*), the *imaginative* world to which belong organs of the same nature in the human being, namely the centers of subtle physiology (the *latīfa*). In a final phase, the *dhikr* is intermingled so intimately with the fundamental being of the mystic that were the latter to abandon the *dhikr*, the *dhikr* would not abandon him. "Its fire does not cease to blaze, its lights no longer disappear. Without interruption you see lights rising and lights descending. The flames of the fire are all around you—very pure, very ardent, and very strong (§51)."

6. *The Green Light*

Lights ascending, lights descending: the *dhikr* sinks down into the well of the heart and at the same time lifts the mystic up out of the darkness of the well. The simultaneity of these concentric movements foretells the birth and growth of the subtle organism of light. The descriptions become more complicated and interwoven until they are resolved, as Najm Kobrā tells us, in the *visio smaragdina* to which these movements are the prelude. "Ours is the method of alchemy," declares the shaykh. "It involves extracting the subtle organism of light from beneath the mountains under which it lies imprisoned" (§12). "It may happen that you visualize yourself as lying at the bottom of a well and the well seemingly in lively downward movement. In reality it is you who are moving upward" (*ibid.*). This ascent (reminding of the vision of Hermes in Sohravardī, his ascent to the battlements of the Throne), is the gradual emergence from the mountains which, as we have already been told (*supra* IV, 2), are the four elementary natures constituting the physical organism. The inner states accompanying this emergence are translated into visions of deserts, even "cities, countries, houses, which come down from above toward you and later disappear below you, as though you were seeing a dike on the shore crumble and disappear into the sea" (§12).

This correspondence is precisely what provides the mystic with a decisive method by which to verify the reality of his visions; it is a guarantee against illusions, for it demands the maintenance of a rigorous *balance*.

> You come to gaze with your own eyes on what you had until then only known theoretically, through the intellect. When you envision yourself as submerged in a sea, and yet making your way across it, know that this is the elimination of superfluous fetal requirements originating from the element Water. If the sea is clear and if suns or lights or flames are drowned in it, know that it is the sea of mystic gnosis. When you envision rain descending, know that it is a dew which falls from the *places* of Divine Mercy to vivify the earths of hearts slumbering in death. When you visualize a flame in which you are first entirely engulfed and from which you then free yourself, know that this is the destruction of the elements surrounding the fetus that originate in the element Fire. Finally, when you see before you a great wide space, an immensity opening onto the far distance, while above you there is clear pure Air and you perceive on the far horizon the colors *green*, *red*, *yellow*, *blue*, know that you are about to pass, borne aloft through this air, to the field of these colors. The colors are those of the spiritual states experienced inwardly. The color *green* is the sign of the life of the heart; the color of ardent pure *fire* is the sign of the vitality of spiritual energy,[79] signifying the power to actualize. If this fire is dim, it denotes in the mystic a state of fatigue and affliction following the battle with the lower ego and the Devil. *Blue* is the color of this lower ego. *Yellow* indicates a lessening of activity. All these are suprasensory realities in dialogue with the one who experiences them in the twofold language of inner feel-

IV. Visio Smaragdina

ing (*dhawq*) and visionary apperception. These are two complementary witnesses, for *you experience inwardly in yourself what you
visualize with your inner sight, and reciprocally you visualize with your
inner sight precisely what you experience in yourself (§ 13)*.

The shaykh formulates in this way the very law of *balance*
which makes it possible to authenticate these visions of colored
lights, and is all the more necessary since it is a matter, not of
optical perceptions, but of phenomena perceived by the organ
of inner sight; *balance* makes it possible to discriminate and distinguish them from "hallucinations." Discrimination is in fact
established to the extent that the inner state experienced in
reality is verified by its correspondence with the state which
would be brought about by the outer perception of such and
such a color. To that extent, what is in question is certainly no
illusion but a real visualization and a sign, that is to say, the coloration of *real* objects and events whose reality, of course, is not
physical but suprasensory, psycho-spiritual. This is why these
colored photisms are in the full sense of the word *witnesses*—
witnesses of what you *are*, of what your vision is worth, and
prefigure the vision of the personal "heavenly Witness." The
importance of the color *green* (the color of the *pole*) derives
from this whole context, since it is the color of the heart and of
the vitality of the heart (§14). Now, the heart is the homologue
of the Throne, of the *pole* which is the threshold of the beyond.
And so we recognize here more than one feature already figur-
ing in Sohravardī's *Recital of the Exile*.

"*Green* is the color that outlasts the others.[80] From this color
emanate flashing, sparkling rays. This green may be absolutely
pure or it may become tarnished. Its purity proclaims the dominant note of the divine light; its dullness results from a return
of the darkness of nature" (§15). Just as the mountain of Qāf
(the psycho-cosmic mountain, *supra* III, 1) wholly takes on the
coloration of the Emerald Rock which is its summit (the pole,
the cosmic north), so "is the heart a subtle organ which reflects
suprasensory things and realities that revolve around it. The
color of the thing is reproduced in the subtle organ (*latīfa*) it
faces, just as forms are reflected in mirrors or in pure water . . .
the heart is a light in the depths of the *well* of nature, like
Joseph's light in the well into which he was thrown" (§16).

And so from then on, in this light, the vicissitudes of the

78

ascent out of the well begin to take shape. The first time that the *well* is revealed to you it shows you a depth to which no depth perceived physically can be compared. Whereas in the waking state you are on the way to becoming familiar with it, when you visualize it in a state where the outer senses are under restraint (or "missing," that is, in the suprasensory *ghayba*), you are shaken by such terror that you think you are about to die. And then, suddenly at the mouth of the well the extraordinary *green light* begins to shine. From then on, unforgettable marvels show themselves to you, those of the *Malakūt* (the world of the *Animae coelestes*, the esoteric aspect of the visible heavens), those of the *Jabarūt* (the world of the Cherubim, of the divine Names). You experience the most contradictory feelings: exultation, terror, attraction. At the end of the mystic way, you will see the well below you. In the course of the ascent, the whole of the well is changed into a well of light or of green color. "Dark at the beginning, because it was the dwelling-place of devils, it is now luminous with *green light*, because it has become the place to which descend the Angels and the divine Compassion" (§17). Here Najm Kobrā testifies to the angelophanies which were granted to him: the emergence from the well under the guidance of four Angels surrounding him; the descent of the *sakīna* (the *shekhina*), a group of Angels who descend into the heart; or else the vision of a single Angel bearing him up as the prophet was borne up (§§19-21).[81]

And then all the spiritual Heavens, the inner Heavens of the soul, the seven planes of being which have their counterparts in the man of light shine multicolored in the rainbow of the *visio smaragdina*.

Know that to exist is not limited to a single act. There is no act of being such that above it one does not discover an act of being even more definite and more beautiful than the one preceding it, until finally one reaches the divine Being. On the mystic journey there is a *well* corresponding to each act of being. The categories of being are limited to seven; it is to this that the number of the Earths and the Heavens alludes.[82] Therefore, when you have risen up through the seven wells in the different categories of existence, lo and behold, the Heaven of the sovereign condition (*robūbīya*) and its power are revealed to you. Its atmosphere is a *green light* whose greenness is that of a vital light through which flow waves eternally in movement towards one another. This green color is so intense that human spirits are not strong enough to bear it, though it does not prevent them from falling into mystic love with it. And on the surface of this heaven are to be seen points more intensely *red* than fire, ruby or cornelian, which appear lined up in groups of five. On seeing them, the mystic experiences nostalgia and a burning desire; he aspires to unite with them (§18).

7. *The Senses of the Suprasensory World*

We shall understand the meaning of these glowing constellations after hearing a description where the theme of the ascent out of the well is repeated from the point of view of the inner states or events visualized in this way. What you visualize, according to the shaykh's teaching, are the stages of your inner ascent, that is, the very facts of your inner experience. Now, what is the content of this experience? It is the growth of the man of light, the transmutation of his senses into organs of light, into "suprasensory senses." Here the physiology of the man of light, involving a whole doctrine of symbolic forms, recapitulates the *itinerarium ad visionem smaragdinam* from another aspect. In other words, the colors characterizing the colored photisms of visionary apperception signify, to put it briefly, the transmutation of the sensory by a transmutation of the senses into "suprasensory senses."

The process is minutely described by Najm Kobrā. It can be no more than summarized here. We already know that there is a strict interconnection between the feeling of a mystic state and visionary apperception, the latter being the visualization of the former.

> But there is a difference in that the visionary apperception presupposes the opening of the inner eye by the removal of the veil which darkened it, whereas the feeling of mystic experience (*dhawq*) is caused by a transmutation of the being and of the spirit. The mystical experience is the intimate feeling that an event is taking place within you. This transmutation includes a transmutation of the faculties of sensory perception. The five senses are changed into *other senses* (§41).

And what is essential here can no doubt be expressed as follows: an inversion which brings about a suprasensory perception of the sensory, that is, perception of the sensory in the *mundus imaginalis* which Sohravardī calls the heavenly Earth of

Hūrqalyā (the *Terra lucida*, in the cosmic north), familiar to all
visonary mystics such as, for example, Ibn 'Arabī,[83] for whom it
is the place of transfigurations, the place where the *imaginative*
power (*Imaginatrix*) operates to produce scenes in which there
is no tinge of demonic, twilight "fantasy."

Looking back briefly, we can see the distance that has been
covered along the mystic Way. At the beginning visonary apperception is directed to the figures and images originating in
the sensory world; later it directly perceives persons, essences
(*dhawāt*), and it is then (and the concomitance must be stressed)
that the colored photisms come about. More explicitly: the intellect, like a hunter, begins by being on the lookout for suprasensory realities (the *ma'ānī*, the hidden, "esoteric" contents).
It has a twofold net for catching them: the imaginative and the
representative faculties. The visual faculty is as it were his dog,
his pointer. The imagination clothes the *ma'ānī* in appropriate
attire; for example, it gives a contemptible enemy the form of a
dog, a noble and generous enemy the form of a lion, etc. The
science of the *ta'bīr* of dreams[84] is founded on this, the interpretation of symbols, that is to say of indirect perceptions.
(§42)

However, should one say the events *directly* perceived in
Hūrqalyā are *only* symbols? If it is more fitting to say "nothing
less" than symbols, thereby referring to the quality that causes a
thing to "symbolize with" another, does this not mean to say
that this synchronism already postulates precisely what follows
from the inversion described above? *New senses* perceive *directly*
the order of reality corresponding to them. At this stage, in
fact, the intellect realizes how deceptive are the senses which
previously suggested to it that nothing is real except what is
physically seen, tasted and touched. Now it has discovered
"another mode of sensory perception" (*ihsās ākhar*), "suprasensory senses" (*hiss ghaybī*—all of this precise terminology must be
noted), and consequently an active Imagination, other than the
imagination that is forced to adhere to the data of the physical
senses. The intellect now refuses to believe in the data from the
previous way of sensing things.[85] It is no longer interested in
"hunting," since it perceives directly. "Henceforth, spiritual
realities are displayed to it in *colors*, because the synchronism of
colors and inner vision is now established."

IV. Visio Smaragdina

In still other words, a decisive event has taken place: the colors are evidence of perfect internalization, perfect concordance between the state experienced and the event visualized, and this is what constitutes the transmutation of the physical senses into "suprasensory senses" or into the "senses of the suprasensory world," into organs of light. The perception of the colored photisms coincides with the moment when these suprasensory senses come into action as the organs of the man of light, of the "particle of the divine light." "All the *ma'ānī* return to their source in the heart; everything becomes fixed in a single color, the *green* which is the color of the vitality of the heart" (§43). Here again, in the inner Heavens of resplendent emerald green, a star emerges, *reddish purple*, the color that, according to Najm Kobrā, heralds the Intelligence in its twofold form:[86] that of the macrocosm (*Insān Kabīr, Homo maximus*), namely the Angel-Logos, the theophany of the Inaccessible, and that of the microcosm, another name for the *nafs lawwāma*, which, as we have seen, being the light-consciousness casting off the *shadow*, thus makes the state of "pacified soul" accessible to the heart whose vitality is proclaimed by the green light. The visionary coherence of the figures and images is striking.

8. *The Orbs of Light*

And so the event experienced (the ascent from the well) and the visualizations (the colored photisms) are synchronic and mutually verify each other, because they take place at the same time as the opening of the man of light, that is, of the organs of light (the suprasensory senses) of his subtle physiology. Other photisms described by Najm Kobrā now tell us of his growth, which will continue until the visualization of the "Invisible Guide," the "heavenly Witness," is reached. This growth is proclaimed by the vision of orbs of light forming the antithesis to the circle of darkness perceived by the mystic in the beginning, when his lower ego (*nafs ammāra*) was still projecting a shadow. Each of the senses transmuted into "suprasensory senses," or rather each of the subtle organs of light corresponding to the physical senses, is heralded by a light which is proper to it. Thus there is a light of speech, a light of hearing, etc.

(§57).[87] However, these latter are not yet experienced in the aspect of the geometrical figures so characteristic of some of Najm Kobrā's visualizations, such as circles which manifest the face in the final stage of the mystic pilgrimage. Amongst other circles, there is the double circle of the eyes, two orbs of light which appear wherever one turns, to the right or to the left. There is the circle of the divine Light which is manifested as equidistant from the two eyes. There is the circle of the vital *pneuma* (*dā'irat al-rūh*), etc. (§57).

The double circle of the two eyes comes to be seen as of predominant significance, for, to the degree that the "Inner Heavens" are purified, it becomes bigger until it shows the circle of the complete face and finally the *aura* of the whole "person of light." The phases of the appearance of this orb of light allow us to make various preliminary comparisons. It passes, in fact, through stages of growth corresponding to the phases of the Moon, starting from the new moon. Because this growth is simultaneously the passage to the "Inner Heavens" (Spirit and Heaven are one and the same thing, we have been told), the mystic thus inwardly experiences the twenty-eight lunar stations which correspond to the twenty-eight letters of the Arabic alphabet, since the latter, interpreted as letters of the "philosophical alphabet," are engendered by the heaven of the Moon (§111).[88]

The double circle of the light of the eyes (or eyes of light) grows as the mystic journey progresses. Allusion was made above (IV, 6 *in fine*) to the seven categories of being, to the seven heavens which have their counterparts in the mystic's inner world. The growth of the orbs of light refers to the inner ascent through seven strata, from each of which proceed the "letters" of each Heaven and which, according to Semnānī (*infra* VI), are the *latīfa*, the subtle organs of the physiology of the man of light. Furthermore, whatever their differences, there is something in common between the circles of which Najm Kobrā speaks and every other vision or diagram in the form of a circle made known to us from other sources (Hallāj, the Druses), just as there is homology of function between the *latīfa* of Semnānī and the *chakras* which are the centers of consciousness and the organs of suprasensory perception in Mahayana Buddhism.

IV. Visio Smaragdina

"When such and such a part of the inner Heaven gradually becomes pure, the color of that Sky and its magnitude in relation to the preceding Heaven become visible to the mystic, until finally the circle coincides with the entire face (§115)." It may even happen, for example, when a state of happiness succeeds distress, or when fear changes to familiarity, or when torpor is succeeded by ardent desire, that all the circles of light of the face are manifested at the same time. It then seems to the mystic that the August Face itself is revealed to him, irradiated by flaming circles which surround it with hymns of praise: "Involuntarily he utters: 'Glory be to me! Glory be to me! How sublime my state!'[89]—when he finds himself wholly immersed in this light. Or else, retaining a sense of himself, he will utter in the third person: 'Glory be to him! Glory be to him! How sublime is his state!'(§115)."

9. The "Heavenly Witness"

And so now we come to the innermost secret of the mystical experience, to the decisive event already pre-sensed in the splendors of the "emerald vision." The alternation between the first and the third person, the substitution of the one for the other, are only another way of stating the same paradox—procreated-procreator, Contemplated-Contemplator—which the theme of Perfect Nature had already allowed us to grasp as being the supreme expression of individual spiritual initiation. In this realization of reciprocity alone can the features of the August Face be fleetingly glimpsed: a face of light which is your own face because you are yourself a particle of Its light. What the mystic, by virtue of his ardent desire, pursues and experiences is not a collective relationship shared by all alike in respect to a singular object, is not a relationship identical for all to which everyone has an equal claim in respect to one and the same object. No, this relationship is unique, individual, unshareable, because it is a relationship of love. It is not a filial relationship, but rather a *marital* one. An individual, unshared relationship of this nature can only be manifested, represented, and expressed by a figure which *attests* to the real presence of one alone to one alone and for one alone, in a dialogue *unus-ambo*. The figure of the "Heavenly Witness," of the suprasensory personal Guide, thus guarantees with such certainty a theophany perceived by love alone, corresponding to a feeling of *marital relationship*, that its most characteristic manifestations—the flaming of photisms bearing witness to the reunion of "like with like"—come about at the moment of a state of love carried to its climax. The mystical experience described by Najm Kobrā thus comes to accord with the forms and experience of celestial love in Iranian Sufism.

> When the circle of the face has become pure [writes the shaykh], "it effuses lights as a spring pours forth its water, so that the mystic has a sensory perception (i.e., through the suprasensory senses) that these lights are gushing forth to irradiate his face. This outpouring takes place between the two eyes and between the eyebrows. Finally it spreads to cover the whole face. At that moment, before you, before your face, there is another Face also of light, irradiating lights; while behind its diaphanous veil a *sun* becomes visible, seemingly animated by a movement to and fro. In reality this Face is your own face and this sun is the sun of the Spirit (*shams al-rūh*) that goes to and fro in your body. Next, the whole of your person is immersed in purity, and suddenly you are gazing at a person of light (*shakhmin nūr*) who is also irradiating lights. The mystic has the sensory perception of this irradiation of lights proceeding from the whole of his person. Often the veil falls and the total reality of the person is revealed, and then with the whole of your body you perceive the whole. The opening of the inner sight (*basīra*, the visual organ of light) begins in the eyes, then in the face, then in the chest, then in the entire body. This person of light (*shakhs nūrānī*) before you is called in Sufi terminology the suprasensory *Guide* (*mooaddam al-ghayb*). It is also called the suprasensory *personal Master* (*shaykh al-ghayb*), or again the suprasensory spiritual *Scales* (*mīzām al-ghayb*) (§66).[90]

It has been given many other names, all reminiscent of the "midnight sun," the witness in the vision of Hermes described by Sohravardī (*supra* II, 1 and III, 1). Najm Kobrā refers to the Guide of light as the Sun of the heart, the Sun of certainty, the Sun of faith, the Sun of knowledge, the spiritual Sun of the Spirit.[91] And more explicitly still he says: "Know that the mystic has a Witness (*shāhid*). He it is who is called the personal Master in the suprasensory world. He carries the mystic up toward the Heavens; thus it is in the Heavens that he appears (§69)."

The personal Guide in the suprasensory world is thus expressly designated as the *shāhid*. It is a characteristic term in the vocabulary of those spiritual seekers who, in Sufism, should rightly be called the "faithful lovers," because of the "divine service" they render to beauty by contemplating it as the greatest of all theophanies.[92] When Najm Kobrā refers more precisely to the "Witness in the Heavens" (*shāhid fi'l samā*), the heavenly Witness, this epithet further accentuates the essential aspect of the *shāhid*, of the "witness of contemplation," meditated similarly by mystics such as Rūzbehān or Ibn 'Arabī, and it immediately places the original expression of the shaykh's visionary apperception in the context of Iranian Sufism; lastly, this designation should make it impossible to distort the idea of the *Shāhid* by an erroneous psychological interpretation and bring it down to the notion of the "Double" as being the *shadow*.

For a "faithful lover" like Rūzbehān of Shīrāz, every beautiful face is a theophanic witness because it is a mirror without which the divine Being would remain a *Deus absconditus*. It is likewise significant that in Najm Kobrā the "Witness in the Heavens" should be pre-sensed in the aspect of an outburst of flame visualized in the Heavens, and accompanied by a state of intense love. Between the heavenly person of the Guide of light and the object—that is to say, the earthly person loved with a celestial love—the relationship is an epiphany, since it even gives rise to the symptom visible to the eyes of the suprasensory senses of the presence of the "witness in the Heavens." Since the latter is visible to the "eyes of light" only to the degree that the man of light frees himself from the crude ore of darkness, there is evidence that celestial love is the teacher initiating this liberation. This is why the idea of the *shāhid* finds its place in a complete doctrine of mystical love, bringing together the earthly loved one and the "witness in the heavens" manifested as the Guide of light. Needless to say the phenomena here again have to do with the physiology of the "suprasensory senses."

> Lo and behold! [writes Najm Kobrā] while sojourning in Egypt, in a small town on the banks of the Nile, I fell passionately in love with a young girl. For many days, I remained practically without food and without drink, and in this way the flame of love within me became extraordinarily intense. My breath exhaled flames of fire. And each time I breathed out fire, lo and behold, from the height of heaven *someone* was also breathing out fire which came to meet my own breath. The two shafts of flame blended between the Heavens and me. For a long time I did not

know *who* it was who was there at the place where the two flames came together. But at last I understood that it was my *witness in Heaven* (§83).

Nothing could illustrate better than this experiental verification what we have been given to understand by the theme of the coming together of "like with like" (*supra* IV, 4): "every time a flame arises from you, behold a flame comes down from the heavens toward you."[93]

Another of Najm Kobrā's confessions suggests to us in a manner no less specific the connection constituting celestial love, by introducing the theme of the *soror spiritualis*.

> I departed[94] [he writes], and behold, there appeared to me a Heaven that resembled the book of the Qorān. Four-sided figures were inscribed therein, outlined by dotted lines. The dots formed some verses from the *sūra Ta-ha* (20:39-41): "I shed thee love from Me; that thou mightest be before my eyes when thy sister came to pass by."[95] Having understood these verses, I began to recite them. And it came to me by inspiration that their meaning related to a woman I knew who bore the name of *Banafsha*,[96] while her name in the suprasensory realm was *Istaftīn* (§160).

Do not look for the meaning of this last name in some Arabic or Persian dictionary; only Najm Kobrā can explain it to us. Returning to the theme of the esoteric Names borne by certain beings in the suprasensory realm (§176), he interprets the name in question as signifying the "'Ayesha of her time." The very fact that the earthly woman bears an "esoteric" name, that is to say, has a *name in Heaven* (a name in the suprasensory world which is the world of the Guide and of the personal master), indicates, in a manner that is as discreet as it is eloquent, what celestial love essentially implies: the perception of a beautiful being in her heavenly dimension, through senses which have become organs of light; precisely, the organs of the "person of light."

And that is why Najm Kobrā's doctrine of love connects essentially with the doctrine of those for whom, like Rūzbehān, human and divine love are by no means opposed to one another as a dilemma demanding that the mystic make a choice. They are two forms of the same love; passages in one and the same book which one must learn to read (with "eyes of light"). To pass from one to another does not consist in the transfer of love from one *object* to another, for God is not an *object*; God is the absolute *Subject*. To pass from one form of love to another implies the *metamorphosis of the subject*, of the *'āshiq*. This is what the entire doctrine of Rūzbehān[97] and that of Najm Kobrā are intended to indicate, so that we should not be surprised if, for the same reason, Najm does not make the same distinction as do some devotees and pious ascetics between divine and human love. For the metamorphosis of the subject resolves the apparent dissonances in the paradoxes, the "pious blasphemies," of ecstatics in love. It may be that the lover, addressing the earthly beauty, the object of his love, cries out: "You are my Lord: I have no Lord but you!" Perhaps those are blasphemous words; however, they arise from an emotional state, from an inner compulsion, which is neither conscious nor voluntary. These words are not uttered by the lover, but by the living flame of love, for the fire of love is fed by the beloved and the lover can but speak in the inspired language of the moment: "For you, I am lost to the religious and profane worlds; you are my impiety *and* you are my faith; you are what I was yearning for *and* you are the end and fulfillment of my desire; *you are myself (anta anā)*." The vehemence of this lyricism is finally appeased in a long quotation from Hallāj: "I am filled with wonder about you and me, that through yourself you make me as nothing to myself, that you are so close to me that I come to think that you are me." (§81)[98]

Still further (§101), Najm Kobrā quotes another couplet attributed to Hallāj: "I am he (or she) whom I love; he (or she) whom I love is me." The anonymous Iranian commentator on Rūzbehān introduces this same couplet to accompany the theme of Majnūn when he has become the "mirror of God"[99] (the state of Majnūn to which the commentator relates the same Qorānic verses as those read by Najm Kobrā in the constellations of the inner Heaven as relating to his *soror spiritualis*, because he knew her heavenly name). The shaykh expresses this further by saying: "It may be that the lover is entirely consumed by love, then he is himself love" (§82). That is exactly the doctrine of Ahmad Ghazālī.[100] When the lover has become the very substance of love, there is no longer any opposition between subject and object, between the lover and the beloved. That is the metamorphosis of the subject expressed by the

Neoplatonic identity of love, lover and beloved, and that is the divine form of love. When Najm Kobrā describes the four ascending degrees of love, he is concerned with this metamorphosis. To wonder why he makes no distinction between human love and divine love would be quite beside the point, would indicate the failure to perceive the meaning of the concomitance experienced in the reunion of the two flames between Heaven and Earth, of the synchronism between the manifestation of the Witness in Heaven, the suprasensory Guide, the Sun of the heart, and the knowledge of the "esoteric" name, of the "name in Heaven," of the earthly beloved. Individual initiation ends here in this inner revelation; these are the steps proclaimed by the colored photisms, from the circle of darkness and the blue light of the lower ego, still given over entirely to sensory and sensual perceptions, up to the *visio smaragdina* of the Throne iridescent in orbs of light. In this way one can foresee what is common to the profoundly original spirituality of Najm Kobrā and that of his great contemporaries, Sohravardī, Rūzbehān, Ibn 'Arabī.

10. The Scales and the Angel

Among the expressions qualifying the heavenly Guide in relation to the colored photisms, there is one, "the suprasensory Scales" (*mīzān al-ghayb*), that shows more particularly the homology between Najm Kobrā's heavenly Witness and the other manifestations of the same archetype analyzed above (*supra* II), especially the manifestation which exemplifies it best of all, namely, the figure of Daēnā-Fravarti in Zoroastrian Mazdeism. Furthermore the theme of the *scales* allows us to recognize for certain *what* the shadow is and *where* the shadow is; it forces us to accept that three-dimensionality of the inner world without which, as previously indicated, orientation toward the *pole* would remain ambivalent and ambiguous, or rather would not in fact guarantee any *sense* of *direction*.

Najm Kobrā stresses this symbolic qualification several times. The entire question for us is to interpret correctly what the *scales* indicate. What in fact happens in the case where it is said that the suprasensory Guide shows himself, or rather hides himself under blackness, darkness? "The suprasensory Wit-

IV. Visio Smaragdina

ness, the suprasensory Guide, the suprasensory Scales: this is what you are shown when you close your eyelids. According to whether what appears to you is light or darkness, your witness (*shāhid*) is light or darkness." Or, to put it more exactly, in the latter case it means that you have no witness, no heavenly partner: he is not there at all. This is exactly why "he is called the *scales*, because by him the states of the soul (or your ego) are *weighed* as to their purity or disfigurement."[101] As a balance, its role is therefore to indicate whether there is excess or deficiency in the spiritual state, that is, whether light prevails over darkness or *vice versa* (§69). If it so happens that at the midpoint of the mystical journey, the two circles of light of the eyes appear, it is the sign of an excellent spiritual state. If they remain hidden, this concealment indicates a lack, a preponderance of the dark nature. Furthermore, they may appear bigger or smaller; more frequently or less: all these variations correspond to an excess or a deficit on the scales (§70).

The phases corresponding to the transmutations of the soul can be recapitulated thus: At the beginning there may be darkness (the man still without light, without a witness, "without a fravarti"). At the midpoint, two circles of light, increasing or diminishing; at the last, complete visibility of the person of light.

> It may happen that this person (the Witness) appears to you at the beginning of the mystical journey; but then you only see a black color, a black figure. Then it disappears. But the other (that is, the person of the Witness revealed to the person of light) will no longer leave you; or, more accurately, you are that person, for it enters into you; it is conjoined to you. If, at the beginning, it appeared to you as black in color, it was because the veil of your own dark existence was hiding it. But when you make this dark existence disappear from before it, and when the flame of the *dhikr* and of ardent desire have consumed this barrier with fire, then the pure jewel is freed from its ore. Then it becomes a person wholly of light (§66).

The text is highly condensed. It echoes in a way the theme of the robe of light, of the *Song of the Pearl* in the *Acts of Thomas*, at least as the Song is rendered in a symbolic recital in the Encyclopedia of the "Brethren of the pure heart" and by Nasîroddîn Tûsî.[101a] Here, once the garment of darkness has been burned and consumed, the person of light becomes visible. There, the garment of wretchedness and dirt having been shed at the moment of the return to the "orient", the mystery of the robe of light is explained in terms that overcome the difficulty of expressing the *unus-ambo*: *two*, distinct from one another, yet but *one* in similar form. Here also there is a distinction: the heavenly Witness can disappear, be absent, while you remain there, without it. The celestial Witness is a person of light and is visible only for and by your person of light (like can be seen only by like). The disc of darkness, the Black figure sometimes visualized by the Spiritual at the beginning of his mystical journey, is *not* the celestial Guide, the Witness in Heaven. The blackness, or darkness, is precisely the absence of the Witness of light; the black color is not the Witness, but the *shadow*; not its shadow, but the Ahrimanian shadow (active negativity) which prevents him from being seen. This shadow is not he, but you, for it is the shadow projected by your *nafs ammāra*, the sensual soul, your lower ego. Seeing only this shadow, you cannot see your heavenly Witness. And if he is not present to you, how would he see you, how would you be present to him? When he is your Witness, it is because you are present to him; he is the Witness who contemplates you, you are what *he* contemplates. But for that very reason he is simultaneously present to you, he is what *you* contemplate. For he contemplates you with the same look with which you contemplate him. Every mystic has attempted to formulate this subtle reciprocity of roles. Here the twofold nuance of the word *shāhid*, the "eye-witness" who attests, and "the one who is present," helps to express the dialogical situation.[102] The Witness can only respond for you in the correspondence of a co-response. This is why one cannot speak of a *shāhid* who is not there; that would be an "absent presence." If he is absent, if only the Black figure is there, it is because you are without a *shāhid*, without a co-respondent, or personal Guide. As a corollary, his appearance and degree of visibility are the *scales* measuring what you truly are: light or darkness, or still a mixture of the two. Thereby (and this is important for understanding the structure of Iranian Sufism) the idea of the *shāhid* in Najm Kobrā unites, as emphasized above, with the idea of theophanic witness, a witness of contemplation, for the mystical "Faithful lovers."

IV. Visio Smaragdina

At that very point, in fact, the *shāhid* denotes the being whose beauty bears witness to the divine beauty, by being the divine revelation itself, the theophany par excellence. As the place and form of the theophany, he bears witness to this beauty to the divine Subject Himself; because he is present to the divine Subject as His witness, it means that God is contemplating Himself in him, is contemplating the evidence of Himself. So, when the mystic takes this theophanic witness as witness to his contemplation, the former is the witness *of* divine Beauty, present *to* the divine Beauty contemplating itself in him; it is God contemplating Himself in this contemplation of the mystic directed toward His Witness.[103] Najm Kobrā's idea of a "Witness in Heaven" and Rūzbehān's idea of a "theophanic witness" meet in the same testimony. In both cases the apparitional form changes according to the state of the contemplator. Either the man has no *shāhid*: he sees nothing but shadow, darkness, the Black; the form of his love is confined to the sensual form because of his incapacity to perceive the theophany. (Just as in our day certain loud assertions that art no longer has to refer to beauty finally crush their authors under the whole weight of the testimony that they are offering against themselves.) Or else the man of light, the "precious gem" having been freed from its ore, "perceives his likeness": the orb of light, the flames rising to the Heavens of the soul. As you look upon the *shāhid*, so does he look upon you, and such you yourself are. Your contemplation is worth whatever your being is worth; your God is the god you deserve; He bears witness to your being of light or to your darkness.

So finally we hear again what was already pre-sensed in the Zoroastrian notion of Daēnā-Fravarti: another dimension of the soul, the dimension of a soul which has a personal Witness "in Heaven," which is vouched for by this Witness to the extent that his own being bears witness to him and for him. It would be impossible to realize what this means if one were limited to the one-dimensional perspective offered by current psychology. The bi-unitary structure, whose symbol, as we have seen, is not $1 + 1$ but 1×1, is the structure that postulates a dimension of *individual* personal *transcendence*, and as an idea quite different, certainly, from the idea of a transpersonal evolution. An Initiation that is typically individual, with degrees and a figura-

92

§10. The Scales and the Angel

tion such as we have just been brought to recognize, is specifically what opens up this other dimension; it does not relate the essential individuality either to collective mediation or to any socialized or socializable religious form. All depends upon whether our *ability to comprehend*, our *hermeneutics*, has or has not sufficient dimensions at its disposal. Accordingly, a spirituality as original as that of Najm Kobrā, attentive to the perception of signs of this essential individuation in suprasensory colored photisms, may either orient our search toward a new horizon or possibly cripple it because of a misinterpretation resulting in disorientation.

Let us try to construct the diagram suggested to us from the outset by the threefold structure of the soul (*supra* IV, 3). On the lower plane: *nafs ammāra*, the lower ego, the imperative *psyche*, apparent in the disk of shadow, the Black figure, the black cloud turning to dark blue. On the upper plane: *nafs motma'yanna*, the pacified soul, the green color, emerald splendor and orbs of light. Between the two: the soul-consciousness (*nafs eawwāma*) perceived in vision as a great red sun; this is the intellect (*'aql*), consciousness proper. In terms of the *scales*: the "witness in Heaven" becomes manifest to the extent that the soul-consciousness, placed in the center, empties the "pan" of the scales containing the lower soul, and gives greater weight to the "pan" of the pacified soul which is the *heart*, that is to say, the subtle organ so named by the Sufis. And this is why it was possible, from that point on, to give an unambiguous answer to a first question: to whom did the shadow, the black color visualized at the beginning, belong? In other words, could the "heavenly witness" ever have *been* darkness? No, this darkness was the darkness of your own nature, whose opacity was opposed to the transparency that conditions the reciprocal presence of the man of light to the guide of light and ultimately the penetration of the Image of the Guide into you to the point where it may be possible to say "you are he" (1 × 1). And so it was your own shadow, your Iblīs or *nafs ammāra* which was projecting and interposing a veil that the flame of the *dhikr* finally set on fire and consumed; this was the only thing that was making the *shaykh al-ghayb*, your partner and heavenly counterpart, invisible.

But the transmutation that is effected by no means signifies

93

IV. Visio Smaragdina

that the old Iblīs, your "Iblīs converted to Islam" has become your *shaykh al-ghayb*, your "witness in Heaven." Conversion of your Iblīs (your *nafs ammāra*) to Islam is the *condition on which* the *shaykh al-ghayb* can become visible; which is not at all to say that Iblīs becomes the "witness in Heaven." Such a notion is untenable because of the fundamental orientation, the polar orientation analyzed here at the beginning: either the soul-consciousness is not freed from its shadow, the *nafs ammāra,* but looks at it and through it, thus seeing nothing but shadow, *its* shadow; or else the shadow has subsided and the soul has risen to the degree of *nafs motma'yanna* and sees its own dimension of light.

If this is stressed to avoid confusion, it is because a question will inevitably arise. It would be very tempting indeed to interpret the triadic diagram of the soul recalled above in terms of consciousness and the unconscious and leave it at that. However, can the phenomena of shadow and light, the inner process of which has been so minutely analyzed by Najm Kobrā and the Sufis of his school, really be translated simply by speaking of consciousness as the region of light and the unconscious as the region of shadow? The soul-consciousness (*nafs law-wāma*) is placed between the two: between the lower soul and the higher soul, to which and by which the "witness in Heaven," the suprasensory Guide, is made manifest. How could one possibly say that the "two souls" between which the soul-consciousness is placed both belonged equally to the same region of *shadow*? The first is the shadow that has to be overcome in order for the bi-unitary structure to be restored. Is it not then this two-dimensionality of the soul (a syzygy of lights) which itself postulates the three-dimensionality of psycho-spiritual spatiality? In other words: does not the *trilogy* of the soul (*supra* IV, 3) force us to admit at least orientation, distinct levels within the unconscious, in order to determine its structure? But how can one introduce positive differentiations into what is negative and negativity? A more serious decision has to be made, namely, to accept all that follows from our diagram, if we wish to avoid the mistake, already pointed out, of confusing complementary elements with contradictory elements, which would lead to interpreting the Fravarti, or the "witness in Heaven," and Iblīs-Ahriman as complementary manifestations of the same Shadow.

§10. The Scales and the Angel

Foreseeing these difficulties, we have avoided here two things in particular. In the first place we have avoided relating the idea of the "witness in Heaven" to what is connoted by the German term *Doppelgänger*, precisely because of the ambiguity, the shadow, attached to this term. In fact what we are speaking of is a counterpart, a celestial, transcendent counterpart, rather than a "double"; the idea of this heavenly partner is antithetic to the Double whose role is suggested in a number of fantastic tales, and there could be no question of bringing these antitheses together to form one Whole. And indeed psychological analysis shows this Double to be the manifestation of the personal unconscious, hence belonging to the functions of the lower psyche, that is, the *nafs ammāra*, the dark envelope, the shadow, exactly what the *dhikr* has to destroy by fire so that the Guide of light may become visible. What prevents the reunion of twin lights cannot be one of its constitutive elements.

In the second place, in the few phenomenological indications outlined here and there, we have avoided any suggestion of a "collective unconscious." One notices in fact a certain tendency to accentuate in this expression the adjective "collective," to the point of giving it the substantiality and virtues of an hypostasis: in so doing, it is simply forgotten that the purpose of psychoanalysis, as therapy for the soul, tends essentially to foster what it calls the process of individuation. For the same reason it would be absurd to explain the kind of individual initiation proper to Sufism by relating it to some collective norm, whereas its whole purpose is to free the inner man from such authority. The predisposition to something like Sufism can exist in a multitude of individuals, but it is not for that reason a collective disposition. The obsessions of the present day will end by obscuring every spiritual or cultural phenomenon that does not fit their case.

As for the construction of the diagram, urgently required, as we foresaw a little earlier, so that our hermeneutics might have the requisite dimensions, we should now amplify it as follows: an anthropogony in which antithetic forces (murderer and victim, for example) objectively represent one divine primordial reality is one thing; an anthropogony situating man between two worlds is quite a different thing. Man according to Ismaelian gnosis is an intermediary—potential angel or potential demon; his complete eschatological reality is not the sum of

95

these two antithetical virtualities. Man in Ibn 'Arabī's anthropogony is likewise intermediate: situated between being and non-being, between Light and Darkness, at the same time responsible and respondent to both sides; he is responsible for the Darkness to the extent that he intercepts the Light, but he is responsible for the Light to the extent that he prevents the Darkness from invading and governing it.[104]

In Najm Kobrā, the soul-consciousness is also placed between the two. This being so, we need a diagram superimposing the planes; it is impossible to suppose that there could be one single invisible area, inevitably and unilaterally situated *below* the visible area, that is, the area of unconsciousness. A number of manifestations surpassing and going beyond the bounds of the conscious activity of the soul have to be placed not below but *above consciousness*. There is a *subconsciousness* or *infraconsciousness*, corresponding to the level of the *nafs ammāra*; and there is a *superconsciousness* or *supraconsciousness*. corresponding to the level of the *nafs motma'yanna*. In the physical order, the invisibility of an object may be due to a lack of light; it may also be due to an excess of light, to the dazzling effect of being too close to it. In the "suprasensory" order, that of the "suprasensory senses" or physiology of the man of light, the same applies. On the one hand invisibility (absence of the *shāhid*), which is the shadow, the Ahrimanian darkness, the negation or captivity of the light; opposed to this the invisibility that the disciples of Najm Kobrā call the "black light," the pre-origin of all that is visible, that is to say, of all light (*infra*, V). For this very reason, the "black light" is the antithesis of the Ahrimanian darkness. In both cases there is something that is beyond the limits of consciousness. But in the first case the invisibility, the absence of light, is a fact pertaining to *subconsciousness*; in the second case, invisibility due to an excess of brilliance, to being too close to the light, is a fact pertaining to *superconsciousness* or *transconsciousness*. And the facts of superconsciousness are individual facts; individually, each soul has to overcome, as well as its own shadow, the collective shadow.

As an "exemplary fact" among the facts of superconsciousness, it is necessary to recall—though the word is generally misused—the fact referred to by the idea of *vocation* with all its mysterious, imperative, irrational and inexorable connotations.

§10. The Scales and the Angel

The idea of vocation serves perhaps better than any other for recapitulating all that is suggested by the idea of the Angel, conveyed to us in the theme of *Daēnā* as glory (δόξα) and destiny (τύχη), in the theme of the Perfect Nature of the Sohravardian Hermes, and finally in the theme of the "Witness in Heaven," of the "Scales of the suprasensory world"[105] by Najm Kobrā. In such a recapitulation, the essential, undeniable idea of individuality is seen in fact as inseparable from angelology because it provides a basis for the idea of the Angel just as the idea of the Angel is its own foundation.

On this basis, the idea of individuality stands firm in face of the attempts to justify "collectivization" and nominalist concepts. It saves us from the illusion of believing that it is enough to escape from the individual sphere and, by reaching the "social" sphere, simultaneously to reach the divine, for it is the reverse of the mystic's view of the gradations of being as he scales the mountain of *Qāf* to the Emerald Rock at its summit, and emerges step by step above and beyond the natural realms— the vegetable world, the animal world and the human species. Step by step, a species is revealed which does not yet include individuals; then the individual coexisting with the species that dominates him; then the individual coexisting with the species he dominates. Finally, from ascent to ascent, the return of the man of light to his original pleroma postulates the idea of a non-specific individual, of archetypal individuality whose soaring flight and power, by assuming all the virtualities of a species, itself becomes a unique example. The idea of an individual who is himself his species is the idea of the Angel.[106] Leibnitz transposed it into the monadic concept of the soul and this is what truly makes it possible to understand the idea of vocation as relationship with the archetype. Here exactly this specificity of an individuality being born at the end of a personal mystical initiation is made manifest as a state of "dualitude," a *unus-ambo* structure. This bi-unity is not a union of two contradictory elements, Ohrmazdean light and Ahrimanian darkness, but a union of Ohrmazd and his own Fravarti, of twins of light, of the "pacified soul" and its "witness in Heaven," of Hermes and his Perfect Nature, of *Phōs* and his guide of light, consciousness and *superconsciousness*. "And it is light upon light."

V. THE BLACK LIGHT

1. Light Without Matter

Essentially, what has just been referred to as "superconsciousness" (*sirr*, *khafī*, in Sufi terminology) cannot be a collective phenomenon. It is always something that opens up at the end of a struggle in which the protagonist is the spiritual individuality. One does not pass collectively from the sensory to the suprasensory, for this passage is the birth and expansion of the person of light. Without doubt a mystical fraternity will result from it, but does not exist before it (Hermes is alone as he enters the subterranean chamber following the instructions of his Perfect Nature, *supra* II, 1). As we have seen, this gradual opening is marked by certain "theophanic lights" corresponding to each stage. The correspondence of these lights, the determination of their degree of presence by and for their "witness" is the very thing that thematizes the motif of the *shāhid*.[107] The "super-individuality" of the mystic, that is to say, the transcendent dimension of the person, is conditioned by this syzygic inseparability. Once the threshold has been crossed, the perspective opens on the peripatetics of a secret history, the stages of the spiritual journey, the perils and triumphs of the person of light, the occultations and re-appearances of his *shāhid*. To follow these to the end in detail would require a thorough study of the whole of Iranian Sufism, whereas we

99

V. The Black Light

must limit ourselves here to pointing out some further essential features borrowed from three or four of the great masters. The dimension of superconsciousness is symbolically heralded by the "black light"; according to Najm Rāzī and Mohammed Lāhījī, this constitutes the highest spiritual stage; according to Semnānī, it marks the most perilous initiatic step, the stage immediately preceding the ultimate theophany, which is heralded by the green light. In any case there are obstacles of the highest significance between the *visio smaragdina* and the "black Light," due to their contiguity.

The idea of "black light" (Persian *nūr-e siyāh*) is above all what obliges us to distinguish between two dimensions which could not be accounted for by a one-dimensional or undifferentiatable unconscious. To the extent that the mystical language comes to "symbolize with" physical experience, it seems that the latter perfectly illustrates the idea of a polarity not so much between consciousness and the unconscious as between a superconsciousness and a subconsciousness. There is one darkness which is matter, and there is another darkness which is an absence of matter. Physicists distinguish between the *blackness* of matter and the *blackness* of the stratosphere.[108] On the one hand there is the *black body*, a body that absorbs all light without distinction of color; this is what is "seen" in a dark furnace. When heated it passes from black to red, then to white, then to white-red. All this light is light absorbed by matter and re-emitted by it. This is also so in the case of the "particle of light" (the man of light, φώς-φῶς) absorbed in the dark well (*nafs ammāra, supra* III, 3), which according to Najm Kobrā and Sohravardī, is compelled by the fire of the *dhikr* to liberate the particle, to "re-emit" it. This then is the black figure, the well or dark furnace; it is the lower darkness, the infraconscious or subconscious. But there is another light, a light-without-matter, which becomes visible when released from this already made matter that had absorbed it. The darkness above is the blackness of the stratosphere, of stellar space, of the black Sky. In mystical terms, it corresponds to the light of the divine Self in-itself (*nūr-e dhāt*), the black light of the *Deus absconditus*, the hidden Treasure that aspires to reveal itself, "to create perception in order to reveal to itself the object of its perception," and which thus can only manifest itself by veiling itself in the object state. This divine darkness does not refer therefore to the lower darkness, that of the black body, the infraconsciousness (*nafs ammāra*), but to the black Heavens, the black Light in which the ipseity of the *Deus absconditus* is pre-sensed by the superconsciousness.

We therefore need a metaphysics of Light whose paths will be mapped by the mystic's *spiritual experience* of colors, especially, in the present case, the experience of the Iranian Sufis. Their visionary apperception of colored lights postulates an idea of *pure color* consisting of an *act of light* which actualizes its own matter, that is, which actualizes in differentiated stages the potentiality of the "hidden Treasure" aspiring to reveal itself. More certain and more direct than any other is the reference in an earlier chapter that takes us back to the distinction established in one of the great mystical Recitals of Avicenna between the "Darkness at the approaches to the *pole*" and the Darkness reigning at the "Far West" of matter. The latter is the darkness whose behavior in regard to light is described by physics; these are the forces of darkness that retain the light, obstruct its passage, the forces of the black object which absorbs light and which in the "oriental theosophy" of Sohravardī is called by the characteristic ancient Iranian term of *barzakh* (screen, barrier). On the other hand, the Darkness at the "approaches to the *pole*" is the region of the "black Light," which exists before all the matter that it will itself actualize in order to be received in it and, in it, to become visible light. The antithesis is established between the black light of the pole and the darkness of the material black body, and not simply between light and the darkness of matter. Between the material black body (typified for example by the *nafs ammāra*) from which the light seeks to escape and the pre-material black light (that of the divine Ipseity) the whole universe of lights extends upwards and in their actuality as lights become colors in an autonomous state of life and substantiality.

Since their entire effort tends to free them from a matter which would be foreign to their action and in which they are sometimes captive (see *infra* VI, 1, the meaning of Manichean painting and its influence on Persian miniatures), they do not even need to settle on the surface of an object which could be their prison in order *to be* colors. These lights, made into colors

V. The Black Light

in the very act of becoming light, have to be represented as creating for themselves, out of their own life and nature, their form and their space (that *spissitudo spiritualis*, to borrow again an expression of Henry More's, which is the place of the suprasensory perceptions described by Najm Kobrā and his disciples). These pure lights (forming, according to Sohravardī, a twofold order, longitudinal and latitudinal, "Mothers" and archetypes) are, in the *act of light* which constitutes them, constitutive of their own theophanic form (*mazhar*). The "acts of light" (photisms, *ishrāqāt*) actualize their own receptacles which make the light visible. "Light without matter" means here the light whose act actualizes its own matter (again according to Sohravardī, material bodies are never the sufficient reasons for the properties which they manifest). In relation to the matter of the black body, invested with the forces of obscurity, Ahrimanian darkness, it is no doubt equivalent to an immaterialization. More exactly it is matter in the *subtle* "etheric" *state* (*latīf*), the act of the light, and not antagonistic to light; it is the incandescence of the *mundus imaginalis* ('*ālam al-mithāl*), the world of autonomous figures and forms, the heavenly Earth of Hūrqalyā "which secretes its own light." To see things in Hūrqalyā, as certain Sufi shaykhs say, is to see them in that state which can only be perceived by the "suprasensory senses" (*supra* IV, 7). This perception is not a passively received impression of a material object, but activity of the subject, that is, conditioned by the physiology of the man of light. In this context the Goethean doctrine of "physiological colors" (*infra* VI, 3) finds its place spontaneously.

We shall learn further (*infra* V, 3) that the "black light" is that of the divine Ipseity as the light of revelation, which *makes one see*. Precisely what *makes one see*, that is to say, light as absolute *subject*, can in nowise become a visible *object*. It is in this sense that the Light of lights (*nūr al-anwār*), that by which all visible lights are made visible, is both light and darkness, that is, visible because it *brings about vision*, but in itself invisible. Henceforth also when speaking of color as a mixture of light and darkness, we should not understand it as a mixture with the Ahrimanian shadow, even if it were only the shadow of the black object. The seven colors emerge on the level of the most transparent of bodies. This mixture is to be understood as the relation of the act of light with the infinite potentiality which aspires to reveal itself ("I was a hidden treasure, I wanted to be known"), that is, as the epiphanic act in the night of the *Absconditum*. But this divine night is the antithesis of the Ahrimanian darkness; it is the source of the epiphanies of the light which the Ahrimanian darkness later seeks to engulf. The world of colors in the pure state, that is, the orbs of light, is the totality of the *acts* of this Light which makes them lights and cannot itself be manifested except by these acts, without ever being itself visible. And all these receptacles, these theophanic forms which it creates in these very acts which make it manifest are always in correlation with the state of the mystic; i.e., with the activity of the "particle of light" in man which seeks to rediscover its like.[108a] Perhaps we can glimpse the correlation which requires us on the one hand to distinguish between the *superconscious* and the *subconscious* and on the other hand between the *black light* and the blackness of the *black object*. And this completes the summary of *orientation* which we have sought to establish in the present essay—admittedly in very imperfect terms.

2. *The Doctrine of Photisms according to Najm Rāzī (1256)*

Najm Rāzī,[109] direct disciple of Najm Kobrā, is the author of a mystical treatise in Persian still in current use today in Iranian Sufism, wherein the chapters particularly related to our subject deal with visionary apperceptions (*moshāhadāt*) and the unveilings of the suprasensory (*mokāshafāt*).[110] Their *leitmotiv* makes the distinction between the theophanies or apparitions of divine lights which are those of the "Lights of Majesty" and the theophanies which are those of the "Lights of Beauty." Majesty (i.e. rigor, inaccessible sublimity) and Beauty (fascination, attraction, graciousness): these are the two great categories of attributes which refer respectively to the divine Being as *Deus absconditus* and as *Deus revelatus*, Beauty being the supreme theophany, divine self-revelation.[111] In fact they are inseparable and there is a constant interplay between the inaccessible Majesty of Beauty and the fascinating Beauty of inaccessible Majesty. The interplay is even such that Najm Kobrā, when comparing their relation to that of the masculine and feminine

V. The Black Light

principles, perceives a transference corresponding to a mutual exchange of the masculine and feminine attributes (§4). And to suggest that their twofoldness is necessary for the spiritual individuality to be born, he quotes this saying of the Sufi Abū-Bakr Wāsitī: "The attribute of Majesty and the attribute of Beauty intermingle; from their union the Spirit is born. The son is an allusion to partial reality; the father and mother an allusion to total reality." (§65). According to Najm Rāzī, photisms, pure lights and colored lights, refer to the attributes of Beauty; the "black light" refers to the attributes of Majesty. He outlines the "physiology of the man of light" concurrently with the theory of the "unveilings of the suprasensory world."

First of all, as a general rule, the capacity to perceive suprasensory lights is proportionate to the degree of polishing, chiefly the work of the *dhikr*, which brings the *heart* to the state of perfect mirror. In the beginning these lights are manifested as ephemeral flashes. The more perfect the transparency (the "specularity") of the mirror, the more they grow, the longer they last, the more diverse they become, until they manifest the form of heavenly entities. As a general rule also, the source where these Lights take shape is the spiritual entity of the mystic, his *rūhānīyat*, the very same, as we have seen (*supra* II, 1), in Sohravardī and the Hermetists under the name of Perfect Nature, the philosopher's "Angel." But besides this we have to take into consideration that every spiritual state, every function, every feeling, every act, has its spiritual entity, its "Angel" which manifests itself in the light proper to it. Prophecy (*nobowwat*), Initiation (*walāyat*), the spirits of the Initiates (*Awliyā*), the great shaykhs of Sufism, the Qorān, the profession of Islam, the fidelity of faith (*īmān*),[112] even every form of *dhikr*, every form of divine office and worship, each one of these realities is expressed in a light proper to it.

In the description given by our author of the suprasensory phenomena of pure light, what we note in short is the following: brief flashes and flames most often originate from the liturgical acts (prayer, ritual ablution, etc.). A longer and brighter light is that from the Qorān or from the *dhikr*. There may be visualization of the well-known verse from the chapter Light (24:35): "The image of His light is that of a Niche wherein there is a lamp, the lamp is in a case of glass . . . " Here the

§2. The Doctrine of Photisms according to Najm Rāzī

"Niche of lights" manifests a light of the prophecy or else of the initiatic quality of the shaykh. Tapers, lamps and live embers manifest the different forms of *dhikr* or else are an effect of the light of gnosis. All the forms of stars which are shown in the Skies of the heart (*āsmān-e del*) are, as in Najm Kobrā, lights manifesting the Angel; i.e., the esoteric aspect of the astronomical Sky that is its homologue (*bātin-e falak*). According to the heart's degree of purity, the star may be seen without its Sky or else with its Sky; in the latter case, the Sky is the "subtle astral mass" of the heart, whereas the star is the light of the Spirit. The Constellated figures manifest the *Animae coelestes*. Sun and moon may appear in various positions, each of which has its meaning. The full moon in the Sky of the heart manifests the effects of the initiation corresponding to the degree of lunar initiation (*walāyat-e qamarīya*); the sun manifests the effects of the solar or total initiation (*w. kollīya*). Several suns together are a manifestation of the perfect Initiates (*Awliyā-e kollī*). Sun and moon contemplated together are the joint manifestation of the form of the shaykh and the form of the absolute initiator.[113] Sun, moon and stars may appear as though immersed either in the sea or in running water or on the contrary in motionless water, sometimes in a well. All the mystics recognize there the lights of their "spiritual entity." These immersions in a transparent element proclaim the extreme purity of the heart, the state of the "pacified soul," which, at the boundary, will allow the rays of the divine Lights to pierce through all the veils. This is the meaning of the verse in the *sūra* of the Star: "The heart does not belie what it has seen (53:11)," the mystical sense which sanctions the Prophet's visions ("My heart has seen my Lord in the most beautiful of forms") and the theophanies vouchsafed to Abraham and Moses.

Najm Rāzī knows it: it may be asked whether all these theophanies take *place* in the inner, esoteric world or rather in the outer, exoteric world? His answer is that anyone who asks this kind of question remains far from the real situation where the two worlds meet and coincide. In one case it may be that the suprasensory perception is awakened and stimulated by a sensory perception; between the sensory (*hissī*) and the suprasensory (*ghaybī*), the exoteric (*zāhir*) and the esoteric (*bātin*), there is synchronism and symbolism; these are even the foundation

V. The Black Light

and criterion of visionary apperception. In another instance, a direct perception of the suprasensory by the organ of the heart may come about without a sensory organ or physical support (see *supra* IV, 1, *aura* and auric perception). In either case this organ of the heart (with the spiritual energy of the *Imaginatrix*, effects a transmutation of the sensory so that it is perceived "in Hūrqalyā," on the plane of the *mundus imaginalis*, the *imaginal* world wherein "what is corporeal becomes spirit and what is spiritual assumes a body" ("our method is that of alchemy,"said Najm Kobrā).[114] This is the meaning derived by spiritual hermeneutics from the verse on the Light: "God is the light of the Heavens and of the Earth" (24:35), for, in reality and in the true sense, what makes *manifest* (that is, light) and that which *is manifested* (*mazhar*, the theophanic form), what sees and what is seen are the divine Being himself. "When the meaning of Abraham's exclamation: *This is my Lord* has been mystically understood, then sensory and suprasensory, exoteric and esoteric, apparent and hidden, will be one and the same thing."

Semnānī perceives in another verse of the Qorān (41:53) the very principle of the inward movement whereby every outer datum becomes an event pertaining to the soul, bringing historical, physical time (*zamān āfāqī*) back to inner, psychic time (*zamān anfosī*). This is the final end toward which all mystic ways converge; it is the spiritual abode where the gaze of the one who contemplates the beauty of the Witness of contemplation (*shāhid*) in the mirror of the inner eye, the eye of the heart, is none other than the gaze of the Witness: "I am the mirror of thy face; through thine own eyes I look upon thy countenance." The Contemplated is the Contemplator and vice versa;[115] we have already attempted here to approach the secret of this mystical reciprocity, a paradox which cannot be better expressed than in terms of light. Najm Rāzī pursues the attempt to the limit:

> If the light rises in the Sky of the heart taking the form of one or of several light-giving moons, the two eyes are closed to this world and to the other. If this light rises and, in the utterly pure inner man attains the brightness of the sun or of many suns, the mystic is no longer aware of this world nor of the other, he sees only his own Lord under the veil of the Spirit; then his heart is nothing but light, his subtle body is light, his material covering is

light, his hearing, his sight, his hand, his exterior, his interior are nothing but light, his mouth and his tongue also.

The photisms of pure light thus described correspond to the state of the heart which is that of the "pacified soul." The colored photisms which Najm Rāzī proceeds to describe rise step by step from the moment when the spiritual individuality is triumphantly freed from the lower ego (*ammāragī*) and, on reaching the degree of consciousness (*lawwāmagī*), makes its way to the degree of the pacified soul, the threshold of the beyond (*supra* IV, 3). Then the mystic enters the first valley, following an itinerary the successive stages of which are marked by the visualization of colored lights, leading him to the seventh valley, the valley of "black light." But here we should note certain features through which the originality of each of the Iranian Sufi masters becomes apparent (paying no heed to the immutable rigidity of a certain "tradition" put together in our day in the West). Whereas Semnānī connects the colored lights to the *seven* centers or organs of subtle physiology (*laṭīfa*), Najm Rāzī relates them simply to spiritual states. He outlines, however, in connection with the "unveilings of the suprasensory," a "physiology" of the subtle organs, of which in his theory there are only *five*. What is more, the colored lights are differently graded and in a quite different order in the respective works of these two masters.

According to the Najm Rāzī the colors visualized by the suprasensory senses are graded in the following order: at the first stage, the light visualized is *white light*; it is the sign of *Islām*. At the second stage, *yellow light*; this is the sign of the fidelity of faith (*īmān*). At the third stage, the light is *dark blue (kabūd)*; it is the sign of benevolence (*iḥsān*). At the fourth stage, the light is *green*; this is the sign of tranquility of the soul (the pacified soul, *motma'yanna*). Perception of the green light thus agrees as to its meaning, if not as to its place in the order of succession, with the perception of the green light in Najm Kobrā's treatise (regarding Semnānī's, see *infra* VI, 1). At the fifth stage, *azure blue light*; this is the sign of firm assurance (*īqān*). At the sixth stage, *red light*; the sign of mystical gnosis, "theosophical" knowledge (in Najm Kobrā, it is the color of the *Noūs*, or active Intelligence). At the seventh stage, *black light (nūr-e siyāh)*; the sign of passionate, ecstatic love.

V. The Black Light

The first six steps thus correspond to the lights which Najm Rāzī describes as lights of the attribute of Beauty, theophanic lights which *illuminate*. The "black light" is that of the attribute of Majesty which sets the mystic's being on fire; it is not contemplated; it attacks, invades, annihilates, then annihilates annihilation. It shatters the "supreme theurgy" (*talasm-e a'zam*), that is, the apparatus of the human organism; this term incidentally occurs also in Sohravardī's vocabulary. Their conjunction is however essential (see Wāsitī's text cited above); thus it is inaccessible Majesty which is revealed in alluring Beauty and Beauty which *is* revealed Majesty. But this revelation presupposes a form, a receptable (*mazhar*) to receive it. Najm Rāzī affirms that there is light and darkness wherever you look, and that this is why the Qorān (in reference to light and darkness) speaks not of a creation or created state (*khalqīyat*), but of a primordial establishment (*ja'līyat*, conditioning the very coming into existence of being). Light and darkness are not things alongside other things, but are categories of things. This preliminary orientation will then save us from confusing the divine Night, the abscondity of the Essence which causes light to be revealed, and the darkness here below, the demonic darkness which holds the light captive and does not allow it to escape. This darkness is not what makes the light manifest; it releases it when forced to do so. But if all light so released is visible as light, if therefore the light calls for a "matter," a receptacle to condition this visibility, then the matter in question is not that of the lower darkness. Here the importance is felt (as we have been reminded many times) of the world of subtle matter, *mundus imaginalis* (*'ālam al-mithāl*), in the cosmology professed by all our Spiritual seekers. "Subtle matter" is the esoteric Heavens of the heart, its "astral mass" and so forth. The suprasensory phenomena of colored lights are produced by this "matter" because it is the act itself of light, not the antagonist of light. Divine Night (*Deus absconditus*), as the source and origin of all light (*Deus revelatus*), is not a compound of the demonic and the divine. But this divine light, once revealed, may well fall into captivity in Ahrimanian darkness. This drama is admirably described by the Manichean cosmogony, as an ever-present drama with inexhaustible variants, up to and including confusion of the social with the divine.

§2. The Doctrine of Photisms according to Najm Rāzī

As to the theory of the *subtle organs* according to Najm Rāzī, while differing from Semnānī's theory, it nevertheless opens the way to the latter. The theory proceeds essentially from the tradition (*hadīth*) which states: "God has 70,000 veils of light and of darkness; if he removed them the brilliance of his Face would burn up all that met his look." These veils are the totality of all the sensory and suprasensory universes (*molk* and *malakūt*, *shahādat* and *ghaybat*). The figure which determines the number *qualitatively*, following the above tradition, is 70,000. But there are variants; some traditions mention 18,000 worlds, others 360,000 worlds.[116] Now, all these worlds are existent in the inner world of man, in his subtle or esoteric (*nahān = batīn*) being, which includes as many "eyes" as there are worlds; through these "eyes" man perceives respectively each of these worlds, by the living experience of the spiritual state in which each of these worlds becomes manifest in him. Thus he possesses 70,000 "eyes", among which are the five outer senses attached to the bodily realities of sensory matter, the five inner senses, the five energies of organic physiology; but these, one suspects already, are only a small part of the energies of the whole man to whom "suprasensory senses" are available. And so the term *mokāshafāt*, "unveilings," is never used by Sufis (as Najm Rāzī points out) in reference to objects of a perception deriving from the three categories of faculties just enumerated, but only in reference to suprasensory realities. It thus implies *eo ipso* the idea of unveilings of suprasensory things that come about in the case of the *sāhib-e kashf*, a term which again cannot be better translated than by the word "clairvoyant."

When the "clairvoyant" commits himself to the *tarīqat* or mystical journey, following the rules of spiritual warfare under the direction of the master of initiation (*wāli*) and the shaykh, he passes in succession through all these veils; at each station (*maqām*) an inner eye opens in him correspondingly, and he perceives all the modes of being or spiritual states relating to that station. This perception is effected by the suprasensory faculties or organs of the subtle physiology of the "clairvoyant," which in each generation are imparted to a small group of humans. While Semnānī enumerates seven subtle organs or *latīfa*, Najm Rāzī takes them as five only: the intellect, the heart, the spirit, the superconsciousness (*sirr*), and the *arcanum* or trans-

V. The Black Light

consciousness (*khafī*). Each of these suprasensory faculties perceives its own world; this is why we hear of an unveiling to the intellect (*kashf-e 'aqlī*; the majority of philosophers have not gone beyond that); an unveiling to the heart (*mokāshafat-e del*, visions of the various colored lights); unveilings to the spirit (*m. rūhī*, assumptions to heaven, visions of angels, perception of past and future in their permanent state); finally, unveiling to the superconsciousness and to the *arcanum*. There "the time and space of the beyond" are revealed; what was seen from this side is seen from the other side. And all these organs are intermediate in regard to the others, each transmitting to the next what has been granted and unveiled to itself, and the next receives this in the form proper to itself; the further the mystic progresses on the seven steps of the heart by conforming his being to the *moribus divinis* (*takhalloq bi-akhlāq Allāh*), the more these unveilings multiply for him.

3. Black Light in the "Rose Garden of Mystery" (1317)

The long Persian poem bearing the title of Golshan-e Rāz (the Rose Garden of Mystery), comprising about 1500 couplets, is the work of Mahmūd Shabestarī.[117] This work has been read closely and continuously in Iran until now, but its extreme conciseness (in it the author answers many questions gathered by one of his friends concerning the high doctrines of Sufism) has motivated the writing of any number of commentaries. Among these the most complete and also the most frequently studied in Iran until today is that of Shamsoddin Lāhījī; its scope and content make it a veritable compendium of Sufism.[118]

A feature reported in the biography of Lāhījī demonstrates to what point the doctrine of colored photisms, showing the mystic his degree of progress on the spiritual way, is reflected in the detail of his daily life; it suggests to him in fact that he can wear garments whose colors correspond to those of the lights successively characterizing his spiritual state; the experience is thus translated practically into the symbols of a personal liturgy, coinciding with the very current of life. Qāzī Nūrollah Shoshtarī[119] relates that during the time when Shāh Esmā'īl (Ismael)[120] established his power in the province of Fārs (Per-

110

§3. Black Light in the "Rose Garden of Mystery"

sis) and Shīrāz, the sovereign wished to visit the shaykh. When he met him, he asked: "Why have you chosen always to wear black clothing?" "In mourning for the Imām Hosayn," answered the shaykh. But the king remarked, "It has been established that only ten days each year should be devoted to mourning the holy Imām." "No," replied the shaykh, "that is a human error. In reality the mourning for the holy Imām is a permanent mourning; it will not end until the dawn of the Resurrection."

Obviously one can hear in this answer testimony to the fervor of a Shī'ite, at the heart of whose meditations remains the drama of Karbala, just as the drama of Christ's Passion is at the heart of Christian piety. But another intention can also be seen in the wearing of this black clothing, an intention corresponding precisely to the practice by certain groups in Sufism of wearing clothing of the same color as that of the light contemplated in the mystic station they had attained. In this way a "chromatic harmony" is established between the esoteric and the exoteric, the hidden and the apparent. Thus in the first stages, blue (*kabūd*) clothing was worn.[121] At the highest stage black clothing would have corresponded to the "black light." Is this then indeed the meaning which we find in this personal practice of Lāhījī, which so astonished Shāh Esmā'īl? A poem composed by one of his own disciples in praise of the shaykh, seems indeed to confirm this.[122]

In any case, the pages where Lāhījī unfolds the theme of the "black light" in commenting on Mahmūd Shabestarī's poem are of capital importance when it comes to making a clear distinction between the divine Night and the Ahrimanian Darkness.[123] The black light is the light of the pure Essence in its ipseity, in its abscondity; the ability to perceive it depends on a spiritual state described as"reabsorption in God" (*fanā fī'llāh*), the state in which Semnanī perceives the danger of a supreme ordeal from which, according to him, the mystic rises again on the threshold of a *visio smaragdina*, the green light then being raised to the rank of the highest light of the Mystery. Comparative study of these visions is of exceptional interest; it would call for ample meditation and can only be outlined here.

While following the exact words of the poet, Lāhījī's commentary as it develops affords a glimpse of the precise lines

111

V. The Black Light

its development as a series of steps. Three moments become distinct; namely, an effort to approach the idea of the black light from all sides, then to describe the superconsciousness it postulates, an unknowingness which, as such, is knowing; lastly this "luminous Night" is identified with the state of mystical poverty in the true sense, the very sense in which the Sufi is described as "poor in spirit" (*darwīsh*, dervish, *supra* III, 3).

To encompass the idea of black light is all the more difficult in that it bursts forth in a twofold way. It irrupts in the presence of things; it means a particular way of seeing them, which provides the author with the theme of the *black Face* of beings (*siyāh-rū'ī*). And it irrupts in the absence of things, when the intelligence, turning away from what is manifested, endeavors to understand *Who* is manifested and revealed. This is the theme of pure Essence, of divine Ipseity as *absolute Subject*, whose inaccessibility the author suggests by speaking of excessive proximity and bedazzlement. This is where the theme of mystical poverty brings a dénouement to a dialectically inextricable situation: the coexistence of the absolute Subject and the individual subjects, of the One and the Many.

As for the first theme, there is no better means of placing it than by referring to Shaykh Lāhījī's own testimony, since on many occasions he illustrates his commentary with facts drawn from his personal experience. Here is his account of a vision:

> I saw myself [writes the Shaykh] present in a world of light. Mountains and deserts were iridescent with lights of all colors: red, yellow, white, blue. I was experiencing a consuming nostalgia for them; I was as though stricken with madness and snatched out of myself by the violence of the intimate emotion and feeling of the presence. Suddenly I saw that the *black light* was invading the entire universe. Heaven and earth and everything that was there had wholly become black light and, behold, I was totally absorbed in this light, losing consciousness. Then I came back to myself.

The recital of this vision at once suggests a comparison with one of the great ecstatic confessions of Mīr Dāmād; there is something in common between the black light swallowing up the universe and Mīr Dāmād's perception of the "great occult clamor of beings," the "silent clamor of their metaphysical distress."[124] The black light reveals the very secret of being, which can only *be*, as *made-to-be*; all beings have a twofold face, a face of light and a black face. The luminous face, the face of day, is the only one that, without understanding it, the common run of men perceive, the apparent evidence of their act of existing. Their black face, the one the mystic perceives, is their poverty: they have nothing with which to be, they cannot be sufficient unto themselves in order to be what they have to be, it is the *inessence* of their essence. The totality of their being is their daylight face and their night face; their daylight face is the making of essence out of their inessence by the absolute Subject. This is the mystical meaning of the verse in the Qorān: "Everything perishes except His Face" (28:88), that is, except the face of light of that thing.

Now what those two faces show the visionary is the twofold dimension of being precisely analyzed in Avicenna's ontology as the dimension of necessary being and the dimension of "contingent" being. In fact, there is strictly speaking no "contingency." There is actualized possibility, and every possibility to be actualized necessarily exists from the very fact that its perfect cause, its sufficient reason, is given. It could not not be. However, this dimension of possibility remains latent in the heart itself of the actualized possibility, in the sense that its dimension of necessary being, its capacity to be, comes to it from its connection with the Source from which it emanates, whereas its dimension of possibility, that is to say, its metaphysical indigence, is perceived as soon as it regards itself—fictitiously, to be sure, and in a hypothetical way—as separated from the Principle whence its necessary being derives. As one knows, the entire Avicennan theory of the procession of the cherubinic Intelligences, the emanators of the Heavens and of the Earth, is based on acts of contemplation directed to these "dimensions" of intelligibility. The visionary irruption of this twofold dimension—positive and negative—is the vision of the black light.

Even from the primordial origin of the pleroma, from the eternal instant of the arising of the first of the Intelligences, the first of the Kerobin, Angel-Logos, the twofold dimension of every existentialized being is already manifested: its face of light and its "black face." This is what led certain Iranian Avicennans[125] to compare the Avicennan cosmology with the *Zervānist* cosmology of ancient Iran. No doubt there is a dia-

V. The Black Light

grammatic homology as regards the form but, as we have already noted elsewhere, this would be correct only if referred to "exorcised," "de-satanized" *Zervānism*. For the "black face" that shows itself from the first act of being is not Ahrimanian darkness, but the secret of the creatural condition that has its origin "in the darkness at the approaches to the *pole*," that is, in the very mystery of the setting up of creation. The Ahrimanian darkness is in the "extreme Occident," the region of materialized matter. That is why Lāhījī and the mystic on whom he is commenting repeat, exactly as Avicenna said in the recital of Hayy ibn Yaqzān, that in "this darkness at the approaches to the pole" is to be found the Water of Life. To find this wellspring demands the penetration of the meaning of the twofold face of things, and to understand that is to understand at the same time the mystical implications of Avicenna's philosophy, attested by the perspectives it opened up to Iranian spirituals. Here alas! is where the impoverished rationalism of modern interpreters of Avicenna in the West reveals its impotence and incurable blindness. As Lāhījī says, one does not learn to find the Water of Life in the Darkness simply by hearsay and by reading books.

The Avicennan analysis of the twofold dimension of established being bore fruit until the time of the renaissance of philosophy in Iran in the sixteenth and seventeenth centuries. It is present in the metaphysics of light elaborated by Sohravardī in terms of a metaphysics of *essence*, as well as in the work of his great interpreter, Mollā Sadrā Shīrāzī (died 1640), who gave the *existential* version of the "oriental theosophy." It is traditionally repeated, from Mollā Sadrā down to Shaykh Ahmad Ahsā'ī, the founder of the Shaykhite school in Shī'ism, that the act of existing is the dimension of light of beings, whereas their quiddity is their dimension of darkness. And this cannot be understood without going back to the Avicennan origins. The metaphysical indigence of beings analyzed in Avicennan ontology is translated and experienced by Lāhījī as a feeling of authentic mystical poverty. By experiencing this, the visionary contemplates the mysterious black Light that permeates the entire universe; it is certainly not the Ahrimanian inversion and subversion that transports him in ecstasy, but the Presence whose suprabeing consists in *causing-to-be* and which for that reason can never itself be *caused-to-be*, nor seen as being—forever invisible while *causing to see* in its permanent actuation of each act of being.

That is why there is a profound connection between the meaning of the black Light perceived in the presence of things when they reveal to the visionary their twofold face, and its meaning as he perceives it when things absent themselves from him and he turns toward the Principle. These two themes are so deeply linked together that the second appears as the basis of the first. It is in the second sense that Lāhījī declares that black is the color of the pure divine Ipseity in Itself, in the same way that to Najm Rāzī this color applied only to the attributes of inaccessible Majesty, to the *Deus absconditus*. When he comments on this verse of the *Rose Garden of Mystery*, "The *black* color, if you follow me, is *light* of pure Ipseity; within this Darkness is the Water of Life" (v. 123)—what does Lāhījī mean in this case by speaking of a bedazzlement and a blindness whose cause is certainly not extreme distance but too great a proximity? The eye of inner vision, the "suprasensory senses" themselves, are darkened thereby.

To understand the shaykh's intention and his terminology, let us first recall the implications of Avicenna's ontology: the metaphysical indigence of beings, their *inessence*, implying that they would have nothing with which to be if necessary Being did not compensate for their lack. We referred just now to the existential version of the Avicenne-Sohravardian metaphysics in Mollā Sadrā: Sadrā gives the determinant metaphysical precedence to the act of existing, not to quiddity or essence. It can be said that Mollā Sadrā of Shīrāz, here as elsewhere, reveals his own formation as an Avicennan strongly imbued with the theosophy of Sohravardī and with that of Ibn 'Arabī. But well before him there were Spirituals in Iran who had read both Avicenna and Ibn 'Arabī. Lāhījī was one of them, and no doubt he was able to give the lie to misinterpretations inflicted in the West on the thought of his two masters, so different, incidentally, from each other. The famous expression *wahdat al-wojūd* does not signify an "existential monism" (it has no connection either with Hegel or with Haeckel), but refers to the transcendental unity of being. The act of being does not take on different meanings; it remains unique, while multiplying itself

V. The Black Light

in the actualities of the beings that it causes to be; an uncon-
ditioned Subject which is never itself *caused-to-be*. So this too-
closeness spoken of by Lāhījī, the bedazzlement of black Light,
is understood when every act of being or every act of light is
related to its Principle.

In other words, light cannot *be seen*, precisely because it is
what *causes seeing*. We do not see light, we see only its receptacles. That is why lights visible on suprasensory planes necessi-
tate the idea of *pure colors*, as previously outlined, which are
actualized *eo ipso* by their act of light as receptacles that are the
"matter" of pure light, and not needing to fall into a matter
foreign to their act of light. This being so, it is impossible to
withdraw enough to *see* the light which is the *cause-of-seeing*,
since in every act of seeing it is already there. This is the proximity that the mystic speaks of when he expresses his amaze-
ment "that you bring yourself so near to me that I come to
think that you are me" (*supra* IV, 9). We can neither see light when
there is nothing to receive it, nor where it is swallowed up. By
trying to place ourselves in front of the *cause-of-seeing*, which itself
can but remain invisible, we find ourselves in front of Darkness
(and that is "the Darkness at the approaches to the pole"), for we
cannot take as an *object* of knowledge precisely what enables us to
know each object, what enables *any object* to exist as such. That is
why Lāhījī speaks of a proximity that dazzles. On the other hand,
the demonic *shadow* is not the light, itself invisible, which *causes
seeing*, but is the Darkness that prevents seeing, as the darkness of
the subconscious prevents seeing. The black light, on the other
hand, is that which cannot itself be seen, because it is the cause of
seeing; it cannot be object, since it is absolute Subject. It dazzles, as
the light of *superconsciousness* dazzles. Therefore it is said in the
Rose Garden of Mystery: "Renounce seeing, for here it is not a
question of seeing." Only a knowledge which is a theophanic
experience can be knowledge of the divine Being. But in relation
to the divine Ipseity, this knowledge is a not-knowing, because
knowledge presupposes a subject and an object, the seer and the
seen, whereas divine Ipseity, black light, excludes this correlation.
To transmute this unknowingness into knowledge would be to
recognize *who* the true subject of knowledge is, in a supreme act of
metaphysical renunciation, where Lāhījī testifies to his sense of
the *poverty* of the dervish and to the fruit of his own meditation on
Ibn 'Arabī.

116

§3. Black Light in the "Rose Garden of Mystery"

Here one will recall certain visionary apperceptions of Najm Kobrā: now the red sun standing out on a black background, now the constellations turning red against the background of an emerald Sky, dazzling to human vision. We have learned from him that this red sun and these reddening orbs announce the presence of the Angel-Logos or of one of the angelic Intelligences. As in Hermes' vision, angelophany is associated with the symbol of the "midnight sun," of luminous Night, because the first Intelligence, the Angel-Logos, is the initial and primordial theophany of the *Deus absconditus*. The profound meaning of an episode in the *mi'rāj* of the Prophet then emerges. The Angel Gabriel, as the angel of Revelation identified by all the *Ishrāqīyūn* with the angel of Knowledge, leads the prophet as far as the *Lotus of the limit*. He cannot himself go further, for he would be consumed by fire. Now, it is unthinkable that his theophanic being should be consumed and annihilated; that would mean self-destruction of the divine revelation. As Lāhījī explains, the Angel does not have to cross this *fanā fī'llāh*, the test of reabsorption into God. The theophanic form must persist in order to be met with again at the emergence from the supreme test, the sun becoming red against a black sky, as in Najm Kobrā's vision. The ordeal of this penetration, comprising an experience of death and annihilation, is for man alone to attempt, and marks his hour of greatest peril. Either he will be swallowed up in dementia or he will rise again from it, initiated in the meaning of theophanies and revelations. This resurgence is later translated by Semnānī as an exaltation from black light to green light. By passing thus through the annihilation of annihilation, by passing to the "Gabriel of your being," the recognition of the Guide is authenticated, of the "witness in Heaven," the reddening sun against the background of divine Darkness. For this recognition implies recognition of the Unknowable, which is to say metaphysical renunciation and mystical poverty.

The poet of the *Rose Garden of Mystery* asks: "What common measure is there between the Terrestrial and the divine worlds, that being unable to find knowledge should already of itself be knowledge?" (v. 125) And Lāhījī comments:

> The perfection of contingent being is to regress to its basic negativity, and to come to know through its own unknowingness.

117

V. The Black Light

It means to know with the certainty of experience that the *summum* of knowledge is unknowingness, for here there is infinite disproportion. This mystical station is that of bedazzlement, of immersion of the object in the subject. It is the revelation of the non-being of that which has *never been*, and of the perennity of that which has *never not been*. . . . In reality, there is no knowledge of God by *another* than God, for *another* than God *is not*. The ultimate end towards which the pilgrims of the divine Way proceed, is to arrive at the mystical station where they discover that the actions, attributes and ipseity of things are effaced and reabsorbed in the theophanic ray of light, and where they are *essencified* by the very fact of their essential destitution, which is the stage of absorption in God (*fanā fī'llāh*), where being is returned to being, non-being to non-being, in conformity with the verse of the Book: "God commands you to render that which is held in trust to whom it belongs" (4:61).

But the one to whom it belongs will be found only on condition that the seventh valley is reached.

> The seventh is the valley of mystical poverty and of *fanā*. After that you can go no further. It has been said that mystical poverty is the wearing of black raiment[126] in the two universes. This saying expresses the fact that the mystic is so totally absorbed in God that he no longer has any existence of his own, neither inwardly nor outwardly in this world and beyond; he returns to his original essential poverty, and that is poverty in the true sense. It is in this sense, when the state of poverty has become total, that a mystic can say that he is God, for that mystical station is where he gives divine Ipseity *absolute* meaning (it is *absolved* of all relativation) . . . So long as the mystic has not reached his own *negativity*, which is complete reabsorption, he has not reached the *positivity* of essencification by absolute being, which is superexistence through God. *To be non-being* by one's own efforts is the very same as *to be* through God. Absolute non-being is manifested only in and through absolute being. For any other than Perfect Man access to this degree is difficult, for Perfect Man is the most perfect of beings and the very cause of the coming into existence of the world.

Thus the metaphysical indigence of the being is transfigured into mystical poverty, absolute liberation from this indigence.

"How shall I find words to describe such a subtle situation? *Luminous Night, dark Midday!*" (v. 125), cries the poet further on in the *Rose Garden of Mystery*. His commentator knows what he means: for one who has experienced this mystical state an allusion is enough, whereas anyone else will be able to understand only to the degree of his proximity to it. And Lāhījī is fascinated by this luminous Night (*shab-e roshan*) which is dark Midday, a mystical aurora borealis in which we ourselves recognize one of these "symbols of the north" which from the beginning have oriented our search toward an *Orient* not to be found in the East of our geographic maps. It is indeed *Night*, since it is *black* light and the abscondity of pure Essence, the night of unknowingness and of unknowableness, and yet *luminous* night, since it is at the same time the theophany of the *absconditum* in the infinite multitude of its theophanic forms (*mazāhir*). *Midday*, middle of the Day, to be sure, that is, high noon of multicolored suprasensory light which the mystic perceives through his organ of light, his inner eye, as theophanies of the divine Names, attributes and acts; and yet *dark Midday*, since the multitude of these theophanic forms are also the 70,000 veils of light and darkness which hide the pure Essence (see *supra* Najm Rāzī's reference to this number). The *Night* of pure Essence, devoid of color and distinction, is inaccessible to the knowing subject as knower, since it precedes all his acts of knowing. The subject thus is rather the organ by which the Essence knows itself as absolute Subject. And *luminous Night* nevertheless, since it is what causes the subject to be by making itself visible to him, what *causes* him *to see* by *causing* him *to be*. *Dark Midday* of theophanic forms, certainly, because left to themselves they would be darkness and non-being, and because in their very manifestation, "they show themselves as hidden!"

But it is impossible to divulge the secrets of theophanies and of divine apparitions, that is to say, the secrets of the *shāhid*. One who does so incurs only violent reproaches and denials. "About the forms in which the traces of theophanies are present,[127] certainly I would have much to say, but to be silent is preferable" (v. 129). The *Rose Garden of Mystery* thus comes to an end. All Sufi visionaries agree with him, for he is alluding to the hypostasis of the divine Lights, whose colors, forms, and figures specifically correspond to the spiritual state and vocation of the mystic. This, therefore, is the very secret of the *shāhid*, the Witness of contemplation, the "witness in Heaven," without which the Godhead would remain in the state of abscondity or abstraction, and there would be no possibility of that *uxority* which is the link between lover and beloved, a link

V. The Black Light

which is individual and unshareable, and to which every mystic soul aspires. God has no like (*mithl*), but He has an Image, a typification (*mithāl*), declares Lāhījī. This is the secret of the Prophet's vision tirelessly meditated upon by so many Sufis: "I have seen my God in the most beautiful of forms,"[128] attesting that the divine Being, without form or modality, is present to the eye of the heart in a particular form, modality, and individuation. For after the experience of the reabsorption of all the epiphanic forms in the "black light" of pure Essence, comes the resurgence from the danger of dementia, from metaphysical and moral nihilism, and from collective imprisonment in ready-made forms, the mystic, having understood what it is that assures the perennity of the determination of apparitional forms, of any given distinct epiphanic form. This is the authentic recognition of the figure of the heavenly Witness, the *shāhid*, whose recurrences we have studied under many and various names (*supra*, II and IV, 9). And that is why, in Semnānī, it is beyond the black light, the crossing of which he regards as perilous in the extreme, that the *visio smaragdina* begins to open.

VI. THE SEVEN PROPHETS OF YOUR BEING

1. Alāoddawleh Semnānī (1336)

His is one of the greatest names in Iranian Sufism. Thanks to his doctrine, the connection finally becomes clear between visionary apperceptions, graduated according to their coloration, and the "physiology of the man of light," that is, the physiology of the subtle organs whose growth is nothing other than the ontogenesis of the "resurrection body." It is the spiritual hermeneutics of the holy Book which give it structure: the spiritual *exegesis* of the revealed text coincides with the *exodus* of the man of light making his way step by step inward toward the *pole*, the place of his origin. In other words, the structure of the *seven* esoteric meanings of the Qorān exactly corresponds to the structure of a mystical anthropology or physiology connecting *seven* subtle organs or centers (*latīfa*), each of which is typified by one of the seven great prophets.

Having already dealt at some length elsewhere with this doctrine of Semnānī, we shall limit ourselves here to pointing out its essential features.[129] We shall recall only that the shaykh belonged to a noble family of Semnān (a city still flourishing today, situated some 200 kilometers to the east of Teheran). Born in 659/1261, he entered the service of Argun, the Mongol ruler of Iran, as a page, at the age of fifteen; when he was twenty-four, while camping with Argun's army in front of

Qazwīn, he underwent a profound spiritual crisis, asked to be relieved of his duties, and thereafter gave himself up once and for all to Sufism. He had his *Khānqāh* at Semnān itself, where a throng of disciples came to him and where his memory is still alive today; his sanctuary, a beautiful Mongol monument of delicate construction, was still extant until quite recently.

That the Qorān has a spiritual meaning, or rather several spiritual meanings, that everything exoteric has an esoteric aspect, and that the mode of being of the true believer depends on his knowledge of these spiritual meanings, was already affirmed from the earliest days of Islam; it expresses an essential aspect of Shī'ism, from which Imāmology is inseparable; this affirmation always provoked the disapproval of the orthodox Sunnite literalists. It is founded amongst other things on the *hadīth*, or reported saying of the Prophet himself: "the Qorān has an exoteric and an esoteric meaning [an outer appearance, a literal sense, and an inner depth, a hidden or spiritual sense]. In its turn, this esoteric meaning itself has an esoteric meaning [this depth has a depth, in the image of the heavenly Spheres enfolded the one within the other], and so forth, up to the seven esoteric meanings [seven depths of depth]."

The foundation and practice of these spiritual or esoteric hermeneutics are in fact bound up with a metaphysics of light, whose principal source is the *Ishrāq* of Sohravardī, and which operates similarly in the case of the Ishrāqīyūn, the Sufis, and the Ismaelians. In Semnānī, the physiology of the organs of light, the mystical anthropology, further accentuates the connection. This phenomenon has its counterpart in Latin Scholasticism, where interest in treatises on optics, the treatises *De perspectiva*, was fostered by the wish to ally the science of light to theology, just as it is allied here to Qorānic hermeneutics. The implication of the laws of optics in the study of the scriptures inspired, for example, the exegesis of Bartholomew of Bologna: "While in optics seven other modes of participation of bodies in light are known, Bartholomew finds seven corresponding modes of participation of the angelic and human intellects in the divine light."[130] Asín Palacios had already noted the essential affinity between the hermeneutics of the Islamic Esoterists and that of Roger Bacon. In neither case is there anything in the least arbitrary in their procedure; all they do, in short, is to apply the laws of optics and perspective to the spiritual interpretation of the holy books.[131] Likewise, it is the application of the laws of perspective that makes it possible to produce diagrams of the spiritual world (as with the Ismaelians or in the school of Ibn 'Arabī). An overall comparative research would, of course, have to include here the procedures employed in the biblical interpretations of Protestant theosophists, such as those of the school of Jacob Boehme.

Unfortunately, what Semnānī was able successfully to achieve is only partially expressed in writing. His *Tafsīr*,[132] introduced by a long prologue in which he expounds his method, actually only begins from *sūra 51*. The author's intention was to continue the unfinished *Tafsīr* of Najmoddīn Rāzī. He himself foresaw clearly what a colossal undertaking it would be to accomplish the project—a complete spiritual interpretation of the seven esoteric meanings of the Qorān. His reader appreciates the magnitude of the task while observing how the author takes care to bring out the seven meanings step by step, not in a theoretical way, but always concerned to relate them to spiritual experience, that is, to authenticate each meaning by relating it to the type and degree of spiritual experience which corresponds to a level of this or that depth (or height). This degree itself refers to the subtle organ which is its "place," just as it does to the color of the light that heralds it, and is the evidence that the mystic has arrived at this degree of visionary apperception.

The law of correspondences that governs these hermeneutics, and which is none other than the law governing all spiritual interpretation, can be stated as follows: there is homology between the events taking place in the outer world and the inner events of the soul; there is homology between what Semnānī calls *zamān āfāqī*, the "time of horizons" or "horizontal time," namely, the physical time of historical computation governed by the movement of the visible stars, and the *zamān anfosī*, or psychic time, the time of the world of the soul, of the *pole* governing the inner Heavens. This is exactly why each outer fact can be "led back" (the literal meaning of the word *ta'wīl*, used technically to describe spiritual exegesis) to the inner "region" corresponding to it. That region is one of the series of subtle organs of mystical physiology, each of which, due to the homology of times, is the typification of a prophet in the human microcosm, whose image and role it assumes. Finally, each of these regions or organs is marked by a colored light which the mystic is able to visualize in a state of contemplation and to which he has to learn to be attentive because it informs him as to his own spiritual state.

The first of these subtle organs (envelopes or centers) is called the subtle bodily organ (*latīfa qalabīya; qalab*, lit. = the "mold"). Unlike the physical human body, it is constituted by direct influx emanating from the Sphere of spheres, the Soul of the world, without passing through the other Spheres, or of the planets or of the Elements. It cannot begin to be formed until after the completion of the physical body: having the form of a body, but in the subtle state, it is, so to say, the embryonic mold of the new body, the "acquired" subtle body (*jism moktasab*). This is why in mystical physiology it is symbolically called the *Adam of your being*.

The second organ is on the level corresponding to the soul (*latīfa nafsīya*), not the one which is the seat of spiritual processes, but of the vital, organic processes, the *anima sensibilis, vitalis*, and which consequently is the center of uncontrolled desires and evil passions; as such, it is called *nafs ammāra* in the Qorān, and its role was described to us in Najm Kobrā's trilogy (*supra* IV, 3). This means that the level to which it corresponds on the subtle plane is the testing ground for the spiritual seeker; in confronting his lower self, he is in the same situation as Noah facing the hostility of his people. When he has overcome it, this subtle organ is called the *Noah of your being*.

The third subtle organ is that of the heart (*latīfa qalbīya*) in which the embryo of mystical progeny is formed, as a pearl is formed in a shell. This pearl or offspring is none other than the subtle organ which will be the True Ego, the real, personal individuality (*latīfa anā'īya*). The allusion to this spiritual Ego, who will be the child conceived in the mystic's heart, immediately makes it clear to us why this subtle center of the heart is the *Abraham of your being*.

The fourth subtle organ is related to the center technically designated by the term *sirr* (*latīfa sirrīya*), the "secret" or threshold of superconsciousness. It is the place and organ of intimate conversation, secret communication, "confidential psalm" (*monājāt*): it is the *Moses of your being*.

The fifth subtle organ is the Spirit (rūh, latīfa rūhīya); because of its noble rank, it is rightfully the divine viceregent: it is the *David of your being*.

The sixth subtle organ is related to the center best described by the Latin term *arcanum* (khafī, latīfa khafīya). Help and inspiration from the Holy Ghost are received by means of this organ; in the hierarchy of spiritual states it is the sign of access to the state of *nabī*, prophet. It is the *Jesus of your being*; it is he who proclaims the Name to all the other subtle centers and to the "people" in these faculties, because he is their Head and the Name he proclaims is the seal of your being, just as in the Qorān (3:6) it is said that Jesus, as the prophet before the last of the prophets of our cycle, was the herald of *the last prophet*, i.e., of the advent of the Paraclete.[133]

The seventh and last subtle organ is related to the divine center of your being, to the eternal seal of your person (*latīfa haqqīya*). It is the *Mohammad of your being*. This subtle divine center conceals the "rare Mohammadan pearl," that is to say, the subtle organ which is the True Ego, and whose embryo begins to be formed in the subtle center of the heart, the *Abraham of your being*. Every passage in the Qorān which defines the relationship of Mohammad with Abraham then offers us an admirable example of the inward movement actualized by Semnānī's hermeneutics, the transition from "horizontal time" to the "time of the soul." It ends by actualizing, in the person of the human microcosm, the truth of the meaning according to which the religion of Mohammad originates in the religion of Abraham, for "Abraham was neither Jew nor Christian, but a pure believer (*hanīf*), a *Moslem* (3:60)," which is to say that the "Abraham of your being" is led through the subtle centers of higher consciousness and of the *arcanum* (the Moses and the Jesus of your being) until he reaches your true Ego, his spiritual progeny.

Thus the growth of the subtle organism, the physiology of the man of light, progresses through the seven *latīfa*, each of which is one of the *seven prophets of your being*: the cycle of birth and initiatic growth is homologous to the cycle of prophecy. The mystic is aware of this growth thanks to the apperception of colored lights which characterize each of the suprasensory organs or centers, to the observation of which Semnānī gave so much attention. These lights are the tenuous veils enveloping each of the *latīfa*; their coloring reveals to the mystic which stage of his growth or journey he has reached. The stage of the subtle body at the level of its birth, still very close to the physical organism (the "Adam of your being"), is simply darkness, a *blackness* sometimes turning to smoke-grey; the stage of the vital soul (Noah) is *blue* in color; that of the heart (Abraham) is *red*; that of the superconscious (Moses) is *white*; that of the Spirit (David) is *yellow*; that of the arcanum (Jesus) is *luminous black* (*aswad nūrānī*); this is the "black light," the luminous Night about which we were informed by Najm Rāzī as well·as by the *Rose Garden of Mystery* and its commentator; lastly the stage of the divine center (Mohammad) is brilliant *green* (the splendor of the Emerald Rock, *supra* III, 1 and IV, 6) for "the color green is the most appropriate to the secret of the mystery of Mysteries (or the suprasensory uniting all the suprasensories)."

We immediately notice three things: first of all that the colored lights, in Semnānī's account, differ in two ways from the account in Najm Rāzī's treatise (*supra* V, 2): their order of sequence is different and their term of reference. Unfortunately, we cannot go into detail here. Second, an explicit distinction is made between the darkness of the *black thing* (the black object which absorbs the colors, holds the "spark of light" captive) and the *luminous black, i.e.,* the black light, luminous Night, dark Midday, on which as we have seen, Lāhījī dwells at length in his Commentary on Shabestarī's *Rose Garden*. Somewhere between the two we glimpsed the situation of the world of colors in the pure state (*supra* V, 1). Lastly, unlike the authors just recalled, Semnānī has it that the final mystical station is marked, not by *black light* but by green light. This corresponds no doubt to a difference in the way each of these depths is innerly attained, *oriented*.

The rule applying to this movement inward, the turning away from the "world of horizons" toward the "world of souls" is pointed out by Semnānī as clearly as one could wish.

> Each time you hear in the Book words addressed to Adam, listen to them through the organ of the subtle body. . . . Meditate on that with which they symbolize, and be very sure that the esoteric aspect of the passage relates *to you*, just as the exoteric aspect relates to Adam in that it concerns the *horizons*. . . . Only then will you be able to apply the teaching of the divine Word to

yourself and to cull it as you would a branch laden with freshly opened flowers.

And he continues in the same strain, from prophet to prophet.

The application of this rule governing the movement inward will itself show us why and how, from the point of view of the Islamic Sufi Semnānī, to pass through the *black light* typified by the "Jesus of your being" is the sign of a decisive, not to say dramatic step, but is not the ultimate stage of growth. The complete fulfillment of personal initiation comes to pass only when there is access to the seventh *latīfa*, the one enveloped in "the most beautiful color of all"—emerald splendor. In fact, Semnānī views the level of the subtle organ typified as the "Jesus of your being" as being exactly the perilous distracting stage whereat Christians in general and certain Sufis in Islam have been misled. It is worth our while to listen attentively to this evaluation of Christianity as formulated by a Sufi, for it differs profoundly from the polemics uttered by the offical heresy-hunting apologists who deny validity to all mystical feeling. Semnānī's critique is made in the name of spiritual experience; everything takes place as though this Sufi Master's aim were to perfect the Christian *ta'wīl*, that is, to "lead it back," to open the way at last to its ultimate truth.

By a striking comparison, Semnānī establishes a connection between the trap into which the Christian dogma of the Incarnation falls by proclaiming the *homoousia* and by affirming that 'Īsā ibn Maryam is God, and the mystical intoxication in which such as Hallāj cry out: "I am God" (*Anā'l-Haqq*). These dangers are symmetrical. On the one hand the Sufi, on experiencing the *fanā fī'llāh,* mistakes it for the actual and material reabsorption of human reality in the godhead; on the other, the Christian sees a *fanā* of God into human reality.[133a] This is why Semnānī perceives on the one side and the other the same imminent threat of an irregularity in the development of consciousness. The Sufi would need an experienced shaykh to help him avoid the abyss and to lead him to the degree that is in truth the divine center of his being, the *latīfa haqqīya*, where his higher, spiritual Ego opens. If not, the spiritual energy being wholly concentrated on this opening, it can happen that the lower ego is left a prey to extravagant thoughts and delirium. The "scales" (*supra* IV, 10) are then completely unbalanced; in a fatal moment of looking back, the newborn higher Ego succumbs to what had been overcome and perishes in the moment of triumph. And this is just as true in the moral domain as in respect to the metaphysical perception of the divine and of being. It is a premature rupture of the process of growth, a "failed initiation." One could say that the mortal danger described by Semnānī on both sides is the very same situation with which the West came face to face when Nietzsche cried out: "God is dead."

This then is the peril which confronts the Spiritual seeker in the mystical station of the *black light* or *luminous darkness*. To sum up briefly Semnānī's conclusion (*Commentary to sūra 112*), one could put it as follows: if both Sufi and Christian are menaced by the same danger, it is because there is a revelation and an opening up of the Ego corresponding to each of the *latīfa*. The danger in this case corresponds to the moment when the Ego makes its appearance (*tajallī*) on the level of the *arcanum* (whose color is black light and whose prophet is Jesus). If in the course of spiritual growth "intoxication" has not been completely eliminated, that is, the subconscious allurements of the level of the two first *latīfa*, then a lower mode of perception continues to function and Abraham's journey may remain forever unfinished. This is why the mystery of the theophany, the manifestation of the Holy Ghost in the visible form of the Angel Gabriel appearing in Maryam, his "breathing into" Maryam by which Jesus is made *Rūh Allah* (*Spiritus Dei*)—all of this—was not perceived by the Christians in their dogma of the Incarnation on the level of the *arcanum* (*latīfa khafīya*). They saw it on the level of data belonging still to the level of the first two *latīfa*. Their dogma would have the birth of the one God take place materially "on earth," whereas the "Jesus of your being" is the mystery of the spiritual birth. *i.e.*, of the assumption to Heaven. They saw the event in the *zamān āfāqī*, not in the *zamān anfōsī*, that is, on the suprasensory plane where the real event takes place which is the advent of the Soul into the world of the Soul. The Sufi likewise, on the same level, deviates from the metaphysical poverty, mystical nakedness, which as we have seen (*supra* V, 3), is the secret of the black light. He shouts *Anā'l-Haqq* (I am God) instead of saying, as Ibn 'Arabi reminds him, *Anā sirr al-Haqq*: "I am God's secret," the secret, that is, which conditions the polarity of the two faces, the face of light and the face of darkness, because the divine Being cannot exist without me, nor I exist without Him.

The symmetry of the dangers is reflected in a corresponding symmetry of spiritual therapeutics. The mystic has to be "carried away" to the higher spiritual Abode (to pass from the black Light to the green light), so that the nature of his True Ego may be revealed to him, not as an ego with the godhead as its predicate, so to say, but as being the organ and place of theophany; this means that he will have become fit to be invested in his light, to be the perfect *mirror*, the organ of the theophany. This is the state of the "friend of God," of whom the divine Being can say, according to the inspired *hadīth*, so oft-repeated by the Sufis: "I am the eye through which he sees, the ear through which he hears, the hand by which he touches . . ." This divine saying corresponds to the mystic's: "I am God's secret." Semnānī finds his inspiration regarding these spiritual therapeutics in a verse which he greatly values and in which the essence of Qorānic Christology is expressed: "They did not kill him, they did not crucify him, they were taken in by the appearance; God carried him off toward himself (4:156)," *i.e.*, he carried him off alive from death. Only an authentic "spiritual realism," suprasensory realism, can penetrate the arcanum of this verse. It demands a *polar* orientation rising above the dimension which is the only thing able to hold us back from the reality of the *event*, namely, the "horizontal" dimension of history. On the contrary, what the Sufi is seeking is not at all what we hypothetically call "the sense of history," but the inner sense of his being and of every being; not the material reality, the datum of earthly history-making (in the *zamān āfāqī*), but the "event in Heaven" which alone can save earthly man and bring him "home."

That being so, when you listen to some of God's sayings to his friend the Prophet, or allusions to them, listen to them, see them through the subtle organ which is the divine in you, the "*Mohammad of your being*" (*latīfa haqqīya*). The formation of heavenly man is completed in that subtle center. It is in that very place that the subtle body grows to its full stature, the body "acquired" by the mystic's spiritual practice and which contains the "essential heart," the spiritual child of the "*Abraham of your being*," the one being who is capable of assuming the theophanic function of pure mirror ("specularity," *mirā'īya*).[134] The connection between spiritual hermeneutics and mystical physiology is fully revealed. The understanding of the hidden meanings and the growth of the subtle organism hidden in the human being develop concurrently—the growth "from prophet to prophet" culminating in the full prophetic stature. All the factors in Semnānī's theosophical cosmology have to be taken into account here. As the hidden meanings gradually come to be understood, the organs of the subtle physiology receive energies from universes preceding the sensory universe; these unite with the organs of the "body of immortality" which are at the core of the mystic's person much better than the "stars of his fate," since they are the "prophets of his being."

At this mystical stage, having reached his perfect spiritual stature, the mystic no longer needs to meditate on the ultimate *latīfa*, since from then on he *is* the "Mohammad of his being." At this very point we see the full meaning, in Semnānī, of the theophanic figure we have come to recognize under many and various names, which Semnānī for his part calls the *ostād ghaybī*, the suprasensory master or personal guide. This figure is clearly the *shaykh al-ghayb*, the Guide, the "witness in Heaven" of whom Najm Kobrā's visions informed us. Semnānī discreetly suggests its further role and function:

> Just as the physical sense of hearing [he writes] is a necessary condition if the hearer is to understand the exoteric meaning of the Qorān and receive the *tafsīr* from his outer, visible master (*ostād shahādī*), so the integrity of the heart, of the inner hearing is a necessary condition if the inspired Spiritual seeker (*molham*) is to understand the esoteric meaning of the Qorān and receive the *ta'wīl* of his inner suprasensory master (*ostād ghaybī*).

This passage, so admirably condensed and allusive, thus makes it clear that the inspired mystic's relationship with his *ostād ghaybī* is the same as Mohammad's relationship with the Holy Ghost which was his inseparable companion, just as it was for Jesus. This is why the supreme *latīfa* of the subtle organism is also related to the "Lotus of the Limit," the place where the Prophet saw the angel Gabriel standing in Paradise (53:14); and also why the pre-eminence of the color *green*, heralding the highest mystical station, is supported by an allusion to the *raf-raf*, the *green* drapery seen by the Prophet covering the horizon of the Heavens, at the moment of his first vision of the Angel. And it is immediately clear also why the *latīfa* or subtle organ known as the "Mohammad of your being" should, from another aspect, be described as the *latīfa jabra'elīya*, the "angel Gabriel of your being." Here the *latīfa jabra'elīya* is, for the mystic, related with the Angel of Revelation just as Perfect Nature is related with the Angel of Humanity in Sohravardī's hermeneutics (*supra* II, 1). It can also be understood why so many Sufis, from Jalāl Rumī to Mīr Dāmād, have seen the annunciation of the Holy Ghost-Gabriel to Maryam in their meditations as an annunciation to every mystic soul. But one can go further also and conclude that the theophanic figure of the Angel of Revelation in prophetology, the Angel of knowledge in the "oriental theosophy" of the *Ishrāqīyūn*, is here the Angel of spiritual exegesis, that is to say, the one who reveals the hidden meaning of previous revelations, provided that the mystic possesses the ear of the heart, "celestial" hearing (*malakūtī*). To this extent the Angel has the same spiritual function as the Imām in Shī'ism, the *walāyat* of the Imām as the donor of the hidden meaning, and it would seem that Shī'ite Sufism alone makes the idea of the *walāyat* clear from all sides. But one can say that Semnānī's spiritual doctrine and method comes in the end to the radical inner realization both of prophetology and of Imāmology. And this alone is what makes a "Mohammadan."

> He who has become conscious of this *latīfa*, who has reached it by journeying, step by step, by winged flight or ecstasy, who has allowed the powers of all his subtle organs to open in freedom from the taint of illusion and relativity, who has allowed them to be demonstrated as they should be demonstrated in the pure state, he it is indeed who can truly be called a Mohammadan. Otherwise, make no mistake; do not believe that the fact of uttering the words "I affirm that Mohammad is God's Messenger" is enough to make you a Mohammadan.

2. *The World of Colors and the Man of Light*

The preceding analyses have repeatedly shown us that there was an affinity, sometimes subtle, sometimes explicit, between Sufism and Manicheism revealed in their physics and

131

metaphysics of light. It would be a fascinating task to pursue the traces of this affinity in iconography; more fascinating still if we notice the cross-references between Sufism and Christianity, which we can easily foresee are leading us toward Christian representations not altogether those of official and historical Christianity. Semnānī's indications would already suffice to put us on the track. The central truth of Christianity may be conceived in terms of hypostatic union of divinity and humanity; it may be thought out in terms of theophany (*tajallī*). The first way was that of the Great Church; we need hardly recall how this appeared in the judgment of the whole of Islamic theology. The second way was followed by those who refused the implied contradiction, whether they happened to be Valentinians or Manicheans, an Apollinarious of Laodicea or, among the Protestant Spirituals, a Schwenckfeld or a Valentin-Weigel. This does not in the least mean that they developed a mythological Christology; they affirmed the idea of a *caro Christi spiritualis*.

If we wish to understand the import of the criticisms voiced by a Sufi like Semnānī, as well as the profound intentions of Shī'ite Imāmology, this way of representing it is what we have to keep in mind, for it implies great consequences for the science of religions in general. This "spiritualized realism" has at its disposal the whole substance of the "heavenly Earth of Hūrqalyā" for *giving body* to the psycho-spiritual and to spiritual events. We have seen Semnānī reveal the danger exactly corresponding to that which threatens Sufism: no longer indeed a *fanā fī'llāh*, but on the contrary a *fanā*, of the divine in human reality. If Semnānī had used a modern man's terminology, he would have spoken of historicization, secularization, socialization—not as of phenomena taking place among others in the *zamān āfāqī*, the "horizontal time" of material historicity, but as of the phenomenon itself of the fall of the *zamān anfosī*, a psycho-spiritual time, into the *zamān āfāqī*. In other words, falling from events which *are made* by the history of the soul to a history which *is made* by outer events. The first are in no way mythology, and the iconography that represents them in no way consists of allegories. But, of course, intentions and procedures differ profoundly according to the one or the other category of events. Already one can get an idea of the contrast by referring on the one hand to the iconography of the *Christus juvenis* of the very first centuries of Christianity (a few types were mentioned above, II, 2) and on the other hand, either, in the Eastern Church, to the iconography of the *pantokrator* endowed with all the attributes of maturity and virility,[135] or, in the Western Church, to the iconography of the suffering and crucified Jesus.

What the latter translates is the tendency to attribute to the divine the human reality of everyday life, even to its confusions and miseries: the idea that God could only save man by becoming man in this sense. In contrast, what the first translates is the idea that God can only come in contact with humanity by transfiguring the latter; that the salvation of man imprisoned in Ahrimanian Darkness can be nothing other than an assumption to Heaven, operated by the all-powerful attraction of the divine Light, without the latter having to nor being able to be made captive, for then the possibility of salvation would be abolished. The preparation and expectation of this triumph are exactly what fill the acts of the Manichean dramaturgy of salvation. This soteriology, the liberation of the "particles of light" taken up from their prison and at last rejoining their like, is exactly that of a Sohravardī and of a Semnānī. Hence their metaphysics of light surrounding their physiology of the man of light, itself centered around the presence or the attraction of a Perfect Nature or of a "witness in Heaven," who is for the individuality of the mystic the homologue of the heavenly Twin of Mānī, that is to say, Christ or the Virgin of light. This return of "light to light" as a suprasensory event is what Manichean painting intended to make available to sensory perception. If iconography reveals an affinity between its methods and those of Persian miniatures, this will show us another affinity in depth.

And so this deep affinity, discernible in the affinity between the technical processes of Manichean iconography and Persian miniatures, is the very one which operated in the eighth and ninth centuries of our era, within the spiritual circles where Shī'ite gnosis was formed.[136] The very same idea which dominates Shī'ite philosophy, that of the Imām and of Imāmology, determines a structure to which three fundamental themes are available, in which the affinity between Shī'ite gnosis and Manichean gnosis is discovered. Of these three themes, the theme of the *walāyat* is perhaps dominant, because it crystallizes around it the theme of the cycles of Prophecy and the theme of the spiritual sciences of nature, alchemy, and astrology, which are the bases of Manichean cosmology and biology.

The theme of the *walāyat* has already come up here, whether apropos of the vision of the seven *abdāl*, the seven stars near the *pole*, according to Rūzbehān, or apropos of the esoteric hierarchy, organized in the image of the celestial dome whose keystone is the *pole* (the hidden Imām) and which fills the function of cosmic salvation (*supra* III, 2 and 3). We saw it appear again, a few pages ago, apropos of the idea of the inner master, *ostād ghaybī*, "the angel Gabriel of your being," who, in his role of initiator in the hidden meaning of the revelations, appeared in Semnānī as the "inner Imām" and besides as an interiorization of Imāmology. We have already pointed out the difficulty of translating simultaneously the aspects connoted by the term: the difficulty is due no doubt to the fact that the implied structure has nothing exactly corresponding to it in the West, except among the Spirituals incidentally referred to above. This religious structure is quite different from all that we habitually designate by the word "Church"; it provides in each of the cycles of Prophecy (*nobowwat*), a cycle of Initiation (*walāyat*) to the hidden meaning of the revealed letter. Shī'ite gnosis, as an initiatic religion, is an initiation in a doctrine. This is why it is particularly unsatisfactory to translate, as is often done, *walāyat* as "holiness." What this term connotes, namely the canonic idea of holiness, is very far from the point. *Walāyat* as an initiation and as an initiatic function, is the spiritual ministry of the Imām whose charisma initiates his faithful in the esoteric meaning of the prophetic revelations. Better still, the Imāmate *is* this very meaning. The Imām as *walī* is the "grand master," the master of initiation (thus transposed to another level, the twofold exoteric acceptation of the word *walī* can be conserved: on the one hand, friend, companion; on the other, lord, protector).

The second theme, that of the cycles of Revelation, is implied in the very idea of the *walāyat*. The *walāyat* postulates in fact, as we have just said, a theory of the cycles of Prophecy: prophetology and Imāmology are two inseparable lights. Now, this theory of cycles of Revelation, although in Ismaelian gnosis

§2. The World of Colors and the Man of Light

it has features reminding of the theme of the *Verus Propheta* in Ebionite Christianity, is well known to be a Manichean theory. On the other hand, the "physiology of the man of light," the growth of subtle organs, is modelled in Semnānī, as we have seen, on this same theory of cycles of Prophecy. The subtle organs are respectively the "prophets of your being": their growth into a "body of resurrection," in striking correspondence with the cycle of resurrections of the adept in Islamic gnosis, is the microcosmic actualization and the knowledge of the cycles of Prophecy.

Finally, as the third theme, alchemy and astrology, as the spiritual sciences of nature, are fundamental to the Manichean soteriology of light; we have also heard Najm Kobrā call the seeker the "particle of light" imprisoned in Darkness, and declare that his own method was none other than that of alchemy. This alchemical operation is what produces the aptitude for visionary apperception of the suprasensory worlds, these being manifested by the figures and constellations which shine in the Skies of the soul, the Sky of the Earth of Light. These spiritual constellations are the homologues of those interpreted in esoteric astronomy (*supra* III, 3), thus exemplifying on both sides one and the same figure dominating the *Imago mundi*: the Imām who is the *pole*, just as in terms of spiritual alchemy he is the "Stone" or the "Elixir."

These are the three themes constructed on parallel lines in Manichean gnosis and in Shī'ite gnosis, which amplify and explicate the fundamental motif of the *theophany*, whose presuppositions and implications have been recalled above. Now, this theophanic feeling common to Shī'ism and to Sufism (and which triumphs particularly in Shī'ite Sufism), determines the Shī'ite apperception of the person of the Imām, as it determines the apperception of beauty in those of the Sufis, disciples of Rūzbehān of Shīrāz for example, to whom in particular we have restricted the designation "fedeli d'amore." Consequently we have to appeal to this same fundamental theophanic feeling in order to account for common pictorial techniques in iconography. The person of the Imām (that is to say, the eternal Imām in his twelve personal exemplifications in the case of Twelve-Imām Shī'ism) is the pre-eminent theophanic form (*mazhar*). The person of the *shāhid*, the beautiful

VI. The Seven Prophets of Your Being

being chosen as the witness of contemplation, is for the "fedele" his personal theophanic form; in the course of this study we have identified this figure under diverse names. There is something in common between the chivalric devotion that binds the Shīʿite adept to the theophanic person of the Imām and the loving service that binds the mystic lover to the earthly form through which the pre-eminent divine Attribute—beauty—is revealed to him. The historical origins of this mutual inclination will perhaps never be definitively clarified; it is established at the time and in the spiritual circles that we have recalled above. What holds the attention of the phenomenologist is the testimony of states experienced; the Manichean feeling of the drama of the universe was particularly fitted to develop the feeling of a personal covenant of fidelity; the whole ethic of Shīʿism and Iranian Sufism culminates in the idea of *javānmardī*, that is to say "of spiritual chivalry."

From here on, it becomes possible to fully evaluate the testimony that we owe to a writer of the eleventh century, Abū Shakūr Sālimī, a writer who describes for us how the Manicheans of Central Asia were marked by a form of worship which was the passionate adoration they professed in regard to beauty and all beautiful beings. In our day objections have been raised to this testimony which cancel themselves out by the fact that they show purely and simply a confusion between the implications of the Manichean physics of light and with what we habitually think of in the West in terms of hypostatic union. Hence the warning that we repeated at the beginning of the present chapter: the pure philologist had better keep out of the closed field of philosophy than enter it with ill-adapted weapons.[137]

If one thinks in terms of theophany (*tajallī, zohūr*), not in terms of hypostatic union, one is speaking only of a corporeal receptacle (*mazhar*), which fills the role and function of a *mirror*. This receptacle, *caro spiritualis*, can be perceived in various ways; the alchemy of which Najm Kobrā speaks produces the aptitude for this perception by working on the organs of perception of the contemplator (for which and through which, as we have heard Najm Rāzī declare, events are at the same time sensory and suprasensory). This is why we have been reminded many times that the vision varies in proportion to the aptitude: your contemplation is worth what you *are*. And so the Ismaelian authors, Abū Ya'qūb Sejestānī among others, lay stress, as though to forestall the above-mentioned ill-founded objections, on the fact that beauty is not an attribute immanent in physical nature, nor a material attribute of the flesh; physical beauty is itself a spiritual attribute and a spiritual phenomenon. It can be perceived only by the organ of light; perception of it effects, as such, from now on the passage from the sensory to the suprasensory plane. Perhaps Abū Shakūr's description exaggerates in detail some of the features common to the Manicheans and the Hallājian Sufis, but, as L. Massignon wrote, "his description summarizes the essential character of that peculiar development of crystalline aesthetic sentimentality, as transparent as a rainbow, which Islam derived from a rather dramatic Manichaean concept, that of the imprisonment of particles of the divine light in the demoniac matrix of matter."

Here we have the fundamental esthetic feeling, persisting in a variety of developments, which is here expressed by a common pictorial technique. Mānī has been traditionally regarded in Islam as the initiator of painting and the greatest master of that art (in classical Persian, the terms *nagārestān*, *nagār-khāneh*, are used as signifying the "house of Mānī" to designate a gallery of paintings, a book of painted pictures). Everyone knows that the purpose of his painting was essentially didactic; it was intended to lead vision beyond the sensory: to incite love and admiration of the "Sons of Light," horror of the "Sons of Darkness." The liturgical illumination so highly developed by the Manicheans was, essentially, a scenography of the "liberation of the light." With this aim in view, the Manicheans were led to represent light in their miniatures by precious metals. If we associate the persistence of the Manichean technique and its decorative themes with the resurgence of the Manichean physics of light in the "oriental theosophy" of Sohravardī, and above all in certain psalms composed by him,[138] then we will be the better able to keep in mind longer all that is still being suggested by these lines of L. Massignon:

> The art of Persian miniatures, without atmosphere, without perspective, without shadows, and without modelling, in the metallic splendour of its polychromy, peculiar to itself, bears wit-

VI. The Seven Prophets of Your Being

ness to the fact that its originators were undertaking a kind of alchemic sublimation of the particles of divine light imprisoned in the "mass" of the picture. Precious metals, gold and silver, come to the surface of the fringes and crowns, of the offerings and cups, to escape from the matrix of the colours.

Escape, ascent and deliverance: this is also what visions of colored lights heralded for Najm Kobrā; colors in the pure state, suprasensory, freed from the Ahrimanian darkness of the *black object* which had absorbed them, and restored, just as they were opened up to the divine Night "at the approach to the pole," in the *Terra lucida* "which secretes its own light" (*supra* III, 1). In this pure luminescence we recognize one Iranian representation above all others: the *Xvarnah*, the light-of-glory which, from their first beginning, the beams of light establish in their being, of which it is at once the glory (δόξα) and the destiny (τύχη) (supra II, 3). This is what in iconography has been represented as the luminous nimbus, the *aura gloriae* which haloes the kings and priests of the Mazdean religion; this way of representing it has been transferred to the figures of Buddhas and Bodhisattvas as also the heavenly figures of primitive Christian art. It is the *Xvarnah* that forms the vermillion-gold background of many Manichean paintings of Turfan and of the paintings in certain Persian manuscripts of the school of Shīrāz, survivals of the celebrated mural paintings of the Sassanids.

Let us make no mistake as to the meaning of these red-gold background colors, when we find them again in the gold background of the Byzantine icons and mosaics. Whether it is a question of the nimbus of personages or of the visionary geography of what has been called "*xvarnah* landscapes" (Strzygowski), it remains always a question of the same transfiguring light: lights returning to their origin or lights descending to meet them as far as the surface of the objects out of which they attract them. There is neither contrast nor rupture in the idea, only the prolongation and persistence of one and the same idea. For in the whole of Eastern Christianity there is always a latent monophysitism in which lies the same and imperative desire for transfiguration, *caro spiritualis Christi*, of which the *fanā fī'llāh* of Sufism is perhaps at once the previsioning or the accomplishment. For contrast and rupture, we have to look elsewhere: there where the Shadow and the shadows have definitively banished this light from iconography.

3. The "Physiological" Colors According to Goethe

We shall not attempt to recapitulate the leading themes of the present study; our concern is not to come to conclusions; the aim of true research is to open the way to new questions. Among the questions which remain to be formulated or developed, there is one that at this very moment spontaneously arises. What we have analyzed referring to visionary apperceptions, suprasensory senses, subtle organs or centers that develop in conjunction with a growing interiorization—in brief, all the themes constituting a "physiology of the man of Light"—have shown us that the colored photisms, the suprasensory perceptions of colors in the pure state, result from an inner activity of the subject and are not merely the result of passively received impressions of a material object. Whoever is familiar with or in sympathy with Goethe's *Farbenlehre* (his *theory* or rather his *doctrine of colors*) inevitably wonders whether there is not a fruitful comparison to be attempted between our "physiology of the man of light" and Goethe's idea of "physiological colors."

Let us keep in mind some of Najm Kobrā's principal themes, for example that the object of the search is the divine Light and the seeker is himself a particle of this light; that our method is the method of alchemy; that like aspires to its like; that like can be seen and known only by its like. It certainly seems then that Goethe had himself mapped out the way for anyone wishing to respond to the Iranian Sufi's invitation to penetrate to the heart of the problem:

> The eye [writes Goethe], owes its existence to light. From an auxiliary, sensory apparatus, animal and neutral, light has called forth, produced for itself, an organ like unto itself; thus the eye was formed by light, of light and for light, so that the inner light might come in contact with the outer light. At this very point we are reminded of the ancient Ionian School, which never ceased to repeat, giving it capital importance, that like is only known by like. And thus we shall remember also the words of an ancient mystic that I would paraphrase as follows:

VI. The Seven Prophets of Your Being

If the eye were not by nature solar,
How should we be able to look at the light?
If God's own power did not live in us,
How would the divine be able to carry us off in ecstasy?"[139]

One can leave it to the Iranian Sufis who have been quoted here to make for themselves the spontaneous association of their testimony with that of the anonymous mystic of old whom Goethe calls as witness. The idea of a "physiology of the man of light," as outlined in Najm Kobrā's theory of the suprasensory senses and Semnānī's theory of subtle organs enveloped in color, links up with Goethe's vast scheme, where the author assigns priority to the "physiological colors" in heading his great work and, in its amplification, even treats explicitly the mystic significance of colors and of the experience of colors. The point is that the term "physiology" in no way refers here to some kind of material organism, but to something that rationalist science tries to do without in accepting nothing apart from sensory, empirical data except abstract ideas available to the ordinary mind. Goethe likewise begins by reminding us that the phenomenon he designates as the phenomenon of "physiological colors" has been known for a very long time; unfortunately, due to the radical lack of an appropriate phenomenology, it has been neither comprehensible nor given its proper value; there has been discussion of *colores adventici*, *imaginarii*, *phantastici*, *vitia fugitiva*, *ocular spectra*, etc. In short, these colors have been regarded as something of an illusory, accidental, insubstantial nature, and relegated to the realm of dangerous fantasies, because a concept of the universe wherein physical reality is regarded as total reality, in fact, no longer allows the suprasensory to be seen otherwise than as spectral. In contrast, we have here learned to see something quite different in the suprasensory world of which our Sufis have been speaking. And this "something quite different" is in accord with what is affirmed in the *Farbenlehre*, which postulates that the colors referred to therein as "physiological" pertain to the subject, to the organ of sight, to the "eye which is itself light," and what is more, that these colors are the very conditions of the act of seeing, which remains incomprehensible if it is not viewed as an interaction, a reciprocal action.[140]

§3. The "Physiological" Colors According to Goethe

The term "physiological," applied to colors for this reason, gradually takes on its full meaning and justification to the degree that the notion of the "subject" in question unfolds. There is essentially a refusal to admit pure exteriority or extrinsicity, as if the eye did no more than *passively* reflect the outer world. The perception of color is an action and reaction of the soul itself which is communicated to the whole being; an energy is then emitted through the eyes, a spiritual energy that cannot be weighed or measured quantitatively (it could be evaluated only by the mystical *scales* of which Najm Kobrā has spoken, *supra* IV, 10). "The colors we see in bodies do not affect the eye as if they were something foreign to it, as if it were a matter of an impression received purely from outside. No, this organ is always so situated as to produce colors itself, to enjoy a pleasant sensation if something homogeneous to its nature is presented to it from outside" (§760). And this because colors only occasionally modify the latent determinative capacity or power which is the eye itself. The affirmation returns continually as a *leitmotiv* to the fact that the eye at this point produces another color, its *own* color. The eye searches at the side of a given colored space for a free space where it can produce the color called for by itself. This is an effort toward totality involving the fundamental law of chromatic harmony,[141] and this is why "if it happens that the totality of colors is presented to the eye from the outside as an object, the eye takes pleasure in it because at such a moment its own activity is presented to it as a reality" (§808).

Is there not a similar phenomenon of totality in the reunion of the two fiery lights issuing the one from Heaven, the other from the earthly person, which Najm Kobrā perceived as the theophanic form of his "witness in Heaven" (*supra* IV, 9), that is to say, of the heavenly counterpart conditioning the whole of his being? And what justifies the comparison are the very words of the old mystic adopted by Goethe and paraphrased in the introduction to his own book.

From the mutual exchange between like and like, from the interaction thus suggested in general, the idea of specific actions begins to become clearer; these actions are never arbitrary and their effects are sufficient to attest that "physiological

141

color" as such is an experience of the soul, that is, a spiritual experience of color itself:

> From the idea of polarity inherent in the phenomenon, from the knowledge that we have reached of its particular determinations, we can conclude that particular impressions of colors are not interchangeable, but that they act in a specific way and must produce conditions having a decisive specific effect on the living organism. The same applies to the soul (*Gemüt*): experience teaches us that particular colors produce definite mental impressions.[142]

These are the impressions on which the meanings of colors are based, rising by degrees to their mystical meaning, the very meaning which has held the whole attention of our Iranian Sufi masters. On the subject of these meanings, the *Farbenlehre* concludes in a series of admirable pages: "All that has been said has been an attempt to show that each color produces a definite effect on the human being and by that very fact reveals its essential nature to the eye as well as to the soul. It follows that color can be used for certain physical, moral, and aesthetic purposes." It can also be used for another purpose which makes use of the effect and expresses still better its *inner meaning*, namely, the *symbolic* use which Goethe carefully distinguishes from the allegorical (in contrast with our habit, which unfortunately is more often than not to confuse allegory and symbol).[143]

> Finally it will be easy to foresee that color can assume a *mystical significance*. In effect, the schema in which the diversity of colors is represented suggests the archetypal conditions (*Urverhältnisse*) that belong equally to man's visual perception and to nature; that being established, there is no doubt that one can make use of their respective relationships, as of a language, if one wishes to express those archetypal conditions, which do not of themselves affect the senses with the same force or with the same diversity.[144]

And this is in fact the language in which the colored photisms spoke to all Najm Kobrā disciples, because color is not a passive impression, but the language of the soul to itself. Thus, in the heptad of colors, Semnānī perceived the heptad of the organs of the man of light, the heptad of the "prophets of his being."

The final point made by Goethe may allow us to perceive

how the spiritual experience of color can initiate in the revelation of the "witness in Heaven," the heavenly Guide of whom Sohravardī, Najm Kobrā, Semnānī, have all spoken.

> If the polarity of yellow and blue has truly been grasped, if in particular their intensification into red has been well noted and it has become clear how these opposites tend toward one another and reunite in a third color, then it cannot be doubted that the intuition of a profound secret is beginning to dawn in us, a foretaste of the possibility that a spiritual meaning might be attributed to these two separate and mutually opposed entities. When they are seen to produce *green* below and *red* above, one can hardly refrain from thinking that one is contemplating here the earthly creatures and there the heavenly creatures of the *Elohim* (§919).

Once again the words of the anonymous mystic adopted by Goethe are what enable us to foresee the total convergence between Goethe's doctrine of color and the physics of light of our Iranian mystics, on whose side it represents a tradition going back to ancient pre-Islamic Persia. The indications we have received were elusive. Quite a number of questions will remain in the air, but it was worth while taking the necessary steps to open them. To the extent that Goethe's optics is an "anthropological optics," it runs counter to the requirements and habits of what is called the scientific mind, and will continue to do so. It is the scientists' business to pursue the aim they have set for themselves. But here we are concerned with a different question, a different aim, common to those who have experienced in similar fashion the "action of Light."

This aim is the superexistence of the higher personal individuality, attained by reunion with the individual's own dimension of Light, his "face of light," that gives the individuality its total dimension. For this reunion to be possible the inclination toward the "polar dimension" must have opened in the terrestrial being, the inclination heralded by fugitive flashes of superconsciousness. The physiology of the man of light tends toward this opening—this is what Semnānī was expressing when he spoke of the spiritual child which the "Abraham of your being" must procreate. Najm Kobrā admits having meditated for a long time before he understood *who* was this light that flamed in the Sky of his soul while the flame of his own being was rising to meet it. If he understood that the light

143

VI. The Seven Prophets of Your Being

sought was there, it was because he knew *who* was *seeking* the light. He himself told us this: "What is sought is the divine Light, the seeker is himself a particle of the light." "If God's own power were not living in us, how would He be able to transport us in ecstasy?" The mystic of old who inspired the prologue of the *Farbenlehre* was asking the same question.

The literal concordance of the evidence allows us, so far, to consider the investigation of the origins and causes of the "physiological colors" as the search for experimental verification of the physiology of the man of light, that is to say of the phenomena of colored lights perceived and interpreted by our Iranian Sufis. On the one side and on the other, the same Quest of the man of light, and the answer to both has been, so to speak, given in advance by Mary Magdalen, in the book of the *Pistis Sophia*, when she says: "The man of light in me," "my being of light," has understood these things, has brought out the meaning of these words (*supra* II, 1). Who is sought? Who is the seeker? The two questions, belonging together, cannot remain theoretical. In every case the revealing light has preceded the revealed light, and phenomenology does no more than uncover later the already accomplished fact. It is then that the five senses are transmuted into other senses. *Superata tellus sidera donat*: "And the earth transcended brings us the gift of the stars" (Boethius).

NOTES

I. ORIENTATION

1. A brief note on the transcriptions adopted: because of the unavoidable necessity for typographical simplification, diacritical marks have been sacrificed; hence, the emphatic consonants of the Arabic alphabet (*d, t, s, z*) are not distinguished from the ordinary consonants either in the Arabic or Persian words. Similarly, the *hamza* and the *'ayn* are both transcribed simply by an apostrophe. As for the others, *h* always represents an aspiration; *kh* = the German *ch* or Spanish *j* (likewise the *x* in words derived from the Avesta). The macron accent represents the *scriptio plena*; *ū* is pronounced as in "food."

2. On the ancient *Mappae mundi* representing an ideal *divisio orbis* in which the East figures at the top, while Jerusalem is in the center, see the evocative remarks of L.-I. Ringbom, *Graltempel und Paradies* (Stockholm, 1951), p. 254 ff.

2a. *The Gospel according to Thomas*, Coptic text established and translated by A. Guillaumont, H.-C. Puech, *et al.* (London, 1959), log. 3, pp. 3, 19-26.

3. See our work on *Avicenna and the Visionary Recital* (hereafter ref. *Avicenna*), translated from the French by Willard R. Trask, Bollingen Series, LXVI (New York: Pantheon Books, 1960) Pt. II, Ch. 12, 13, and 18, comm. 4. At the time of publication this work appears to have caused some surprise, because it was entirely conceived in the Iranian perspective, with all its implications. Some people do not *see* Avicenna except clothed in his Latin scholastic armor. Furthermore, full comprehension of any author demands that one take into account the manner in which his thought was in fact a living part of the experience of the spiritual environment in which he was recognized; the pretext of taking into account only earlier texts (which he himself may not have known) is a device used for erroneous, historical "explanation." Still worse, anyone is free to profess the rationalism which suits him, but this does not authorize him to advance misinterpretations, particularly in reference to the word "esoteric" (τά ἔσω, *bātin,* as opposed to τά ἔξω, *zāhir*). Avicenna's visionary recitals form a trilogy; to isolate one or another of them is the surest way of not seeing their meaning. As the authors quoted in the present book frequently remind us, like can only be known by like; every mode of understanding corresponds to the mode of being of the interpreter. I am too convinced of this not to recognize how hopeless it is to try to convey the meaning of symbols to people who are blind to them. The Gospel parable of the Feast (Matt. 22:2-10; Lk. 14:16-24) means precisely what it says, even from the scientific point of view. It would be ridiculous to engage in polemics against the men or the women who refuse to come to the feast; their refusal inspires only sadness and compassion.

II. THE MAN OF LIGHT AND HIS GUIDE

4. See *Avicenna*, Pt. I, pp. 231-234; W. Scott, *Hermetica*, IV (Oxford, 1936):106 (Greek text), 108, 122, 124-125; J. Ruska, *Tabula Smaragdina* (Heidelberg, 1926), pp. 26-28 (German translation).

5. ’α=ἀνατολή (rising, east);δ=δύσις (setting, west); α=’ἄρκτος (the Bear, north); μ = μεσημβρία (midday, south).

6. See Carl Schmidt, *Koptisch-gnostische Schriften, I, Die Pistis Sophia . . . ,* 2ᵗᵉ

Notes

Auflage bearbeitet . . . von Walter Till (Berlin, 1954), pp. 189, l. 12; 206, l. 33; 221, l. 30.

7. See our *En Islam iranien: aspects spirituels et philosophiques* (Paris: Gallimard, 1971), II, Bk. II, Ch. VI, "Le Récit de l'exil occidental et la geste gnostique"; Hans Söderberg, *La Religion des Cathares* (Uppsala, 1949), p. 249. See also the rather obscure verse 30 in *The Gospel according to Thomas*, p. 21 of the edition cited above (and the anxiety provoked in Aphraate, the "Persian Sage," trans. J. Doresse, p. 167).

8. Pseudo-Magrītī, *Das Ziel des Weisen*, *I*, Arabischer Text, hrsgb. v. Hellmut Ritter, *Studien der Bibliothek Warburg*, XII (Leipzig, 1933). This is the work of which a medieval Latin translation was published under the title of *Picatrix* (Arabic *Būqratīs* = Ἱπποκράτης, Hippocrates). See also our study *Rituel sabéen et exégèse ismaélienne du rituel*, *Eranos-Jahrbuch*, XIX (Zurich: Rhein-Verlag, 1951).

9. *Ibid.*, p. 193. The entire chapter concerning the Perfect Nature is supposed to be derived from a *Kitāb al-Istamakhīs*, in which Aristotle pours out advice to Alexander and instructs him how to invoke his Perfect Nature, following the example of Hermes.

10. *Ibid.*, p. 194; See *En Islam iranien*, *loc. cit.*

11. These are the very words which are reported in the well-known "*hadīth* of the vision" to have been uttered by the Prophet; See our *Creative Imagination in the Sūfism of Ibn 'Arabi*, trans. from the French by Ralph Mannheim, Bollingen Series, XCI (Princeton, N.J.: Princeton University Press, 1969), p. 272 ff. (hereafter abbreviated as *Sūfism of Ibn 'Arabi*).

12. *Das Ziel des Weisen*, p. 188.

13. See the well-known verse in the Qorān, the Light (24:35), part of which has been included here as the epigraph to Ch. I: "The image of His light is as a niche wherein is a lamp. The lamp is in a glass. The glass is as it were a shining star. . . . "

14. See J. Ruska, *Tabula smaragdina*, pp. 134-135 (Arabic text) and pp. 138-139 (German trans.). The "Guarded Tablet" (*lawh mahfūz* 85:22) on which the archetype of the Qorān is written, has been identified by some adepts with the *Tabula smaragdina*. Regarding the emerald brilliance shining here in the night, compare the relationship between the green light and the "black light" in Semnānī, *infra* VI.

15. See the texts cited in our *En Islam iranien*, II, Bk. II, Ch. III and VI.

16. See *Avicenna* Pt. I, pp. 88-90. Regarding Abū'l-Barakāt, see principally S. Pinès, *Nouvelles études sur . . . Abū'l-Barakāt al-Baghdādī*, *Mémoires de la Société des Etudes juives*, I (Paris, 1955); *Studies in Abū'l-Barakāt al-Baghdādī's Poetics and Metaphysics*, *Scripta Hierosolymitana*, VI (Jerusalem, 1960).

17. See our edition of this work in Sohravardī, *Opera metaphysica et mystica*, I, *Bibiliotheca Islamica*, XVI (Leipzig-Istanbul, 1945):464.

18. In the *Book of Elucidations* (*Kitāb al-Tālwīhāt*) ed. *ibid.*, p. 108, # 83.

19. See *En Islam iranien*, II, Bk. II, Ch. III.

20. For the context of this theme, see our *Sūfism of Ibn 'Arabi* (supra, n. 11), pp. 169-173 and p. 346, n. 70. See also *En Islam iranien*, III, Bk. V. Ch. I, "Confessions extatiques de Mīr Dāmād."

21. See *Avicenna*, Pt. I, p. 157 ff., and M. R. James, *The Apocryphal New Testament* (Oxford, 1950), pp. 411-415.

22. H. Leisegang, *La Gnose*, trans. J. Gouillard (Paris, 1951), p. 249.

Notes

23. Both the Arabic text and the paraphrase in Persian were published in vol. II of our *Oeuvres philosophiques et mystiques* of Shihāboddin Yahyā Sohravardī, Bibliothèque Iranienne, II (Teheran-Paris, 1952); see the *Prolégomènes* in French at the beginning of the book, p. 85 ff., and *En Islam iranien, II, Bk. II, Ch. VI*. We have published a translation into French of the whole cycle of Sohravardī's mystical recitals under the title *L'archange empourpré*, Documents spirituels, 14 (Paris: Fayard, 1976).

24. The text entitled *Khawd al-Hayāh* (The Cistern of the Water of Life), *la version arabe de l'Amrtakunda*, was published by Yusuf Hosayn in the *Journal asiatique* 213 (1928): 291-344. There is also an unpublished version of it in Persian. Regarding the attribution to Avicenna, see G. C. Anawati, *Essai de bibliographie avicennienne* (Cairo, 1950), p. 254, no. 197.

For further details on the content of this brief Irano-Indian spiritual romance, parts of which already exist in Sohravardī and which clear titling of the mss makes it impossible to attribute to Avicenna, see our study *Pour une morphologie de la spiritualité shī'ite*, *Eranos-Jahrbuch*, XXIX (Zurich, 1961), Ch. V. and *En Islam iranien*, II, Bk. II, Ch. VI, 5.

25. The formula 1 x 1 is also given by Rūzbehān as that of the esoteric *tawīd*. See our study on the Sufism of Rūzbehān Baqlī of Shīrāz in *En Islam iranien*, III, Bk. III, Ch. VI, 6.

26. *Poimandres*, §§ 2-4, 7-8: *Corpus Hermeticum* (ed. A. D. Nock, trans, A. J. Festugière) I (Paris, 1945): 7 and 9.

27. Martin Dibelius, *Der Hirt des Hermas*, (Tübingen, 1923), p. 491. Greek text ed. Molly Whittaker, *Die apostolischen Väter*, I (Berlin: Akademie-Verlag, 1956): 22, *Visio* V, 1 ff.

28. See the psychological commentary of M.-L. von Franz, *Die Passio Perpetuae*, following C. G. Jung, *Aion, Untersuchungen zur Symbolgeschichte* (Zurich, 1951), pp. 436-438. On *Christos-Angelos* see Martin Werner, *Die Entstehung des christlichen Dogmas*, 2nd ed. (Bern, 1953), pp. 322-388.

29. *Fravarti* is the original form of the word, which, due to an erroneous association with a similar term, was traditionally spelt *Fravashi* (in modern Persian, *farvahar, forūhar*).

30. For what follows, see our two studies in which references to the original texts are given: *Le Temps cyclique dans le mazdéisme et dans l'Ismaélisme*, *Eranos-Jahrbuch*, XX (Zurich, 1952: 169 ff. (cited hereafter as *Temps cyclique*) and our book *Spiritual Body and Celestial Earth*, trans. from the French by Nancy Pearson, Bollingen Series, XCI:2 (Princeton, N.J.: Princeton University Press, 1977): 40 ff. (cited hereafter as *Spiritual Body*).

31. Regarding this question we could spell out the anthropology given in the *Bundahishn* (the Mazdean Book of the Creation), wherein man is said to be composed of five forces: body, soul, spirit, individuality, and guardian spirit (for the texts see H. S. Nyberg, *Questions de cosmogonie et de cosmologie mazdéenes*, in *Journal asiatique* 214 (1929):232-233). This is, in short, the effort attempted by the dastur J. J. Modi, in *The Religious Ceremonies and Customs of the Parsees*, 2nd ed. (Bombay, 1937), pp. 388-401. But his analysis of the "spiritual constitution of man" fails to give a satisfactory picture of the posthumous relation of the fravarti to the soul; what is more, it says nothing about the episode of the meeting with and recognition of *Daēnā*. So it seems that there is a defect in his schematization, and that the solution has to be thought out in another way.

32. See H. W. Bailey, *Zoroastrian Problems in the Ninth-Century Books* (Oxford,

Notes

1943), pp. 110-115 (texts of *Zātspram* 29:9 and *Dātastān ī dēnik* 23:3). Of course, much more stress than is possible here should be placed on the data of the problem posed and the meaning of the solution proposed.

33. On this topography, see our *Spiritual Body*, p. 27 ff.

34. G. van der Leeuw, *Phänomenologie der Religion* § 16 (Tübingen, 1933), p. 125.

35. Nasîroddîn Tūsī, *The Rawdatu't Taslīm commonly called Tasawwurāt*, Persian text ed. by W. Ivanow (Leiden-Bombay, 1950), pp. 44, 65, 70; see our *Temps cyclique*, p. 210 ff., nn. 86, 89 and 100.

36. See also the theme of the heavenly *hourī* in Nasīr Tūsī, *Aghāz o anjām*, Ch. XIX, Publications of the University of Teheran, CCCI (Teheran, 1335 s.h.): 47-48.

37. E. S. Drower, *The Mandaeans of Iraq and Iran* (Oxford, 1937), pp. 54-55.

38. See Henri-Charles Puech, *Le Manichéisme, son fondateur, sa doctrine* (Paris, 1949), pp. 43-44; and our *En Islam iranien*, II, Bk. II, Ch. VI, 4.

39. *A Manichaean Psalm-Book*, Pt. II, ed. C.R.C. Allberry (Stuttgart, 1938): 42, 1. 22.

40. See principally the texts collected by Georgio Widengren, *The Great Vohu Manah and the Apostle of God* (Uppsala, 1945), pp. 17 ff., 25 ff., 33 ff.; Hans Söderberg, *La Religion des Cathares* (Uppsala, 1949), pp. 174 ff., 211 ff., 247 ff.

41. See *En Islam Iranien*, II, Bk. II, Ch. VI, 4; and Widengren, *op. cit.*, pp. 19-20. Particularly relevant are the homologies among the triads issuing from each of the five "Fathers" or fundamental archetypes (*Kephalaia*, Ch. VII, pp. 34-36). It is the image of light (homologue of the Virgin of Light) that "evokes" the three Angels or deities coming to meet one of the Elect at the moment of death. A far lengthier study than is possible here could be made concerning the Gnostic theme of the Angel as the heavenly *Alter Ego* and savior. Note the correspondence between the Gnostic terms ψυχαγωγός, ψυχοπομπός, ὁδηγός, ἡγεμών (*rector*) and the fundamental Iranian term designating the function of the savior and guide of the soul: *parvānak* (in Mandean, *parwanka*; Widengren, *op. cit.*, p. 79 ff.). In modern Persian: *parwardan*, to nourish, to educate; *parwā kardan*, to take care of.

42. Philo, *Quod deterius potiori insidiari soleat*, English trans. by F. H. Colson and G. H. Whittaker, II, *The Loeb Classical Library* (Cambridge, Mass., 1950): 216-219.

43. Namely *Svetāsvatara-Upanishad* and *Kāthaka-Upanishad*, cit. by Fritz Meier, in the great work quoted below in note 64.

III. MIDNIGHT SUN AND CELESTIAL POLE

44. For the "Earth of seven keshvars," the cartographic process, and the references to the texts, see our *Spiritual Body*, pp. 17-24.

45. For the texts, see *ibid.*, pp. 32-36.

46. *Ibid.*, p 73 ff., 84 ff.; See our *Prolégomènes II aux oeuvres philosophiques et mystiques de Sohravardī* (*supra* n. 23), pp. 39-55, concerning the structure of the pleroma of Lights, and p. 85 ff. on the connection between the *Recital of the Occidental Exile* and the Avicennan *Recital of Hayy ibn Yaqzān*. We also intend to publish shortly a translation of Sohravardī's great book *Hikmat al Ishrāq* (the "oriental" theosophy), together with the Glosses of Mollā Sadrā Shīrāzī (d. 1640), the latter being equal in importance to an original work (see our ed. and

Notes

trans. of the *Livre des pénétrations métaphysiques* (*Kitāb al-Mashā'ir*), Bibl. Iranienne, X (Teheran-Paris, 1964), Intr., p. 40.

47. As Mohsen Fayz (an Iranian Shī'ite theologian of the seventeenth century) repeats; See our *Sūfism of Ibn 'Arabī*, p. 351 f. See the translation of this text in our *Spiritual Body*, pp. 176-179 ff.

48. In no. 83 of the *"Book of Elucidations"* (above n. 18), a text of the highest importance.

49. See our *Introduction* to the great work of Rūzbehān, *Le Jasmin des Fidèles d'amour*, Bibliothèque Iranienne, VIII, Persian text published in collaboration with Moh. Mo'in and trans. of the first ch. (Teheran-Paris: Adrien-Maisonneuve, 1958), p. 37 ff. See also *En Islam iranien*, III, Bk. III, Ch. II.

50. *Banāt Na'sh*, the constellation of the Bear (Ursa Major and Ursa Minor).

51. Compare the text used as an epigraph by an alchemist of the seventeenth century in his edition of Nicholas Flamel: *Et videbant lapidem stanneum in manu Zorobabel. Septem isti oculi sunt Domini, qui discurrunt in universam terram* (cit. by C. G. Jung, *Der Geist der Psychologie*, in *Eranos-Jahrbuch*, XIV) (1947: 436-437). One cannot help relating the theme of the seven *Abdāl* (who nightly traverse the world to inform the pole) to the text of Zechariah, "Those seven are the eyes of the Lord, which run to and fro through the whole earth" (4:10), or again " . . . the stone that I have laid before Joshua, upon one stone shall be seven eyes" (Zech. 3:9).

52. For the context of this doctrine in Rūzbehān, see *En Islam iranien*, III, Bk. III, Ch. III. It contains the Shī'ite of Walāyat and the current Sufi idea of *Wilāyat*. There will be further occasion below (*infra* VI, 2) to recall why the frequent translation of the one or the other word by "sanctity" and of *walī* (plural *Awliyā*) by "saint" is inadequate. The term *Initiation* seems to recapitulate best the implications of the word *walāyat*. In Twelve-Imām Shī'ite gnosis, the "cycle of Initiation" (*dā'irat al-walāyat*) dominated by imāmology succeeds the cycles of prophecy which were completed with the "Seal of the Prophets." On the development of this theme in Lāhījī (the work cited below in note 118) and on the relationship suggested with Goethe's poem and "the Friend of God of Oberland," see our work *En Islam iranien*, IV, Bk. VII, Ch. III.

53. For the text of this tradition, see *op. cit.* III, Bk. III, Ch. III. There are numerous variations in the enumeration and classification of these mystical hierarchies.

54. J. C. Coyajee, *Cults and Legends of Ancient Iran and China* (Bombay, 1936), pp. 161-183.

55. *Yazata* (Persian *Izad*) literally: "adorable." When, in conformity with post-Islamic tradition, the equivalent given for it is the notion of *Angel* (Persian *fereshta*), what must be remembered are not so much the angels of the Bible as the *Dii-Angeli* of Proclus.

56. See the diagram set up by J. C. Coyajee, *op. cit.*, p. 166.

57. Drower, *op. cit.* (*supra* n. 37), pp. 9, 56, 325. It seems fitting to mention here the form of worship practiced by an ideal sect of philosophers, referred to in the Encyclopedia of the *Ikhwān al Safā* (the "Brethren with pure hearts"). These philosophers appear to be at once Sabeans permeated by Neoplatonism and, as it were, pre-Ismaelian theosophers. In the course of each month they celebrate three holy nights corresponding to the phases of the Moon (the first night, the mid-month night, and lastly the night between the twenty-fifth day of the month and the first day of the following month). The ritual on each

Notes

night is divided into three periods: the first third is devoted to meditation in one's private oratory; the second third to meditation on the "cosmic scripture" under the sky, turning one's face toward the *pole Star*. The last period is devoted to chanting from a philosophical hymnology (the "prayer of Plato," the "prayer of Idris-Hermes," the "secret psalm of Aristotle," etc.). The choice of the *pole Star* as *qibla* (the axis of orientation of the prayer) seems to point to the Sabeism of these Sages; their calendar confirms this impression. See also *Rasā'il Ikhwān al-Safā* IV (Cairo, 1928): 303-304, and for further details our study *Rituel sabéen et exégèse ismaélienne du rituel*, *Eranos-Jahrbuch*, XIX/1950 (1951): 209 ff.

58. See *Sūfism of Ibn 'Arabī*, pp. 46-53 ("The Pilgrim to the Orient"), and p. 306 n. 37.

59. This treatise of 'Alī Hamadānī has been studied by Fritz Meier, *Die Welt der Urbilder bei 'Alī Hamadānī*, *Eranos-Jahrbuch*, XVIII (1950): 115-172; see particularly p. 167. Fritz Meier quotes (p. 92 of the work cited below n. 64) a treatise also by 'Alī Hamadānī entitled *Hashrio al-rūhānīya wa-maghrib al-jismānīya:* the *Orient* of spiritual realities and the *Occident* of material realities.

60. See our *Avicenna*, Pt. I, p. 137 ff., particularly § 3, 10, 21 and 22; Pt. II, p. 319 ff.

IV. VISIO SMARAGDINA

61. It is the brief anonymous treatise studied more than a century ago (*Zeitschrift der Deutschen Morgenländischen Gesellschaft*, Vol. 16 [Leipzig, 1862]: 235-241) by Fleischer, *Ueber die farbigen Lichterscheinungen der Sufi's*, according to the Leipzig Ms. 187: *De variis luminibus singulorum graduum Suficorum propriis.*

62. See our edition of *Hikmat al-Ishrāq* (*Oeuvres philosophiques et mystiques de Sohravardī*, II, *supra* n. 23, § 272). In this work, fifteen categories of photisms which mystics can experience are described and the author's conclusion is that "all this pertains to the laws of the *eighth* climate, where the marvelous cities Jabalqā, Jabarsā, and Hūrqalyā are to be found."

63. See Gerda Walther, *Phänomenologie der Mystik* (Olten, 1955), pp. 68-71 and 151-155, and our analytical review of this work in the *Revue de l'histoire des religions* (January-March 1958), pp. 92-101. See also Mircea Eliade's valuable study, *Significations de la "lumière intérieure"*; *Eranos-Jahrbuch*, XXVI (1958): pp. 189-242. Victor Zuckerkandl's substantial work, *Sound and Symbol* (New York, 1956), also contains original phenomenological observations of the "intentions" of color (p. 61 ff.). There are cross-references in all these studies which have a bearing on our purpose. Not being able to go into them further here, we shall have to return to them at some other time.

64. All the parenthetical references in the text of the present chapter refer to the excellent edition by Fritz Meier, *Die Fawā'ih al-jamāl wa-fawātih al-jalāl des Najm ad-dīn al-Kubrā*, Akademie der Wissenschaften und der Literatur, Veröffentlichungen der Orientalischen Kommission, IX (Wiesbaden, 1957). This valuable edition, together with a German commentary, is a major contribution to the studies of Sufism. We have a slight reservation as to the form of the title adopted by the editor in contrast to that of the majority of the manuscripts. We also would prefer: *Fawātih al- jamāl . . .* and thus take it to mean: *The blossoms of Beauty and the perfumes of Majesty*, which means that without the blossoming of Beauty as theophany man could not approach the sublimity of the *Deus absconditus*. Concerning these two categories of attributes see again *infra* V,

Notes

2. The aspects of *Freundlichkeit* and *Erhabenheit* derive respectively from the two fundamental Attributes, but it seems to us essential to preserve their primary meaning (without which all the texts relating to beauty as theophany in Rūzbehān and Ibn 'Arabī would be incomprehensible). We can give here only the briefest glimpse of Najm Kobrā's biography. Born in 540/1145, he spent the first part of his life in long journeys (Nishapur, Hamadān, Ispahan, Mecca, Alexandria) in the course of which he acquired his spiritual training. But the traditions concerning the order and itinerary of his travels diverge to the point that they are difficult to reconstruct with perfect coherence. He returned to Xwārezm in about 580/1184. From then on, all his activity took place in Central Asia, where he had a throng of followers, several of whom bear illustrious names. There is some evidence to indicate that he recognized only twelve great disciples as such (see *infra* n. 109). Traditions relate his heroic death during the horrible siege of Xwārezm by the Mongols in 617/1220-1221. We ourselves devoted an entire course at the Ecole des Hautes-Etudes (1958-1959) to the important treatise by Najm Kobrā made accessible to us in Fritz Meier's edition. Here it has only been possible to indicate its principal themes. See *Annuaire de la Section des Sciences Religieuses*, Ecole pratique des Hautes-Etudes, 1959-1960, p. 75 ff. As for the bipolarity of the divine attributes *Jamāl* and *Jalāl*, there is an exact equivalence in Kabbalah, see Gershom G. Scholem, *On the Kabbalah and its Symbolism*, trans. by Ralph Manheim (London, 1960), p. 79 ff.

65. Concerning this term, see our *Sūfism of Ibn 'Arabī*, pp.153, 179 ff., 187 ff., where the need for this neologism is explained.

66. On the three aspects of *nafs* (the soul) see *infra* §3. Taken by itself the word *nafs* expands beyond our current notion of soul. In its higher aspect, the soul is the heart (Arabic *qalb*, Persian *del*, German *Gemüt*). In its intermediate aspect, it is the intellect (*'aql*), consciousness. In the present context, it designates the lower psyche.

67. Among many other examples (it may also be recalled here how Zarathustra put Ahriman to flight by reciting the *Ahunavairya*, see *Vendidād* XIX), Fritz Meier recalls (*op. cit.*, p. 162) an episode that figures in the Slavic version of the *Vita Adae et Evae*: when the Devil tries to lure Eve away from the Tigris by his talk, Eve does not utter a single word in reply.

68. On the mystical exegesis of this verse from he Qorān see our *Sūfism of Ibn 'Arabī*, p. 132.

69. A perfectly polished mirror (*speculum*) in which the image that is reflected is both what sees and what is seen: it is the *leitmotif* of all *speculative* mysticism attempting to express the "duality" of the *unus-ambo*, the secret of the heavenly *alter ego*, from the finale of the *Song of the Pearl* to the motif of the *shaykh al-ghayb* in the present treatise.

70. See the text of the *Risālat al-insān al-kāmil* (Treatise on the perfect man) of 'Alī Hamadānī (*supra* n. 59), given by Fritz Meier, *op. cit. Anhang*, p. 283, no. 5.

71. *Himma*. Concerning this notion, see our *Sūfism of Ibn'Arabī*, p. 222 ff.

72. As an illustration of the same theme, we should cite a remarkable case of "synchronicity" between one of Najm Kobrā's dreams and a dream of his own shaykh, 'Ammār Badlīsī: "I was in my retreat and behold, I experienced ecstasy (lit., "I went away," as the author always says in such cases). I was raised to the heights and behold, there was a rising sun before me. I was led into this sun,

Notes

after having experienced the tremendous intensity of its energies. Later I questioned the shaykh ('Ammār) about this. He said to me: 'Glory be to God! I myself had the following vision in a dream: I seemed to be strolling in the sacred territory of Mecca. You were with me and the sun was in the middle of the Sky. Then you said to me: O shaykh! Do you know who I am? I said: Who are you? You said: *I am that sun in the Sky*. Then my shaykh rejoiced that our two visions had synchronized. He said: 'I was ushered into the world of the heart. I carried on the battle for God night after night. I observed the Sky attentively until it entered into my inner world, and I experienced that *I am the Sky*. And I observed the Sky throughout other nights until I saw it below me, just as I had seen it above me. And I observed the Earth night after night, and I sought to discover it as it is, until it was engulfed in an orb of light (§58)."

73.   Concerning this extremely important comparison see Fritz Meier, *op. cit.*, p. 79, and Carl Schmidt, *Koptisch-gnostische Schriften* I (Berlin, 1954): *Das erste Buch des Jeu*, Ch. 39, p. 294; *Das zweite Buch des Jeu*, Ch. 42, p. 303.

74.   In the *Risālat al-sā'ir* (F. Meier, p. 201, n. 5) Najm Kobrā recommends adding from time to time the second part: "And Mohammad is God's Messenger." We should take into account, on this point, the increasing complexity of the formula in certain Shī'ite circles; the Imām is mentioned as the *walī Allāh*, "Friend of God," "initiator," even Fātima as "Light of God." Generally speaking, Shī'ite doctrine and practice include a triple *shahādat*: 1) attestation of the Divine Unity; 2) attestation of the prohetic mission; 3) attestation of the *Walāyat* of the Imāms.

75.   See Herzog, *Realencyklopädie für protestantische Theologie und Kirche* 3rd ed., XVI, 251, 1. 49 ff.; E. Tisserant, *Ascension d'Isaïe* (Paris, 1909), p. 211, note on 11:34 (reminiscence of the *Revelation of Elijah* in St. Paul, according to Origen; reminiscence of Isaiah, according to St. Jerome: *Ascensio enim Isaiae et Apocalypsis Eliae hoc habent testimonium*).

76.   Najm Kobrā's *Risālat ilā'l-hā'im*, quoted by F. Meier, *Anhang*, p. 295, no. 20.

77.   *Ibid.*, p. 202; L. Massignon, *L'idée de l'esprit dans l'Islam, Eranos-Jahrbuch* XIII/1945: 279 (the Taoist influence was pointed out by H. Maspero; see also *supra* III, 3, concerning another possible Taoist influence).

78.   F. Meier, *op. cit.*, p. 204; Rudolf Otto, *Sünde und Urschuld* (Munich, 1932), p. 140 ff.

79.   The *himma*: see *supra* n. 71.

80.   Majdoddīn Baghdādī (quoted by F. Meier, p. 244), in his *Tohfat al-barara*, also mentions a shaykh's saying, wherein the green color is characterized as the last veil of the soul. On the pre-eminence of this color in Semnānī, see *infra* VI, 1.

81.   "Know that four angels raise the mystic towards this mystic station—the Abode of the lordly condition and of power: one on his right, one on his left, one above him, one below him . . ." (§19). On this quaternity representing a symbolism of the center, see our commentary on the "Confessions extatiques de Mīr Dāmād" (*supra* n. 20); a similar angelic tetrad figures in the *Summum Bonum* of Robert Fludd, 1629 ed. "Usually the Angels come from behind. Sometimes they come from above. The same for the *Sakīna*: this is a group of Angels who descend into the heart; their advent brings an experience of quiet and peacefulness into the heart. They transport you out of yourself so wholly that you have no longer any freedom to move or speak, no possibility of thinking of anything other than the divine Being" (§21). "An Angel carried me away.

Notes

He came up behind me, took me in his arms and carried me off; then he turned toward my face and gave me a kiss. His light sparkled in my inner view. Then he said: In the name of God, than whom there is no other, the Compassionate, the Merciful. Then he rose up with me a little higher. Then he set me down again" (§23).

82. Concerning the seven Heavens, see Qorān 67:3 and 78:12; concerning the seven Earths, *Safīnat Bihār al-Anwār*, I, 661. For an amplification of this theme in the Shaykhite School, see our *Spiritual Body*, p. 302, n. 86.

83. This is the general theme of our book, *Spiritual Body*, referred to in the previous note; see also *Sūfism of Ibn 'Arabī*, p. 350, n. 10.

84. Compare the text of the *Risālat ilāl-hā'im*, quoted by F. Meier, p. 97, n. 2.

85. The same theme is fundamental in Sohravardī and his great commentator, Mollā Sadrā Shīrāzī: spiritual realities must be observed in a proper manner, just as material realities call for an appropriate method of observation.

86. See §§44 and 70. Attention should be drawn here to an important treatise by one of the masters of the Iranian Shaykhi school of the last century, Shaykh Mohammad Karīm Khān Kermānī, on the color red: the optical phenomenon, its essence and nature, its symbolic and mystical meanings, etc. (*Risāla-ye yāqūta-ye hamrā*). Compare this with the red light that is the dominant note in the visions of Rūzbehān: "One night I saw something enveloping the Heavens. It was a sparkling red light. I asked: What is that? He told me: It is the cloak of Magnificence." See *En Islam iranien*, III, Bk. III, Ch. IV.

87. So in each case we are told about a light projected by its corresponding organ, one of the subtle organs of the body of light, the visualization of which corresponds to the moment when these organs become independent of the physical body's sensory organ. "The light of hearing does not have a circular form: it consists only of two points of light which make their appearance behind the double circle of the two eyes" (§57). As in the case of the other senses, this "visualization" of the acoustic phenomenon will be observed in terms of suprasensory physiology. The "physiology of the man of light," according to Semnānī, is established on a basis common to all the senses, but develops quite differently in each case.

88. On this correspondence, see F. Meier, *op. cit.*, p. 67, n.1; Paul Kraus, *Jābir ibn Hayyān*, II (Cairo, 1942), index; our own study on *Le "Livre du Glorieux" de Jābir ibn Hayyān*, *Eranos-Jahrbuch*, XVIII (1950): 75 ff.; Ps. Majrītī (*supra* n. 8), *Das Ziel des Weisen*, p. 46.

89. This is one of the well-known "outrageous sayings" of the great Iranian mystic, Abū Yazīd Bastāmī (d. 261/875), in our edition of Rūzbehān Baqlī-Shīrāzī, *Commentaire sur les paradoxes des soufis (Sharh-e Shathīyāt)*, Persian text with French introduction, Bibl. Iranienne, XII (Teheran-Paris, 1966).

90. Considerable research remains to be done on the various ways of naming this figure in the school of Najm Kobrā. The *shaykh al-ghayb* appears again in 'Azīz Nasafī, see the text *Tanzīl al-arwāh*, quoted by F. Meier, p. 188, n. 1, and *Anhang*, pp. 293-294, no. 18. In *Semnānī (infra,* VI, 1) it is called *ustād ghaybī*.

91. See the text of the *Risālat ilā'l-hā'im* quoted by F. Meier, pp. 185-186 and *Anhang*, p. 293, no. 17.

92. On this idea of the *shāhid*, according to Rūzbehān, see our work *En Islam iranien*, III, Bk. III, Ch. III, V, VI-6.

93. 'Aynal-Qozāt Hamadānī (d. 525/1131), Ahmad Ghazālī's favorite disciple (and who, like Sohravardī, died a martyr's death), relates an analogous

Notes

vision in his book, the *Tamhīdāt:* "At this mystic station," he said, "I saw a light emanating from the divine being, and simultaneously I saw a light rising from myself. The two lights met and blended together, and there appeared a form of such beauty that for some time I remained dazzled thereby" (cit. F. Meier, p. 114, n. 1). It is significant that 'Aynal-Qozāt ends this personal recollection by an allusion to the well-known *hadīth* of the vision, where the Prophet declares: "I saw my God in the most beautiful of forms." See our *Sūfism of Ibn' Arabī*, p. 272 ff.

94. *Ghibto*: As we have already pointed out, this is the technical term by which Najm Kobrā refers to each of his visionary experiences: "departures" from the sensory world; "entrances" into the suprasensory world.

95. These Qorānic verses refer to the episode of Moşes being rescued from the waters. The way in which the verses are repeated in isolated fragments is in accordance, of course, with the visionary's intention. Rūzbehān also gives us to understand that the words "I shed on thee love from Me" characterize celestial love: the exegesis of this verse is to be found in the fact that Majnūn has become a "mirror of God," because his being has become the pure substance of love (*Jasmin*, §270 *in fine*). Besides, the passage contains another *leitmotiv* important in Najm Kobrā, that of the "suprasensory books" written by God in Heaven. Najm knows several of their titles; one may be able to read them (just like the Qorānic verses quoted here) in the lines and figures outlined by the stars in the Heavens of the soul (§71-72). F. Meier (pp. 134-135) reminds us in this connection of the case of Justinus Kerner's Seeress of Prevorst.

96. This Persian word designates the violet (flower and color). Concerning this other important theme of the esoteric names, or heavenly names, borne by certain beings, see F. Meier, pp. 135-136.

97. See *En Islam iranien*, III, Bk. III, Ch. VI, 7, and my *Introduction* to *Jasmin* (*supra* n. 49) and the translation of the first chapter of that book.

98. *Dīwān d'al-Hallāj*, ed. Louis Massignon in *Journal asiatique* 218 (1931), no. 30. The text given by Najm Kobrā has some variants, see F. Meier, p. 39 of the Arabic text.

99. *Dīwān, ibid.* no. 57. See our edition of the *Jasmin, Gloss*. 95, p. 170. The two lines are sometimes attributed to Hallāj, sometimes to Majnūn, sometimes quoted anonymously as they are by Rūzbehān's commentator: "When the mystic reaches perfection in love," he says, "the two modes of being become one whole in him. Then he cries out: 'I am the one whom I love and the one I love is I; we are two spirits immanent in one body.'" That these lines may have been addressed to an earthly person, as Sarrāj testifies, no more than bears out, far from contradicting it, the theophanic idea of love, see *En Islam iranien* III, Bk. III, Ch. VI, 7.

100. The great mystic, fiery soul, not to be confused with his brother, the theologian, Abū Hāmid Ghazālī. The Persian text *Sawānih* by Ahmad-e Ghazālī (d. 520/1126) (*Aphorismen über die Liebe*) was edited by Hellmut Ritter, in *Bibliotheca Islamica*, 15 (Istambul-Leipzig, 1942). We have made a translation of it, as yet unpublished.

101. The analogy with the Mazdean idea makes itself felt in context, especially in certain interpretations which Najm Kobrā gives of Bākharzī's visions. See the passage in the latter's *Waqā'i al-khalwat*, quoted by F. Meier, p. 186 and *Anhang*, p. 292, no. 16: "At that moment the force of the individuality (*qowwat al-'ayn*) is revealed, that is called the *suprasensory sun*, and which is the *scales* for weighing actions and thoughts. A man can recognize by means of these scales

154

Notes

whether his inner state shows an excess or a deficit, whether he is safe and sound or in danger of perishing, whether he is on the right path or has strayed, whether he is faithful or unfaithful and dissolute, whether his heart is dilated or distressed, whether his goal is near or is still far off, whether he is rejected or accepted, whether he is making progress or is standing still. In short, he can discriminate between light and darkness."

101a. We are referring to the symbolic recital developed by Nasīr Tūsī at the end of one of his books in Persian (*Koshāyesh-Nāmeh*, unpublished).

102. See references above in note 92.

103. *Ibid.*; the whole of Rūzbehān's book, *The Jessamine of the Faithful in Love* (*supra* n. 49), forms a setting for this theme, of which only the bare outline can be given here.

104. Ibn 'Arabī, *Kitāb al-Fotūhāt al Makkīya*, Ch. 360; Cairo edition, 1329, Vol. III, p. 274 ff.

105. Further to n. 101 above, one will recall here the connection in Christian iconography between the symbol or attribute of the *scales* and the Archangel Michael (whose liturgical feast, September 29, also comes under the zodiacal sign Libra). This weighing of the souls was what led the Zoroastrian scholar, J. J. Modi, to make a comparative study of the figure of the Archangel Michael and that of Mithra in Zoroastrianism: *St. Michael of the Christians and Mithra of the Zoroastrians. A comparison (Journal of the Anthrop. Soc. of Bombay*, Vol. VI, pp. 237-254).

106. All these connections have been admirably indicated in a little book with which we do not entirely agree on all points but towards which we feel sympathetic because it is one of the rare treatises on angelology written in our time and because it is for the most part inspired by heartfelt daring: Eugenio d'Ors, *Introducción a la vida angélica, cartas a una soledad* (Buenos Aires, 1941), especially pp. 37-40 and 62-63.

V. THE BLACK LIGHT

107. This is a corollary of the theme of the knowledge of like by like; in Rūzbehān as well as 'Ibn Arabī, a fundamental theme is that the theophanies of the Names and Attributes always and essentially correspond with the spiritual state of the one to whom they are revealed.

108. See the excellent article by Jean-Louis Destouches, *L'ombre et la lumière en physique,* in the volume *Ombre et Lumière,* publ. by the Académie septentrionale (Paris, 1961), pp. 15-20.

108a. Here it is fitting also to bring to mind the correlation between the acts of light or of illumination (*ishrāqāt*) and the acts of contemplation (*moshānadāt*) in the cosmogony of Sohravardī.

109. Najmoddīn 'Abdollah ibn Mohammad ibn Shāhāwar Asadī Rāzī, known as Dāyeh (d. 654/1256), one of the twelve great disciples whom, according to one tradition, Najm Kobrā accepted as such by name (see the writings of Hosayn Xwārezmī, quoted by F. Meier, p. 44, n. 1); he lived later in Hamadān; at the time of the Mongol invasion he retreated to Ardabīl (the cradle of the Safavid dynasty, on the present Russo-Iranian frontier, west of the Caspian Sea), then in Asia Minor; he was in contact with Sadroddīn Qonyawī and Jalāl Rūmī's circle. Buried in Baghdād. His chief work as a mystic, besides a Qorānic commentary, is quoted below.

110. Chapters XVIII and XIX of the *Mirsād al-'Ibād,* publ. by Shamsol-'Orafā (Teheran, 1312 s.h. [= 1352 l.h. = 1933 A.D.]), pp. 165-173.

Notes

111. Concerning these two categories of divine attributes, see above n. 64, remarks concerning the title of Najm Kobrā's treatise.

112. There is an important theological distinction between the two ideas of *Islām* and *īmān*, the second being the perfection of the first. In Shī'ite theology *īmān*, faith (as in fidelity and confidence), implies the adherence of the heart to the person of the holy *Imāms* as *Awliyā*, the initiators to the hidden meaning of the prophetic revelations; total faith in the Shī'ite sense presupposes the threefold *shahadāt* (above, note 74).

113. *Walī-e motlaq*. In Shī'ite terminology *walāyat* is the prerogative of the Imāmate, the charisma of the Imām as *walī*, including the Imām of our day who is hidden and invisible (see *supra* III, 2 and 3, and *infra* VI, 2). It is impossible to discuss here the relationships between Shī'ite terminology and that of Sufism as such, nor the Shī'ite presuppositions, at least latent, in every theosophy where the idea of *walāyat* enters. Naturally the Shī'ite Sufis hold a precise opinion on this point and on the extensive use of the term *Awliyā*. Here we note the emphasis on the symbols of the sun and moon, which in general symbolism figure respectively the masculine and feminine. In Ismaelian Shī'ite gnosis (where the expression *dā'i-e motlaq* is somewhat reminding of the expression in question here), the Imām as initiator to the hidden meaning, dispensator of the "light of the *walāyat*," is represented as "spiritual mother of the adepts." Fātima, the daughter of the prophet and the mother of the holy Imāms, is the "confluent of the two lights," that of prophecy and that of initiation. In Twelve-Imām Shī'ite gnosis, the solar *walāyat* is that of the Imām, the lunar *walāyat* that of the adepts (Lāhijī, *op. cit. infra* n. 118, pp. 316-317), see *En Islam iranien* I, Bk. I, Ch. VI, 2 and IV, Bk. VII, Ch. I, 3.

114. See ref. *supra* note 47.

115. See refs. *supra* note 92.

116. What is in question here are the planes or universes of a transcendental cosmography, while the 18,000 worlds in Ismaelian gnosis, denote universes following one another from a cycle of epiphany (*dawr al-kashf*) to a cycle of occultation (*dawr al-satr*), or from one religion to another, one civilization to another. Each of these forms a separate universe, and only by speaking of one in particular can one say that it had a beginning (see Nasīr Tūsī, *Tasawworāt*, p. 48 of the Persian text). The figure 360,000 refers to a mega cycle (*Kawr*, Α'ιών) and concurrently to the 360 degrees of the Sphere; see in Rūzbehān the figure 360 refers to the number of Initiates who from one period to another are the "eyes" through which God looks at the world. As for the figure 70, see *En Islam iranien*, III, Bk. III, Ch. III. On the theme of 18,000 worlds in Kabbalah, see Gershom Scholem, *Les Origines de la Kabbale*, pp. 476, 490.

117. Mahmūd Shabestarī, great mystic shaykh of Azerbaijan, lived principally at Tabrīz and died in 720/1320, at the age of 33, in Shabestar, where his tomb still exists. His great poem was motivated by the questions of Mīr Hosaynī Sādāt Harawī. It is significant that both of these men were regarded by the Ismaelians as having been of their persuasion; see our edition of an unfinished Ismaelian commentary on *Golshan-e Rāz*, published in our *Trilogie ismaélienne*, Bibl, Iranienne, IX, Teheran-Paris, 1961, Ismaelism having survived in Iran under the *khirqa* (the cloak) of Sufism, or if one prefers, Sufism having taken on certain aspects of a crypto-Ismaelism.

118. This commentary, re-edited several times in Iran, has again been the object of a recent edition under the care of Mr. Kayvān Samī'ī, *Mafātih al-i'jāz* (Teheran, 1957), in a beautiful volume of 96 + 804 pages. Shamsoddīn

Notes

Mohammad Gīlānī Lāhījī, native of the region to the southwest of the Caspian Sea, was an eminent shaykh of the Nūrbakhshīyah Order; he was even one of the successors of Sayyed Nūrbakhsh as head of the Order. He died and was buried at Shīrāz in 912/1506-07. Numerous pages of this commentary are to be found translated in our *Trilogie ismaélienne*.

119. Qāzī Nūrollah Shoshtarī is one of the great figures of Shī'ism in the Safavid period (his lineage was traced back to the fourth Shī'ite Imām 'Alī Zaynol-'Abidīn). He died a martyr in India, by the order of Jahāngīr, in 1019/ 1610. See our *Introduction* to the *Jasmin* of Rūzbehān, p. 73, n. 124. In his great collection of biographies, *Majālis al-Mu'minīn*, he gives valuable information about our author.

120. Shāh Esmā'īl (born 892/1487, died 930/1524, great-grandson through his mother of Kalo Joannes Comnenus, last Christian emperor of Trebizond) was, as we know, the restorer of Iranian national unity some nine hundred years after the collapse of the Sassanids before the armies of Islam. It was he who made Twelve-Imām Shī'ism the national religion of Iran. He was only fourteen at the time of his coronation in Tabriz (905/1500); the night before the ceremony, some of those close to him, and even some Shī'ite theologians, warned him against the danger of formulating the Shī'ite profession of faith in a city the great majority of whose inhabitants were Sunnites. To this the adolescent answered: "I am committed to this action; God and the Immaculate Imāms are with me, and I fear no one" (see E. G. Browne, *Literary History of Persia*, IV, p. 53).

121. *Kabūd-pushān*, the "blue-clothed," is a current Persian way of naming Sufis, referring to their custom of wearing blue clothing; various explanations have been given of this practice. Here it has a precise meaning, being in accord with a general symbolism of the color of clothing. Thus the meaning of the color blue (in Najm Kobrā as in Semnānī) makes blue clothing appropriate to those who are still in the first stages of the mystic life. For that very reason one can understand the malicious humor of Hāfez with regard to those of the Sufis who made a regular habit of wearing clothing of that color: were they to be taken as people who never got beyond the first stages of the mystic life? On the other hand, when the great mystic poet of Shīrāz describes the status of his master as "rose-colored" (*Pīr-e Golrang*) as opposed to the wearers of blue, he was alluding to this custom of changing the "liturgical" color of personal clothing to accord with progress on the spiritual path. See our *Introduction* to *Jasmin* of Rūzbehān, pp. 56-62 (where exactly the clue to the identity of the *Pīr-e Golrang* perhaps allows us to connect Hāfez to the *tarīquat* of Rūzbehān of Shīrāz; in it are also recalled several essential ideas in the symbolism of Hāfez which has been so unfortunately misunderstood in the West by simply forgetting how and why his Dīwān could have been used as a Bible by the Iranian Sufis until our day). This practice is expressly attested to by Najm Kobrā, who distinguishes two categories of the color blue: *kabūd* (deep blue) and *azraq* (sky blue, azure), see the passage from his *Adāb al-Morīdīn* quoted by F. Meier, p. 126, n. 7: black and blue (*siyāh o kabūd*) colored clothing are to be worn when, thanks to the spiritual warfare, the lower psyche (*nafs ammāra*) has been overcome, as though one were in mourning for it. The meaning is therefore not the same as in the case of Lāhījī; here black does not refer to the higher stage where one speaks of "black light." In a higher spiritual Abode where the mystic gains access to the translunar worlds by concentration of his spiritual energy (*himmat*), Najm Kobrā connects this with the wearing of azure colored clothing. In every case we must take into account the symbolic scale of the colors, but

157

Notes

they can vary, as we have seen here, from one master to another. In Semnanī the highest color is the color green.

122. This is the poem of Mulla Banā quoted by Mr. Kayvān Samī'ī, p. 95 of his introduction to the *Golshan-e Rāz* (*supra* n. 118). Other works referred to therein show how visions of colored lights have never ceased to interest the Iranians.

123. Pp. 94-102 of the commentary in the edition referred to, which we shall now analyze without particular references; couplets 123-129 (not mentioned in this edition) of the *Rose Garden of Mystery*.

124. See the second of the "Ecstatic Confessions" of Mīr Dāmād, *En Islam iranien*, IV, Bk. V, Ch. 1, 4.

125. Sayyed Ahmad 'Alawī, pupil and son-in-law of Mīr Dāmād, see our *Avicenna*, pp. 58-60.

126. Literally, "the black color of the aspect"; this statement can be related to the fact that Lāhījī habitually wore black clothing, this being the outward sign of the metaphysical poverty which is the greatest of riches for the being essentialized by the divine being of the Godhead. The theme of "black light" reminds us here of the paradoxical form in which one of the most ancient Shī'ite gnostics, Hishām ibn Sālim Jawālīqī, propounded his doctrine: God has human form and a body, a subtle body, not composed of flesh and blood, but of sparkling, radiant light. Like the human being, He has five senses, but they are subtle organs. He has abundant black hair which is *black light* (*nūr aswad*). See the context in our *Sūfism of Ibn 'Arabī*, p. 381 f., n. 12.

127. *Mashhad*: place of the presence of the *shāhid*, where the witness testifies to his presence and to the presence to which he is present (hence the place of testimony of the *martyrs*). Therefore it is the *shāhid* as place and form (*mazhar*) of theophany (*tajallī*): the being of perfect beauty chosen as witness of contemplation.

128. On the mystical context of this *hadīth*, see our *Sūfism of Ibn 'Arabī*, p. 272 ff.

129. For more details on the doctrines of Semnānī, see our work *En Islam iranien*, 2 III, Bk. IV, Ch. IV. In it can be found in detail all the references to the works of Semnānī, still in manuscript, in Persian and in Arabic; these references will not be repeated here.

130. Et. Gilson, *History of Christian Philosophy in the Middle Ages* (New York: Random House, 1955), pp. 341-342.

131. See Miguel Asín Palacios, *Obras escogidas I* (*Ibn Massarra y su escuela*) (Madrid, 1946), pp. 159-160, on the *Opus majus* of Roger Bacon and the spiritual interpretation of the Ishrāqīyūn. Concerning the science of perspective as the most fundamental of the sciences of Nature, see Raoul Carton, *L'expérience physique chez Roger Bacon* (Paris, 1924), pp. 72-73, and *L'expérience mystique de l'illumination intérieure chez Roger Bacon* (Paris, 1924), pp. 214 ff. (the seven degrees of inner science), 265, 306 ff.

132. In fact the word *tafsīr* designates the literal exegesis centered around the canonical Islamic sciences. Although one generally refers to Semnānī's *Tafsīr*, it would be more appropriate to speak of his *Ta'wīl* (*ta'wīl*, etymologically, means "to reconduct," to lead something back to its origin, to its archetype). On the three degrees of hermeneutics: *tafsīr*, *ta'wīl*, and *tafhīm*, see *En Islam iranien*, index s.v.

133. In Islamic exegesis the word *Parakletos* is taken to be a deformation, by

Notes

the Christians, of the word *Peryklitos* (*laudatissimus* = Ahmad = Mohammad). The verses (14:16 and 28; 15:16) of St. John's Gospel would thus read as the announcement of the advent of the Seal of the Prophets. In Shī'ite gnosis, the Paraclete (*farāqlīt*) is identified with the Twelfth Imām (the hidden and awaited Imām) who will reveal the esoteric meaning of the Revelations; see our report on *L'idée du Paraclet en philosophie iranienne*, presented at the Congress on Iranology, Rome, Academy of the Lincei, April 1970, and published in *Atti del Convegno internazionale sul tema: La Persia nel Medioevo* (Rome: Accademia nazionale dei Lincei, 1971), pp. 37-68.

133a. This interpretation, in going to the very root, proceeds equally from a deep penetration of Islamic theology. It would be interesting to make a comparative study of the Pauline theme of κένωσις (Phillip. 2:6 ff.), the *"semetipsum exinanivit"* which was such a thorny problem for Lutheran theologians in the nineteenth century; see article by Loofs, *Kenosis*, in Herzog, *Realencycl. f. prot. Theol. und Kirche*, 3rd ed., X, 246-263.

134. On the three bodies of the human being: body of origin, earthly and perishable; body of acquisition or fruition; body of resurrection, and on the analogy with the "physics of resurrection" in the Shaykhis, see *En Islam iranien*, III, Bk. IV, Ch. Iv, 5.

135. On these observations concerning iconography, see our *Sufism of Ibn 'Arabī*, pp. 275 ff. and 379 ff., n. 7 to 12.

136. See Louis Massignon, "The Origins of the Transformation of Persian Iconography by Islamic Theology: the Shī'a School of Kūfa and its Manichean Connexions" (in Arthur Upham Pope, *A Survey of Persian Art*, Vol. V, Pt. IX, Ch. 49 [Oxford University Press, 2nd ed., 1964-196], pp. 1928-1936, particularly pp. 1933-1936), who was the first to throw light on the role of Kūfa at the origin of painting in Islam, and to show the value of the testimony of Abū Shakūr Sālimī quoted below. The Iranian motif of the *Xvarnah* leads us however here to a different interpretation of the connection of this iconography with what the gold backgrounds of Byzantine iconography suggest.

137. See our *Introduction to Jasmin*, pp. 6 and 20.

138. This one, for example: "Raise up the *dhikr* of the Light, help the people of Light, guide the light toward the Light." See our *Prolégomènes I* to the Works of Sohravardī (supra n. 17), p. 45.

139. *Farbenlehre*, Kröners Taschenausgabe, Vol. 62: Schriften über die Natur geordnet und ausgewählt von Günther Ipsen (Stuttgart, 1949), *Einleitung*, p. 176. (We came across too late to be able to use it here a very interesting number of the review *Triades* III, 4, winter 1955, dedicated to "the spiritual experience of colors." The articles in this number offer striking correlations with the present research.)

140. *Ibid.*, §§ 1 to 3. Let us recall very briefly one of the simplest experiments described at the outset of Goethe's work. On a pure white sheet of paper place or draw a disc of uniform color, blue for example; concentrate your gaze fixedly and attentively on this disc. Soon the periphery begins to glow with a reddish-yellow light that is very brilliant but extremely delicate, so delicate that it is not always possible to give it a name. This iridescent light (physiological color) seems to be trying to "escape" from the colored disc (recall here the technique of Manichean painting). It succeeds and becomes a complete "orb of light" which, having become detached, seems to flutter on the white paper around the colored disc. If one abruptly removes the disc (assuming it to be a separate piece) one then perceives only the orb of this physiological color.

Notes

141. *Ibid*., §805: "When the eye sees a color it is immediately activated and is fitted by nature to produce unconsciously, necessarily, another color, which, together with the given color, includes the totality of the circle of colors. A single color provokes in the eye, through a specific sensation, the effort toward generality." §806: "In order to become conscious of this totality and satisfy itself, it seeks at the side of each colored space a space without color in order to produce the color it requires." (See the example given above in note 140.) §807: "There exactly one finds the fundamental law of the whole harmony of colors, of which each one of us may become convinced through personal experience, by trying the experiments indicated in the section of this book devoted to *physiological colors*."

142. *Ibid*., §§751-756. §753: "To experience perfectly these definite and meaningful effects, one must completely surround the eyes with a single color; one is, for example, in a room all of one color, or one looks through a colored glass; one is then oneself identified with the color; the color brings the eye and also the mind into unison." This may remind us of Nezāmī's great poem (of the twelfth century), *Haft Paykar* (The Seven Beauties), in which the Sassanid prince Bahram Gōr visits seven palaces, each of which respectively is entirely the color of one of the seven planets; in each of the seven palaces, a princess of one of the seven climates, dressed also in the corresponding color, tells the prince a long story containing many indications. The poem illustrates the adage *Vita coelitus comparanda*, and provides one of the motifs most frequently used in Persian miniatures.

143. *Ibid.,* 915-917. (N. 86 above refers to an important study by an Iranian shaykh of the last century on the symbolism (*ta'wīl*) of the color red.)

144. *Ibid.*,§819, ending as follows: "The mathematicians learned the value and the use of the triangle; the triangle is held in great veneration by the mystics; many things can be schematized in the triangle, and in such a way that by duplication and intersection we get the ancient and mysterious hexagon."

BIBLIOGRAPHY

Allbery, Charles Robert Cecil, ed. *A Manichean Psalm-Book*, II, Stuttgart 1938.

Asín Palacios, Miguel. *Obras escogidas I (ibn Masarra y su escuela)*, Madrid 1946.

Bailey, Harold Walter. *Zorastrian Problems in the Ninth-Century Books*, Oxford 1943.

Carton, Raoul. *L'expérience physique chez Roger Bacon* and *L'expérience mystique de l'illumination intérieure chez Roger Bacon*, Paris 1924.

Destouches, Jean-Louis. Article entitled *L'ombre et la lumière en physique* in the volume entitled *Ombre et Lumière* publ. by the Académie Septentrionale, Paris 1961.

Dibelius, Martin. *Der Hirt des Hermas* (Tübingen 1923); Greek text ed. by Whittaker, Molly—*Die apostolischen Väter* I, Berlin, Akademie-Verlag 1956.

Drower, Ethel Stefana. *The Mandaeans of Iraq and Iran*, Oxford 1937.

Eliade, Mircea. Study entitled *Significations de la "lumière intérieure,"* *Eranos-Jahrbuch* XXVI/1957 (1958), pp. 189-242.

Festugière, André-Jean, trans. *Poimandres* in *Corpus hermeticum* I, ed. by Arthur Darby Nock, Paris 1945.

Fleischer, Heinrich Leberecht. *Ueber die farbigen Lichterscheinungen der Sufi's* after Leipzig manuscript 187: *De variis luminibus singulorum graduum Suficorum propriis* in *Zeitschrift der Deutschen Morgenländischen Gesellschaft* 16, Leipzig 1862, pp. 235-241.

Franz, Marie-Louise. *Die Passio Perpetuae* following C. G. Jung's *Aion, Untersuchungen zur Symbolgeschichte*, Zurich 1951, pp. 387-496.

Gilson, Étienne. *History of Christian Philosophy in the Middle Ages*, New York, Random House 1955.

Ivanow, W., ed. Nasîroddîn Tûsî, *The Rawdatu't Taslîm commonly called Tasawwurāt*, Leiden-Bombay 1950.

Jung, Carl Gustav. *Der Geist der Psychologie*, *Eranos-Jahrbuch* XIV/1946 (1947), pp. 385-490.

Kraus, Paul. *Jābir ibn Hayyān* II, Cairo 1942.

Massignon, Louis. *L'idée de l'esprit dans l'Islam*, *Eranos-Jahrbuch* XIII/1945 (1946), pp. 277-282.

Meier, Fritz. *Die Fawā'ih al-jamāl wa-fawātih al-jalāl des Najm ad-dîn al-Kubrā*, Wiesbaden 1957.

Nyberg, Henrik Samuel. *Questions de cosmogonie et de cosmologie mazdéennes*, *Journal asiatique* 214/1929, pp. 193-310.

Ors, Eugenio de. *Introduccíon a la vida angélica, cartas a una soledad*, Buenos-Aires 1941.

Otto, Rudolf. *Sünde und Urschuld*, Munich 1932.

161

Bibliography

Pinès, Salomon. *Studies in Abū'l-Barakāt al-Baghdādī's Poetics and Metaphysics (Scripta Hierosolymitana VI)*, Jerusalem 1960.

Puech, Henri-Charles. *Le Manichéisme, son fondateur, sa doctrine*, Paris 1949.

Ringbom, Lars-Ivar. *Graltempel und Paradies*, Stockholm 1951.

Ritter, Hellmut, ed. Pseudo-Magritī, *Das Ziel des Weisen* I (*Studien der Bibliothek Warburg* XII), Leipzig 1933; Ahmad-e Ghazālī, *Aphorismen über die Liebe* (*Bibliotheca Islamica* 15), Istanbul-Leipzig 1942.

Ruska, Julius. *Tabula smaragdina*, Heidelberg 1926.

Schmidt, Carl. *Koptisch-gnostiche Schriften* I, Berlin 1954.

Scholem, G. *Les origines de la Kabbale*, Paris 1966.

Scott, Walter. *Hermetica* IV, Oxford 1936.

Söderberg, Hans. *La religion des Cathares*, Uppsala 1949.

Van Der Leeuw, Gerardus. *Phänomenologie des Religion*, Tübingen 1933.

Walther, Gerda. *Phänomenologie der Mystik*, Olten 1955.

Werner, Martin. *Die Entstehung des christlichen Dogmas*, 2nd ed., Bern 1953.

Widengren, Geo. *The Great Vohu Manah and the Apostle of God*, Uppsala 1945.

Zuckerkandl, Victor. *Sound and Symbol*, New York 1956.

INDEX

Abathur Muzania, 33
abdāl: the seven, 52, 53, 134; the
   forty, 56
Abū'l-Barakāt Baghdādī, 19 ff.
Abū'l-Ma'ārī, 66
Abū Shakūr Sālimī, 136, 137, 159
   n.136
Abraham, 55, 105, 125; "of your being," 124-126, 128, 130, 143
absolute subject, 102, 112, 113
act: of light, 101, 102, 116; acts of illumination (*ishrāgāt*), of contemplation, 103 ff.; of the Light, 103,
   143
Active Intelligence, *see* Intelligence
Acts of Thomas, *see* Song of the Pearl
Adam, 48, 55; carnal, 28; corporeal,
   14; earthly, 14, 15, 28, 43;
   esoteric, 58, 126; and Eve (Mandeism), 33; and *Phōs*, 14 ff.; "of
   your being," 124, 126
Ahmad Ahsā'ī, Shaykh, 114
Ahmad 'Alawī, Sayyed, 158 n.125
Ahriman, 29, 47, 48, 151 n.67;
   Ahrimanian counter-powers, 29
Ahunavairya, 151 n.67
Air (element), 65, 66, 77
'ālam al-mithāl, *see* mundus imaginalis
alchemy, 3, 77, 106, 134-139
'Alī Hamadānī, 58, 68
'Alī Zaynol-'Abidīn, Fourth Imām of
   Shīism, 157 n.119
Allberry, Charles Robert Cecil, 148
   n.39
alone with the alone, 84
alter ego (heavenly), 8, 10, 33, 59, 151
   n.69. *See also* Angel; Perfect Nature
Amahraspands (Zoroastrian archangels), 41 ff., 55
'Ammār Badlīsī, 151 n.72
Amrtakunda, 24 ff.
Anā'l-Haqq (Hallāj), 127, 128; *anā sirr
   al-Haqq* (Ibn 'Alabī), 129
androgyny, 48
Angel (the), 32, 97, 104; archetype
   of humanity, 16, 20, 27, 33-40 (*see
   also* Gabriel; Holy Ghost; Active
   Intelligence); of knowledge and
   of revelation, 14 (*see also ibid.*);
   esoteric Angel of each Heaven,
   105; Angel-Logos, 7, 48, 113, 117

angelology, 6, 20, 97; Zoroastrian, 43
angelophanies, 79
Angels: the four, 147 n.31; of Christ,
   16
animae caelestes, 105
anta anā (you are I), 88, 116
anthropogony, 95-96
Antimimon, 48
Apocalypse of Elijah, 75
Apollinarious of Laodicea, 132
Apollonius of Tyana (Balīnās), 18 ff.
Apuleius, 35, 45
'aql, see intellect
aqtāb (poles), the seven, 52
arcanum, transconsciousness (*khafī*),
   69, 109-110. *See also latīfa*
archetype: Figure (*mabda', dmutha*),
   33, 42 (*see also mundus imaginalis*);
   Images, 5. *See also* Angel
Argun, 121
Ascension of Isaiah, 152 n.75
Asín Palacios, Miguel, 122
assumption to Heaven, 133
astrology, 134-135
astronomy: esoteric, 52, 135;
   Ptolemaic, 60
'Attār, Farīdoddīn, 66
Attestor/Attested, 72
Attis, 27
aura, 62, 135; *gloriae*, 138
aurora borealis, 4, 5, 46 ff., 59, 119
Avesta, 55
Avicenna, 34, 113, 114; (apocryphal)
   Epistle of the Origin and Return, 24
   ff.; mystical recitals, 6; *Recital of
   Hayy ibn Yaqzān*, 22, 25, 59, 101,
   114, 148 n.46
Awliyā-e Khodā (Friends of God),
   54-55, 105
awtād, the four, 57
'Ayn al-Qozāt Hamadānī, 153 n.93

Bacon, Roger, 122
Bahrām Gōr, 160 n.142
Bailey, Harold Walter, 147 n.32
Banafsha, violet, 87
Bartholomew of Bologna, 122
barzakh, 101
Bastāmī, Abū Yazīd, 153 n.89
Bear, constellation of the, 49, 52, 53
Bearing/Born, 17, 19, 21, 30, 84
beauty, 36, 86-88, 92, 103-104, 108,

Index

135-136, 158 n.127; as
theophany, 63 ff.; spiritual essence of, 137

being: the being beyond, 10 ff.; "the one who never has *not been*," 118

"be-tween," man as a, 33, 95

birth (spiritual), 128

bi-unity, 7, 9, 23, 31, 49, 68; *see also unus-ambo*

black, 93; body, object, 100-103, 126, 138; color, 115; the black face of beings, 112; luminous, 7, 126, 128

blackness: of the stratosphere, 100; without light, 47

blazes, rejoining of the two, 63, 65-66, 72-73, 85-87, 89, 141, 143-144

blindness (spiritual), 66

blue-clad (the), Sufis, 157 n.121

body: acquired subtle, 124, 129, 159 n.134; of immortality, 130; of origin, 159 n.134; resurrection, 121, 135, 159 n.134; subtle body of light, 41, 106, 153 n.87

Boethius, 144

Boehme, J., 123

Books (suprasensory), written in Heaven, 87

Brünnhilde, 32

Buddhas and Bodhisattvas, 138

Buddhism (Mahayana), 83

Buddhists of Central Asia, 50

Bundahishn, anthropology of, 147 n.31

Byzantine icons, mosaics, 40, 138, 159 n.136

cardinal points, the four, 1, 14 ff.

caro spiritualis, 132, 136, 138

Carton, Raoul, 158 n.131

Catharism, 34

center, 5, 18, 21, 26, 41 ff., 49

chakras, 83

Chinvat Bridge, 30-33, 41, 44, 51

chivalry (spiritual chivalry, *javān-mardī*), 136

Christ, 16, 47, 55, 133; and Mānī, 27; *Christos-Angelos*, 27, 34; *Christus juvenis*, 132-133; *Christus-Pastor*, 27

Christianity, 47, 127, 132; Ebionite,

135; oriental, 138

Christians, 127, 128

Christology, 27; Qorānic, 129

Chromatic harmony, 111, 141

cities of the oppressors, 23-24, 45, 47, 49-51; personal city, 25

circumambulation, 49

Climate, The Eighth, 2, 44, 57, 60. *See also mundus imaginalis*

clothing, symbolism of color of, 110-111; azure, sky blue, 157 n.121; black, 111, 118, 157 n.121; blue, 111, 157 n.121; *see also* symbolism of colors

cloud: black, 65, 67, 93; glowing, 65; of unknowing, 7, 10; white, 65

cognitio: matutina, 59; *polaris*, 59; *vespertina*, 59

coincidentia oppositorum, 47, 50

collective, collectivity, 10; collectivization, 31, 51, 97

color: language of the soul to itself, 142; mystical meaning of, 140, 142-143; pure, 101; spiritual experience of, 142-143, 159 n.139

colors: archetypal conditions, 142; auric, 62; blue (*kabūd* and *azraq*), 157 n.121; blue and yellow, polarity of, 143; green, 143, 157 n.121; harmony of, 160 n.141; lights made colors, 101; mental impressions of, 142; "physiological," 62, 102, 139-144; in the pure state, 103, 116, 126, 138, 139; red, 142-143; the seven, 102, 142; symbolic, not allegorical, use of, 142 ff.; synchronism of, 81; the world of, 131-139. *See also* symbolism of colors

Column: of Dawn, 45; of Light, 70; *columna gloriae*, 5, 34, 45

Communicatio idiomatum, 71

complementaries and contradictories, 47, 50, 94

conscious, 6

consciousness, 47, 93-94, 96-97, 99-100

Contemplator/Contemplated, 72, 84, 106

correspondences, law of, 123

Coyajee, J. C., 149 nn.54, 56

Cross of Light, 45

164

Index

16, 32, 34, 37, 42, 100, 108, 115, 122, 133, 134, 155 n.108a; *Opera metaphysica I*, 146 n.17; *Opera metaphysica II*, 147 n.23, 150 n.62; *Psalm to the Perfect Nature*, 21-22, 46; *Recital of the Occidental Exile*, 22 ff., 43-45, 59, 63, 70, 148 n.46
Song of the Pearl (from the *Acts of Thomas*), 22-24, 34, 44, 48, 58, 63
Sons of Light, Sons of Darkness, 137
Sophia (heavenly), 35, 48
soror spiritualis, 87, 88
soteriology, 133
soul (*nafs*), 68, 69; lower soul or lower ego (*nafs* ammāra), 63, 65, 66, 67, 74, 82, 91, 93, 94, 101, 107, 124; consciousness (*nafs* lawwāma), 66, 67, 82, 93, 94, 107; pacified soul or higher ego (*nafs* motma'yanna), 66, 67, 82, 93, 94, 105, 107
Soul of the world, 124
south, the side of shadow, 62
spatiality, spatialization, 1, 5
specularity (mirā'īya), 130
speculum, see mirror
Sphere of Spheres, 42, 43, 46, 124
spirit (*rūh*), 68-70, 110. *See also latīfa Spiritus sanctus angelicus, Spiritus principalis*, 34
spissitudo spiritualis, 102
Sraosha (angel), 55 ff.
star: North, 56; pole, 1, 8, 49, 56
Stone (alchemy), 135
stones (precious), 69-71, 73
Stranger, gnostic theme of the, 22, 24, 46
Strzygowski, Josef, 138
stupas, 42
subconsciousness, 7, 96, 100, 103, 116, 128
substance of light in you, 73
Sufis, Sufism, 11, 13, 64, 95, 122, 132; Central Asian, 56; Iranian, 2, 8, 47, 55, 85, 86, 99, 107, 139; Shī'ite, 54, 131, 135, 156 n.113
Sun: in the middle of the sky, 151-152 n.72; of the Spirit, 9, 46, 85; of certitude, of knowledge, of faith, 85; midnight, 4, 5, 7, 10, 45-48, 50, 85; of high knowledge, 9; of the heart, 9, 17, 46, 85; of

the mystery, 9, 17; Northern, 50; glowing, 67; rising in the west, 46; suprasensory, 46, 154 n.101; sun and moon, 105, 106
superconsciousness, supraconsciousness, 7, 10, 48, 96, 97, 99, 100, 101, 103, 109, 110, 116, 126, 143
superexistence, 143
superindividuality, 99
symbolism of colors, 61 ff.; ardent fire, 77; black, 67, 89-91, 126; blue, 65, 77, 93, 126; darkness and fire, 65; green, 77, 78, 79, 82, 93, 126, 130, 131; glowing orb, red sun, 117; luminous black, 126; red, 77, 80, 82 (purple star), 93, 126, 160 n.143; smoke grey, 126; violet, 87; white, 126; yellow, 77, 126; *See also* colors; light
symbols of the north, 21, 36, 37, 45, 119
synchronism, 105
syncretism, 13
Syzygy, 19, 21; of lights, 29, 94, 95

Tabarī, 32
Tablet, *see* Emerald Tablet; Guarded Tablet
Tabrīz, 157 n.120
tafsīr, 158 n.132
Taoism, 56, 57, 75
ta'wīl, 123, 130; of Christianity, 127
Temple of the light, 42, 45
tent (cosmic), 57
Terra lucida, 5, 11, 23, 35, 57, 58, 71, 138
theogony (Iranian, Nordic), 32
theophanic knowledge, 116
theophanies, 11, 50, 53, 72, 92, 103, 105, 117, 132, 136; of Names and Attributes, 119, 155 n.107
therapeutics (spiritual), 129
theurgy (supreme), 108
Throne (the), 66, 72, 73; in the microcosm, 66
Till, Walter, 146 n.6
Timaeus, 35
time: outward of the physical world (*zamān āfāqī*), 106, 123, 128, 129, 132; inward of the world of the

Index

Mēnōk (subtle state), 29; Mēnōkih
(subtle organism), 30
Mephistopheles, 48
Meru, Mount, 56
Ming-Tang, mystical palace of, 57
metaphysics of Light, 101, 122, 132,
133
Michael (archangel), 27, 55, 155
n.105
Mīr Dāmād, 21, 112, 131, 152 n.81
Mi'rāj (heavenly assumption of the
Prophet), 3, 58, 60, 70
Mirror, 104, 106, 129, 151 n.69
Mīthāq (pre-eternal covenant), 3
Mithra, 155 n.105
mixture (cosmogonic period), 29
Modi, J. J., 147 n.31, 155 n.105
Mohammad: the Prophet, 34, 130;
"of your being," 125, 129-131
Mohammad Karīm Khān Kermānī,
153 n.86
Mohammadan (the true), 131
Mohsen Fayz, 149 n.47
Mokāshafāt (unveilings of the supra-
sensory), 103, 107, 109-110
Monophysitism, 138
Mons Victorialis, 22
Moon, 67, 83
More, Henry, 102
Morīd and Morād (the seeker and the
sought), 63, 68, 139, 144
Moses, 55, 105, 154 n.95; "of your
being," 124, 126
"Mothers," world of the, 42, 102
Mount Salvat, 22
Mountain: cosmic, 41, 56 (see also
Qāf); of dawns, 41
Mshunia Kushta, 33, 58
Mundus imaginalis ('ālam al-mithāl), 6,
42 ff., 46, 58, 76, 80, 102, 106,
108

Najmoddīn Kobrā, 7, 8, 11, 17, 28,
36, 37, 46, 60, 61-97, 100, 102,
117, 139, 140
Najmoddīn Rāzī (Dāyeh), 61, 100,
103-110, 115, 123, 126
names (esoteric), names in heaven,
87, 88, 154 n.96
Nasafī, 'Azīz, 153 n.90
Nasīroddīn Tūsī, 33, 90, 156 n.116
Natural existence, 64, 66

Nature, 63; spiritual sciences of, 134,
135
Neoplatonism, 13
Neryoseng, 56
Nezāmī, 160 n.142
Nicotheos, 14
Nietzsche, 128
Night, 7; the world of, 4; of light,
luminous, 4, 5, 7, 12, 18, 47-49,
112, 117-119, 126; esoteric, 48;
of pure essence, 119; of symbols,
48; divine, 19, 103, 108, 111, 138;
divine night of unknowing, of the
ineffable, 9-10, 46, 48; of superconsciousness, 10, 48; Ahrimanian, 48; of the demoniacal
depths, 49; without light, 49;
dark, 7
"Noah of your being," 124, 126
north, 3, 4; as qibla, 50, 57; as symbol, 40, 50; cosmic north, abode
of the Angel Sraosha, 56-57;
cosmic north, threshold of the
beyond, 2, 5, 6, 7, 23, 39, 45, 49,
50, 53, 56, 58, 78; heavenly, 1, 23;
the side of light, 62. See also far
north
Noūs (the), 34; of Hermes, 26; according to Philo, 35
Nūrbakhsh, Nūrbakhshīyah (order
of the), 157 n.118
Nyberg, Henrik Samuel, 147 n.31

observation (irtisād) of the spiritual,
153 n.85
Occident, 4; symbol of the shadow,
the world beneath, 43-45, 50,
58-59. See also far west
Ohrmazd, 29, 41, 47
optics: laws of, 122; anthropological,
143
orbs of light, 67, 82 ff., 93, 103, 152
n.72; circle of the divine light, of
the vital pneuma, 83; double circle of the two eyes, 83 ff., 90; circle of the face, 85-86; the August
Face, 84
organs or centers (subtle), organs of
light, 68, 80, 82, 121, 123 ff., 130,
138; the five subtle organs (Najm
Rāzī), 107, 109-110. See also latīfa
Orient: symbol of the suprasensory

Index

Cycle: of epiphany, of occultation, 156 n.116; of Initiation, 149 n.52; of initiatic growth, 125; of prophecy, 12, 54, 125, 134-135; of the *walāyaṭ*, 134

Daēnā, 97; in Manicheism, 35; in Mazdeism, 30 ff.; The Soul on the Way, 30-31; eschatological vision of, 30 ff., 33, 41; and Fravarti, 30, 31, 89, 92
daïmōn paredros, 27, 35
darkness, 4-5, 14, 28, 96; twofold, 6 ff.; Above, 100; at the skirts of the Pole, 6-7, 11, 18, 100-101, 114, 116, 138; divine, 7, 100, 117; Beneath, 100; Ahrimanian, 31, 96, 97, 102-103, 108, 111, 114, 133, 138; demoniacal, 9, 108; of the Far West, 101; of the Subconsciousness, 116. *See also* Night
dark noontide, 5, 118, 119, 126
darwīsh (*drigōsh, daryōsh*), dervish, 57, 112, 116. *See also* poverty
David "of your being," 125
Day: the world of, 4, 7; exoteric, 10, 24, 46-49; deliverance of the "particles of Light," 133, 137
Destouches, Jean-Louis, 155 n.108
Deus absconditus, 48, 53, 86, 100, 103, 108, 117, 150 n.64
devil (*shaytān*), 63, 65 ff.
dhikr (*zekr*), 64, 67, 73-76, 104; blaze of the, 90 ff.; fire of the, 95, 100; immersion into the heart, into the *sirr*, 75 ff.; light of the, 104-105; techniques, 75 ff.; of the Light, 159 n.; Hermetist, 19; Sufic *dhikr* and Taoism, 75; and the monks of Athos, 75
Dibelius, Martin, 147 n.27
Dii-Angeli, 149 n.55
dimension: beyond, 2, 4; of light (being), 4; of darkness (quiddity), 114; of the north, 3; polar, 7, 8, 143; transcendent, personal, 6, 10, 20, 47, 49, 64, 92, 100; vertical, 1, 3, 42, 50, 51, 62
disorientation, 7, 47-50; of symbols, 51
divine attributes, 69, 71-72. *See also jalāl, jamāl*

dmutha (tutelary Spirit, Image), 58
Doppelgänger, 95
dreams (*ta'bir* or science of), 81
Drower, Ethel Stefana, 148 n.37
Druses, 83
dualism, 48
dualitude, 97
dyads, 16

Earth: element, 65; of light, 11, 35, 57; of visions, 40-41; heavenly, 57; and loci of the suprasensory, 70-71. *See also Terra lucida*
Ecclesia spiritualis, 53
Eckhart, Meister, 19, 68
ego, 9-10; lower, 66-67 (*see also* soul); the true, 124-125, 127-128
Elburz (Alborz), 43, 55
elements, the four, 65
Eliade, Mircea, 150 n.63
Elijah, 55
Elixir, 135
ellipse, symbol, 10
Elohim, 143
Emerald: Rock, 6, 23, 43-46, 59, 70, 78, 97, 126; Tablet, 18
Empedocles, 68
energy (spiritual), 70, 77, 141, 157 n.121
Enoch (Idrīs, Hermes), 55
Epimetheus, 15
Ērān-Vēj, 39 ff.
esoteric, 48, 105-106, 111; of each Heaven, 60; meaning of the Qorān, 121-122; hierarchy, 46, 52, 55, 57, 134
Espahbad, 31
events: in Heaven, 10, 129; of the soul, 106, 128-129
Evil, 65
Exodus: of the man of light, 60, 121; out of Egypt, 23, 24
exoteric, 105-106, 111, 122
experience (mystical), 70, 80
eye (the): itself light, 139-140; produces its own color, 141; of the heart, 106, 120; inward, 80
eyes: of God in this world, 53-54; inward eyes of man, 109

face: of light, 113, 143; black, 112-113

Index

fanā fī'llāh (resorption into God),
111, 117 ff., 127 ff., 132, 138
far east (spiritual), 43-44; far north,
40; far west (non-being, hell), 6-7,
101, 114
Farbenlehre, 139-144
Fate, 15
Fātima, 21, 156 n.113
Faust, 48 ff.
fedeli d'amore, 8, 91, 135
feminine, 103-104, 156 n.113
Festugière, André-Jean, 147 n.26
Fire: element, 65-66, 77; dark fire of
the devil, 74; fiery light of the
dhikr, 73 ff.; infernal fire (inward
to man), 69
Flamel, Nicholas, 149 n.51
Fleischer, Heinrich Leberecht, 150
n.61
Fludd, Robert, 152 n.81
forms, 4; apparitional, 64 ff., 120; of
light, 27, 34-35, 49, 57;
theophanic, 102-103, 106, 117,
119, 136, 141
Franz, Marie-Louise von, 147 n.28
Friend of God (in the Oberland), 54
Friends of God, *see Awliyā-e Khodā.*
Fravarti (forūhar), 22, 28-32, 94, 97;
and Walkyries, 31-32
Fylgja, 32

Gabriel (archangel): Holy Ghost, Active Intelligence, Angel of humanity, 16, 27, 34, 55, 128, 130;
Angel of knowledge and revelation, 20, 117, 131; "of your being," 117, 131, 134. *See also latīfa
gebra'ēlīya*
Garōtmān (Abode of Hymns), 30, 42
Gemistus Pletho, Georgius, 8
geocentrism, 3
gētīk (material state), 29
Ghazālī, Abū Hāmid, 154 n.100
Ghazālī, Ahmad, 88
Gilson, Etienne, 158 n.130
gnosis: in Islam, 50; Ismaelian, 95,
134, 156 n.116; Manichean, 133,
135; Shī'ite, 133-135, 159 n.133;
Valentinian, 16, 58
Goethe, 12, 54, 68, 139-144
Gondophares, 22
Good, 65

Gospel according to Thomas, 3-4, 146
n.7
Green island, 58
Guarded Tablet (*Lawh Mahfūz*), 146
n.14
Guide of light, personal inward
guide, suprasensory guide
(*moqaddam al-ghayb, ostād ghaybī,
shaykh al-ghayb*), 9-11, 15, 27, 36,
48, 50, 63, 64, 82, 85, 130-131
Guiomar, Michel, 7

hadīth: of the vision, 105-106, 120,
154 n.93; of the seven esoteric
meanings, 122
Hafez of Shīrāz, 157 n.121
Hākim Termezī (898), 56
Hallāj (al-), 83, 88, 127
hallucinations, 62, 78
hearing of the heart, 131
heart (*qalb*), 65, 66, 68, 69, 73, 78, 82,
93, 104, 109, 151 n.66. *See also
latīfa*
Heaven: black, 101, 117; inward, 70,
82; of the heart, 69, 105; of the
robūbīya, 79; of the soul, 45, 59,
69
Heavens: inward, 79, 83, 123; of the
heart, 105, 108; of the Earth of
light, of the Soul, 135; spiritual,
69, 79; suprasensory, 60; the seven, 83
hegemonikon, the, 31
Hermas, 26-27, 31
hermeneutics (spiritual, esoteric), 93,
121-122; and mystical psychology, 130
Hermes, 8, 26, 68; *Creophoros,* 27; ecstatic ascension of, in Sohravardī,
5, 45, 47, 50-52, 70, 77, 85; and
the underground chamber, 18,
24, 45, 99; and the Perfect Nature, 17-19, 21, 31-32, 45-46,
48-49; Sacred Books of, 14;
Shaykh of the personal city, 25;
vision of Apollonius of Tyana, 18
Hermetism, 11, 13; in Arabic language, 14, 16
hexagon, 160 n.44
Hibil Ziwa, 58
hierocosmology, 56, 57, 68
hierocosmos, 57 ff.

166

hierognosis, 6, 56, 68
hierophanies, 41
hikmat al-Ishrāq, see "oriental"
theosophy
himma, 77, 151 n.71, 157 n.121
historicization, 132
history of the soul, 132
Holy Ghost, in man, 11, 69. *See also*
Gabriel, Holy Ghost
homo verus, the man in man, 35
homoousia, 127
Hosayn ibn 'Alī, third Imām of
Shī'ism, 111
hourī (heavenly), 148 n.36
Hūrqalyā, 11, 23, 39, 42-44, 46, 57,
80-81, 102, 106, 132
Hyperboreans, 40
hypostatic union, 132

Iblīs, 43, 94; converting Iblīs to Islām, 66, 94
Ibn al-'Arabī, Mohyīddīn, 22, 53, 81,
86, 89, 96, 115, 123, 151, n.64,
155 n.107; pilgrim to the Orient,
58
Ibn Kammūna, 46
iconography, 132-133, 135, 138-139
Ieu, Gnostic books of, 71
*Ikhwān al-Safa ("The Brethren with
Pure Hearts"),* 90; *ritual of the
Philosophers,* 149-150 n.57
illuminatio matutina, 45
Image: of light, 34-35, 52; primordial Images, 4-5, 32, 39. *See also*
archetype Images
"imaginal," *see mundus imaginalis*
imaginary, 5
Imagination, 81; active, 5, 43, 81;
transcendental active Imagination, 80
imaginative faculty (Imaginatrix),
64, 81, 106
Imām (in the Shī'ite sense), 131, 134,
135; the Imām as pole, 46, 48,
156 n.112; the hidden twelfth
Imām, pole of poles, 52, 54, 56,
58, 159 n.133; the inward, 134;
Imāmate, 134, 156 n.113, Imāmology, 54, 122, 131-134
immaterialization, 102
immersion of the object into the subject, 118

Incarnation, 127, 128
individual and species, 97
individuality (spiritual), 16, 20, 99,
104, 107, 143
individuation (essential), 93, 97
Infernum, 50
infraconsciousness, 96, 101
initiation, 53, 54; individual, 95;
failed, 128
intellect *('aql),* 66-68, 93, 110, 151
n.66. *See also latīfa*
Intelligence: the First, the *Noūs,* 7,
82; Active, 20, 59. *See also* Gabriel
Intelligences, theory of the, 60, 113
internalization, 60, 75, 82, 106, 127,
139; of Imāmology, 131, 134
Invisibles (the), 11
inward master *(ostād ghaybī),* invisible, 85, 93-94, 130, 134. *See
also* Guide of light
inwardness of light, 5
Ionian school, 139
'Isā ibn Maryam, 72, 127. *See also*
Jesus
Ishrāq, 8; Isrāqīyūn, 31, 42, 45, 117,
122
Islām and *imān,* 164
Ismaelians, 122, 156 n.117; an-
thropology, 33
Istaftīn (esoteric name), 87
Istamakhīs (kitāb al-), 146 n.9
Ivanow, w., 148 n.35

Jābalqā, Jābarsā, 41
Jabarūt, 59, 79
Jābir ibn Hayyān, 153 n.88
Jalāl (divine attributes of rigor,
majesty), 103, 108, 136, 151 n.64
Jalāloddīn Rūmī, 21, 131, 155 n.109
Jamāl (divine attributes of grace,
beauty), 103, 108, 136, 150-151
n.64
Jawālīqī, Hishām ibn Sālim, 158
n.126
Jerusalem (heavenly), 41, 42
Jesus: *Rūh Allah,* 128, 130; "of your
being," 125-128. *See also latīfa*
Jung, Carl Gustav, 147 n.28, 149
n.51

Kabbalah, 156 n.116
Kay Khostaw, 60

Index

kenōsis (fanā of the divine into the human reality), 127
Kerubim, 79, 113
Keshvar (orbis, zone), 39; the seven, 42, 148 n.44; the central, 42; the eighth, 43
Khezr (Khadir, Khidr), 55
Kraus, Paul, 153 n.88
Kūh-e Khwājeh, 22

Lāhījī, Shamsoddīn Moh., 100, 110, 114-116, 126; his visions of the black light, 111-112
latīfa (subtle organs or centers), 12, 64, 83; the seven, 42, 107, 109; *qalabīya, nafsīya,* 124, 129; *qualbīya, anā'iya,* 124; *rūhīya,* 125; *khafīya,* 125, 128; *haqqīya,* 125, 127, 129-130; *jabra'elīya,* 131
latitudinal and longitudinal order of Lights, 102
Leibniz, 97
ligature of the senses, 26, 79
like with like, 64, 69-72, 87, 139, 141
Light, 4, 8, 96; and darkness, 108; white, 107 ff.; blue, 89, 107 ff.; in your heart, 65; of fire, 76; of the tongue, of hearing, 82; of prophecy, 104; of pure Essence, 101, 111, 115; of theophany, 118; of the *walāyat,* 104; of lights, 103; of the *dhikr,* 67; the northern, 4, 11, 45, 47; of the Throne, 66; inward, 18, 40, 43, 45, 46, 139; yellow, 107 ff.; black (*nūr-e siyāh,* the antithesis of Ahrimanian darkness), 5, 7, 11-12, 47, 49, 96, 100-103, 107-108, 110-120, 126-129; Ohrmazdian, 31, 97; of origin, 44-45; that makes one see (absolute subject), 102, 116; revealing, revealed, 144; red, 107; without matter, 100, 102; upon light, 29, 31, 72, 74, 97; green, 7, 9, 37, 64, 76-79, 93, 100, 107, 111, 117, 126-127, 129
lights: ascending and descending, 72-73, 138; colored, 61, 104, 108, 112 (red, yellow, white, blue), 124, 126 (*see also* photisms); of Beauty, Majesty, 103-104; of the heart, of the Throne, 72-73; un-

created, 40; infinite, 31, 60; pure, 102, 104; suprasensory, 119; theophanic, 99, 108
"loci": of Mercy, 77; of the true God Ieu, 71; divine, 76
Lotus of the limit, 117, 130
Love: four degrees of, 89; human and divine, 87-88; mystical, 86-87
Luther, Martin, 4

Ma'ānī, 81, 82
Macrocosm, 16, 82
Magi, 22
Man: outward, carnal (*sarkinos anthropos*), 14; Perfect, 118; universal, 16. *See also homo verus*
Man of light (*photeinos anthropos, Shakhs nūrānī*), 12, 14, 18, 25, 28, 36, 47, 59, 63, 64, 85, 100, 106, 131-139; and the Perfect Nature, 25; ascent of, 42; physiology of, 41, 62, 74, 80, 82, 83, 102, 121, 139-140, 143. *See also Phōs, latīfa*
Majdoddīn Baghdādī, 152 n.80
Majnūn, 88, 154 n.95
Majrītī (pseudo-) 16-17, 46, 153 n.88
Malakūt, 53, 59, 79
Mandala, 3, 41
Mandeans, Mandean gnosis, 33 ff., 50, 58
Mānī (the prophet), 34, 133, 137
Manichean: cosmogony, 62; dramaturgy of salvation, 133, 136; painting, 12, 101-102, 133, 137-139, 159 n.140; physics of light, 136, 137
Manicheans, 11, 16, 20, 33, 34, 45, 50, 57, 58, 131, 137; of Central Asia, 136
Manvahmed, 34
Mary Magdalene, 15-16, 144
Maryam, 21, 76, 128, 131
masculine, 103-104, 156 n.113
Maspero, Henri, 152 n.77
Massignon, Louis, 137, 152 n.77, 159 n.136
Matter (subtle), 44, 102, 108
Mazdeism: triad of thought, speech, action, 33; triad of soul on the way, soul outside the body, soul within the body, 30-31
Meier, Fritz, 150 n.64, 151 n.67, 152 nn.73, 78, 153 n.88, 154 n.96

Index

soul (*zamān anfosî*), 106, 123, 128, 132
Tobias, 31
Turfan, 138
transconsciousness, 68, 96, 109-110
transfiguration, 133; transfiguring light, 138
transmutation: of being, 80; of the senses, 80, 82, 144
Treasure, the hidden, 54-55
Treasury of Light, 71
triangle, 160 n.144
tridimensionality (psycho-spiritual), 6, 89, 93, 94, 96
Twin: heavenly (*taw'am*), 33; heavenly Twin of Mānī, 27, 133; of light, 58, 97

unconscious, 6, 47, 48, 94, 95, 100; collective, personal, 95; negativity of the unconscious, 94
unconsciousness, 7, 10
universal (logical), 6
unknowingness that is knowledge, 116, 117, 118, 119
unus-ambo, 7, 9, 17, 84, 97, 151 n.69
Upanishads, 35
Ursa Major, Ursa Minor, *see* Bear, constellation of the
Uttara-kurus, 40, 43
uxoriality, 85, 119

Valentinians, 132
Van der Leeuw, Gerhard, 32
Veils of Light and of Darkness, the 70,000, 109, 119
Verus Propheta, 135
Virgin (the) of Light, 34, 35, 133
visio smaragdina, 11, 12, 77, 89, 100, 111, 120
visionary: apperception, 62, 64, 67, 68, 70, 72, 80, 81, 86, 101, 103, 106, 135, 138; geography, 39, 43, 44
visions of colored lights, 77; *see* photisms
visualizations of inward states, 77, 78, 80, 107, 124. *See also* photisms
Vita Adae et Evae, 151 n.67
vocation, 97
Vohu Manah (Bahman), 34, 41

Wagner, Richard, 32
wahdat al-wojūd, 115

Walāyat, 53, 131, 134, 149 n.52, 152 n.74, 156 n.113; solar, 105
walī, 134
Walkyries, 32
Walther, Gerda, 150 n.63
Wāsitī, Abū Bakr, 104, 108
Water: element, 65-66, 77; of Life, 25, 114, 115
warfare (spiritual), 63, 64, 67, 109, 111
Weigel, Valentin, 132
well: image and theme of the, 23, 24, 37, 45, 47, 49, 51, 60, 62, 64; ascent out of the, 70, 76, 77, 78-79, 80; Joseph's, 78; of nature, 75; of green light, 79
Werner, Martin, 147 n.28
Whittaker, Molly, 147 n.27
Widengren, Georgio, 148 n.40
wilāyat, 149 n.52
Witness (*shāhid*), contemplator/contemplated, 28, 36, 91, 92, 99; of contemplation, 19, 36, 72, 86, 106, 119, 120, 136; in Heaven (*shāhid fī'l-samā*), 9, 10, 15, 17, 36, 46, 63, 64, 66, 72, 78, 82, 84, 85, 86, 91-94, 97, 117, 119, 120, 133, 141, 143; Theophanic, 36, 86, 92; absence of the, 90, 91. *See also* scales of the suprasensory; Perfect Nature
World: of the Angel, 6; of the Soul, 126; suprasensory (*ghayb*), 73-74, 79
worlds, the 18,000, the 360,000, 109

Xvarnah, 31, 138, 159 n.136; of the *Saoshyants*, 41; landscapes, 138
Xwārezm, 151 n.64
Xwārezmī, Hosayn, 155 n.109

Yazata, 55
Yima (*var* or paradise of), 5, 11, 40, 41, 42, 43, 46, 48, 50, 57
you, 9, 59

Zarathustra, Zoroaster, 8, 29, 41, 60, 151 n.67
Zechariah, 149 n.51
Zervānism, 48, 50, 113
ziqqūrāt, 41
Zoroastrian: individual eschatology, 28; spirituality, 55, 56; Iran, 8

Index

Zoroastrianism, 11, 13, 47, 50, 55,
    57, 92
Zosimos of Panopolis, 14, 15
Zuckerkandl, Victor, 150 n.63